THE QUAKER OF THE OLDEN TIME

The Life and Times of
Israel Thompson (d. 1795)

His Land, Plantation, Mills, Tanyard & Mansion House
and the Rise of Wheatland, Loudon County, Virginia

Roberto Costantino

HERITAGE BOOKS
2006

HERITAGE BOOKS
AN IMPRINT OF HERITAGE BOOKS, INC.

Books, CDs, and more—Worldwide

For our listing of thousands of titles see our website
at
www.HeritageBooks.com

Published 2006 by
HERITAGE BOOKS, INC.
Publishing Division
65 East Main Street
Westminster, Maryland 21157-5026

Copyright © 2004 Roberto Costantino

Other books by the author:

Colonial Catoctin: The Fairfax Family and Freeholders of Piedmont Manor and Shannondale Manor, Loudoun County, Virginia Land Book, 1743-1820, Volume I

Colonial Catoctin: Colonial Developmental Dynamices on or about the Potomac River at Catoctin Creek up to Waterford, Volume II

Miscellaneous Road Cases, Loudoun County, Virginia, 1758-1782, Loudoun County Circuit Court, Clerk of Circuit Court, Archives, Miscellaneous Road Cases, Files No. 38 to 48, Leesburg, Virginia

All rights reserved. No part of this book may be reproduced or transmitted in any form or by any means, electronic or mechanical, including photocopying, recording or by any information storage and retrieval system without written permission from the author, except for the inclusion of brief quotations in a review.

International Standard Book Number: 978-0-7884-2541-2

The Quaker of the Olden Time

The Quaker of the olden time!
  How calm and firm and true!
Unspotted by its wrong and crime
  He walked the dark earth through!
The lust of power, the love of gain,
  The thousand lures of sin
Around him, had no power to stain
  The purity within.

With that deep insight, which detects
  All great things in the small,
And knows, how each man's life affects
  The spiritual life of all,
He walked by faith and not by sight,
  By love and not by law;
The presence of the wrong or right,
  He rather felt than saw.

He felt that wrong with wrong partakes,
  That nothing stands alone,
That who so gives the motive, makes
  His brother's sin his own.
And pausing not for doubtful choice
  Of evils great and small,
He listens to that inward voice
  Which called away from all.

Oh spirit of that early day!
  So pure and strong and true,
Be with us in the narrow way
  Our faithful fathers knew.
Give strength the evil to forsake,
  The cross of Truth to bear,
And love and reverent fear to make
  Our daily lives of prayer!

                    J.G. Whittier

Table of Contents

Chapter 1 5

Chapter 2 12

Chapter 3 17

Chapter 4 31

Chapter 5 46

Appendix I 55

Appendix II 58

Appendix III 62

Appendix IV 65

Appendix V 75

Endnotes 89

Index 106

Chapter 1

There is a place in Northern Virginia named Wheatland that is on or about an old millseat on the North Fork of Catoctin Creek. There was once a gristmill or a merchant mill there. From the time the gristmill was developed in 1762 by Israel Thompson, until about 1917 when the old watermill started to collapse and operations came to a halt, there had been a steady and consistent demand for the types of wheat flour turned out there. The demand for the flour was such that it was met by husbandmen and farmers with toil and trouble to produce various strains of wheat for the mill to grind into types of flour. Wheat meant ready money and money was "dough" or "bread". A working mill was an economic engine affording folk the ways and means to earn a living as a husbandman or farmer in an agrarian society. This was a land of wheat or a wheat-land. This is a record of the life and times of Israel Thompson and his land, plantation, mill, tanyard, mansion house, and the rise of Wheatland, Loudoun County, Virginia.

Israel Thompson had originally moved to the Colony of Virginia about 1746 to settle in an area of the Upper Potomac River Valley between Catoctin Mountain and Blue Ridge Mountain commonly known as the Loudoun Valley. He had come to this place on the edge of the south with a party of others including his parents and siblings and probably others, in search of some combination of opportunities and fellowship. The members of his party were primarily made up of free men and women of middling means. They had come to the Loudoun Valley to live amongst a scattered community of Quakers who resided in the proximity of the recently established Fairfax Monthly Meeting (est. 1745). The Fairfax Meetinghouse was in such a place it fell under the jurisdiction at the time in civil law of the County of Fairfax est. 1743 (Loudoun County est. 1757) and under the jurisdiction in ecclesiastical law of Truro Parish est. 1732 (Cameron Parish est. 1749: Shelburne Parish est. 1781). The Fairfax Monthly Meeting had lately grown out of the Fairfax Preparative Meeting, which had preceded it by about a dozen years.

The members of Israel Thompson's party were outsiders in the Colony of Virginia as they had recently removed themselves from a relatively great distance away in the Delaware River Valley, Province of Pennsylvania. They would remain outsiders in the practical sense of the word as they had come to Virginia to be located in the backwoods, on the western fringes of the Atlantic Eastern Seaboard, and at least two to three days away from the most convenient deepwater port in Alexandria, Virginia. They were outsiders in the social sense of the word in Virginia as they were Quakers and popularly considered to be "nonconformists". They were outsiders in the cultural sense of the word as well as they were distinctive Anglo-Irish folk who'd developed social habits and characteristics while in Ireland that distinguished them from others. They would come to find some degree of safety and comfort within the community of relatives, acquaintances, and others, who'd preceded them to the environs of the Fairfax Monthly Meeting.

In Israel Thompson's view of things, probably, there were in the Loudoun Valley choice land holdings for sale or rent in every direction. There would be opportunities there for him to practice mixed husbandry and to engage himself in his trade as a tanner, and to undertake personal spiritual growth under the care of the Fairfax Monthly Meeting. The ties of kin and friendship had an important bearing on the selection of lands and as a consequence, the Fairfax Monthly Meeting would become a congregation in which the Anglo-Irish element was especially strong. In such a neighborhood where the clan element was strong and where intermarriage was not uncommon, these Friends preserved much of their ethnic identity for generations. Albert Cooke Myers opined that in those meetings in which the Irish (Anglo-Irish) element was strong there was a tendency to be more liberal in belief and less stringent in the administration of some of the rules of justice.[1]

Myers wrote about the early history of the movement of Quakers in Ireland in a book entitled, Immigration of the Irish Quakers to Pennsylvania, 1682-1750: With their Early History in Ireland, originally published in 1902. The converts to Quakerism in Ireland had originally been drawn from, mostly, the English, Welsh, and Scot. Most of them had previously been in membership with other Protestant denominations such as the Baptists, Presbyterians, Independents, and Church of England. The majority of Quakers in Ireland were of English descent, or English.[2]

Many Irish Friends removed themselves to several American Colonies because of religious and economic causes. The Irish Friends at an early date were on the Chesapeake Bay in Maryland. In 1682 a shipload of them settled in West Jersey. They were also known to have gone to Quaker settlements in Carolina, and Virginia. But by far the greatest migration of the Irish Quakers was to Pennsylvania during the period from 1682 to 1750. The principal ports wherefrom the Irish immigrants embarked for Pennsylvania were Belfast, Dublin, Cork, and Waterford. Typically, passengers were taken on ships originally from Whitehaven, Liverpool, or Bristol, in England, which would dock in Ireland to take on passengers and cargo bound for Pennsylvania. The principal port of entry was Philadelphia, but many landed in New Castle on the Delaware River, and fewer in Maryland and Virginia.[3]

During the Colonial Period, it was the practice of savvy merchants, artisans and peddlers in the backwoods, to position themselves along wagon roads and around mills and ferries so to be at the point or locus of points common to travel and transportation and, hence, to prevail upon folk to stimulate the occurrence of trade. And, perhaps, that would explain how a common farmer and artisan such as Israel Thompson, a member of the Society of Friends, would come to receive the patronage of such esteemed men as Lawrence Washington, and later of his younger half-brother, George Washington.

During most of his adult life, Israel Thompson (d. 1795) lived and worked principally out of his dwelling plantation or "Home Plantation" in the Blue Ridge Uplands of the Piedmont Region, and in close proximity to the Vestal's Gap Road approximating modern day Charles Town Pike (Route 9), which went back and forth through the Great Gap in Short Hill Mountain. His plantation was situated around a bottom of the North Fork of Catoctin Creek, within ten miles of Leesburg and about three and a half miles west of Waterford and the Fairfax Monthly Meeting. In 1802, a United States post office was established on the site of the late Israel Thompson's home plantation, named "Wheatland".

Israel Thompson was the master as well of land and a plantation located at the foot of the eastern face of Short Hill Mountain and on the spring drains of the Beaverdam Branch of Catoctin Creek, which he called "Cold Spring". He would become heir-at-law to the land and plantation of the late Edward Thompson on the Northwest Fork of Goose Creek, and in the vicinity of the Goose Creek Meeting (Lincoln). Also, from time to time, he owned various different indentures of lease for messuage tenements on or about the Branches of Catoctin Creek. He possessed a town lot in Leesburg and another landholding on the Catoctin Mountain. Additionally, he owned rights to vast landholdings in the District of Kentucky and on the Monongahela River. Israel Thompson was a man of material substance.

The expression "plantation" would have been a part of Israel Thompson's parlance. He would have understood the term in the context of his Anglo-Irish ancestors as meaning a place in which a residential community was planted in a region inhabited by colonists, during the early years of settlement. It was a tract of cultivated land owned or rented by an individual. Throughout the colonial era and, at least in the upper South, the term remained synonymous with farm. It was also used to designate the component quarters of larger holdings. Agricultural development of the land, not necessarily sustained with the labor of slaves, was the principal characteristic of the plantation.[4]

According to Asa Moore Janney and Werner Janney, settlers looked for stands of black locust trees and black walnut trees to recognize lands especially suitable for kinds of agricultural development, and to this day, one may still find such trees in abundance on or about the site of Israel Thompson's one time home plantation.[5] On that old field, the earth's surface is an undulating and hilly landscape with elevations of from 400 to 550 feet above sea level lying between broad upland ridges. The ground is made up primarily of well drained deep to very deep sandy loam soil interrupted by rocky outcroppings, with fair to good potential for agriculture and good potential for grassland. It's supplied with an abundance of accessible spring water. In its natural state, most of it was covered with an oak-hickory flora community.

During 1747 and 1748 Lawrence Washington bought 1,433 acres of land on the western shore of the Shenandoah River in then Frederick County, Virginia. Apparently, Lawrence Washington would have crossed through the Loudoun Valley on his way to and from his lands on the Shenandoah River, as his final estate turned out to be liable to one Israel Thompson for "Negroes shoes". According to an administrative account of the deceased's, Israel Thompson affirmed the same in 1752 and was subsequently paid the sum of three pounds and six shillings by January of 1755.[6]

The Catoctin Creek watershed runs through the Loudoun Valley. All of its waters flow into the Potomac River. Today, this area occupies most of the northwest quadrant of Loudoun County. Although there had been colonial settlements further westward all the way to Winchester, nevertheless, this region lagged behind and suffered because it was composed of, mostly, the vast unimproved land holdings of a small number of either undercapitalized or uninspired real estate speculators such as Francis Awbrey, Catesby Cocke, Catesby Cocke & John Mercer, John Tayloe, John Colvill, William Fairfax, and William Henry Fairfax. These lands also fell under the dominion of the Northern Neck Proprietary and thus they retained the residual interest of Thomas, Lord Fairfax and Baron Cameron, as he was the proprietor.

The speculators were by and large in it for the money as they had wished to somehow transform their land holdings into sources of perpetual income. They used their lands for hunting and raised monies from the trade in skins and pelts. They worked towards evicting all unauthorized poachers and squatters from their private property. They sought the evacuation of the American Indian population so to establish absolute control over the given land as private property. They desired to survey their lands for ready sale or rent and enclosure. They explored and surveyed the surface of the earth to identify and control important landscape sites such as mineral deposits, roadbeds, mill seats, spring heads, river landings, mines, tree stands and so on, which might become sources of income or wealth. They sought the establishment of the authority of the Anglican Church over their land holdings under the jurisdiction of a parish authority.

The most conspicuous feature in the topography of this region is its broad upland ridges or ranges of mountains. The Blue Ridge Mountain, bordering this area on the west, rises to an elevation of from about 1,000 to 1,400 feet above sea level. About three miles easterly, the parallel Short Hill Mountain is about equal in elevation to the Blue Ridge but only about eleven miles long. This range is broken at the Great Gap by the waters of the North Fork of Catoctin Creek. About six miles easterly across the grassland of the Loudoun Valley is the parallel Catoctin Mountain, which rises to an elevation of from about 300 to 700 feet above seal level. These broad upland ridges are eastern elements of the Blue Ridge Mountain System.

As stated, Israel Thompson and others had originally migrated to the Potomac River Valley from the Delaware River Valley, Pennsylvania. There is not any record, apparently, of Israel Thompson's place or date of birth. The author estimates he was born by circa 1718 in the Province of Pennsylvania, between the Brandywine Creek and the Christiana River in modern day southeastern Pennsylvania or northern Delaware. Israel Thompson was a Quaker by birthright. During his youth, apparently, he would have accompanied his parents and siblings as they sojourned from place to place in the Province of Pennsylvania in Edgmont[7] and elsewhere, and under the care of various places of worship including the Newark Monthly Meeting or Kennett Monthly Meeting[8], Uwchlan Monthly Meeting,[9] Chester Monthly Meeting[10], Concord Monthly Meeting[11], Philadelphia Monthly Meeting[12], Haverford Monthly Meeting[13], Bradford Monthly Meeting[14], and the Monocacy Meeting and Fairfax Monthly Meeting[15].

Albert Cooke Myers wrote that the immigration of Irish Quakers to America was encouraged in part by the return to Ireland on short trips of those who had already gone over to settle in Pennsylvania some time before. There were many such instances as numerous Friends made the return journey to see the country and to visit friends and relatives.[16] Israel Thompson may have been such a traveler, possibly, as there was one "Israel Thompson" recorded in 1736 with the Monthly Meeting held at Grange, near Charlemont in County Armagh in the north of Ireland (Northern Ireland).[17] The time coincides with circumstantial evidence to support such a case, notably; his family's contemporary migration from the Concord Monthly Meeting, formerly Chester County now Delaware County, to a seaport, Philadelphia, under the care of the Philadelphia Monthly Meeting, which would have coincided with such a supposed voyage.[18]

There was a contemporary Friend named Thomas Willson (Wilson) who migrated to a settlement in York County, Pennsylvania (Warrington Monthly Meeting), from Grange, near Charlemont, Ireland, about 1748, before shortly later removing to Fairfax Monthly Meeting, Virginia.[19] Thomas Willson was an Irish Quaker and weaver who would become the master of an improved 360 acres plantation on or about the South Fork of Catoctin Creek, immediately adjacent to Jacob Janney's land[20], and on Colvill and Fairfax's line. In fact, Israel Thompson served as one of the witnesses for the subject indentures of lease and release.[21] It seems that, Israel's brother, Edward Thompson (Junior), married a Rebecca Willson in 1747, under the care of the Fairfax Monthly Meeting.[22]

In the early church records of old Chester County, Pennsylvania, in the records of the Bradford Monthly Meeting, is contained the earliest published reference known with certainty to be of the said Israel Thompson dated in 1739, denoting that Edward Thompson and wife and sons, Edward, Israel and Joseph to Haverford MM, "he being settled there."[23] Later, it was recorded by the Bradford MM that Israel Thompson moved around 1745 to the Fairfax Monthly Meeting, Virginia. At the time, Edward Thompson, his father, had renewed his request for a certificate for himself and his wife and sons, Israel and Joseph, directed to the Fairfax MM, Virginia, "his family already being there and he intending to follow in the spring".[24]

It's not clear who it was who was already there. Possibly, it was a William Thompson and or a Forest Thompson, although the familial evidence is lacking.[25] Another early Thompson was a Joshua Thompson, who was, possibly, a cousin.[26] In any case, Israel Thompson's brother, Joseph Thompson, eventually would leave the Fairfax Monthly Meeting for the Hopewell Monthly Meeting, Frederick County, Virginia, by 1757.[27] It sounds as if another sibling, Edward Thompson Junior and wife, Rebecca, left for the Wrightstown Monthly Meeting, Pennsylvania, about 1748. Another brother, Isaac Thompson, would become affiliated with the Fairfax Monthly Meeting.[28] His wife, Hannah Thompson, and children, joined him from the Uwchlan Monthly Meeting, by 1764.[29]

Israel Thompson's parents, Edward and Mary Thompson, had at least seven surviving children including Prudence (b. 1714), Jane (b. 1716), Sarah (b. 1718), Edward (b. 1720), Israel, Isaac, and Joseph. Eventually, Israel Thompson's father, Edward Thompson, would survive his wife whereupon his son-in-law and daughter, Jesse and Prudence Woodward[30], came to join him on the parcel of land and plantation that had been lately conveyed to him by Mahlon Janney by indentures of lease and release, dated May 9 and 10, 1759.[31] Edward's plantation was on or about the Northwest Fork of Goose Creek and in the vicinity of the Goose Creek Meetinghouse, in present day Lincoln, Virginia.

Upon the time of Edward Thompson's death in 1773 he would devise the same land and plantation to his son, Israel Thompson, at the time of the death of his daughter, Prudence Woodward, who possessed a life estate interest.[32] Israel Thompson owned the subject real property at the time of his own decease in 1795. He would refer to it in his last will and testament as a tract of land and plantation near Goose Creek Meeting House joining the lands of Nathan Spencer containing 150 acres.[33] Additionally, by a separate indenture of Deed and Power of Attorney dated 1770, Edward Thompson left to his grandson, Jesse Woodward Jr., all of his late wife's real and personal estate in New Castle County, Pennsylvania.[34]

There is an old anecdotal account that has survived time of a Mrs. Browne who accompanied her brother from London, England, all the way to Fort Cumberland, Maryland, and kept a journal of the same from late 1754 to early 1757, during the French and Indian War. He was attached to a company of troops under the command of Sir Peter Halkett. They were marching through Northern Virginia on their way westerly to meet with the rest of General Braddock's expedition at Will's Creek, when on June 4th to 6th, 1755, they halted for a time at Edward and Mary Thompson's earlier place of domicile in the Loudoun Valley, presumably, Israel Thompson's too, and she recorded the occurrence in rich detail. Apparently, they each left a strong impression on Mrs. Browne. She described Edward Thompson as in the manner of an old sage Quaker with silver locks deliberating on the virtues of temperance, along with Mary Thompson, his wife, musing about the condition of human mortality.[35]

One may make an estimate of the location of Edward and Mary Thompson's place of domicile at the time based on information and data published contemporaneously in the Fairfax County Court Order Book, which contains references to Edward Thompson's place of habitation. Apparently, Edward Thompson's dwelling house or post was in the vicinity of an improved roadway connecting it thereby with Thomas Davis's dwelling house or post, which was probably on the western side of the Catoctin Mountain[36]. Mrs. Browne had estimated in her diary that Edward and Mary Thompson's dwelling place was about fourteen miles west of Mr. (Nicholas) Minor's place (Leesburg). In the estimation of the author, the site may have been on or about the North Fork of Catoctin Creek, in the vicinity of the later Israel Thompson's home plantation. Also, the Court Order Book record includes references to an ongoing case of law to recover a debt from Edward Thompson due Cameron Parish, apparently, for tithing.

When those troops marched up to Edward and Mary Thompson's place of habitation they may have been greeted by the steady and heavy beat of the loom at work, as he was a weaver.[38] The weaver took in yarn and thread to weave on their looms to be made into fabric material for trade. The loom was an ingenious pre-industrial machine consisting of a frame of four square timber posts set apart as in the manner of the posts of a bedstead, and joined at the top and bottom by a frame. The structure was mounted with a yarn beam, cloth beam and iron axle and numerous appurtenances. The operation of a loom required a good deal of dry space so it was not uncommon for the weaver's house to be of considerable size. Also, weavers were itinerant tradesman sometimes traveling with their looms for many miles at a time. The weaver's capital equipment usually made by carpenters was considered valuable and was highly treasured.

According to Alice Morse Earle, weavers were a universally respected and popular element of society. While traveling from place to place in the process of performing work and taking in yarn and thread to weave, they came into contact with a multitude of folk and networked with various members of a given community. Earle has estimated that ten or more spinners had to be calculated to supply yarn for one weaver. Although the weaver's fabrics were readily salable or exchangeable in kind, nonetheless, the supply of yarn was normally limited thus weavers could manage their time enabling them just as well to farm or as in Edward's case, apparently, to serve as a lay preacher.[39] Additionally, Earle noted that weavers were the ancestors to many of the wealthiest and most influential citizens of her time.[40]

The earliest surviving tithing record overlaying this geographic region, specifically, comes from Cameron Parish, 1749. For many years preceding the formation of Cameron Parish in 1749, that part of Truro Parish which lay over Goose Creek was generally referred to as the "Upper Parish". Because at the time the formation of Cameron Parish was then imminent, the Reverend Charles Green annotated the 1749 list of old Truro Parish for the purpose of showing exactly which tithing resided in the area to become Cameron Parish, above Goose Creek. This record bears the title, *"Fairfax County List of Tithables for 1749"*, and notes the religious preferences of each householder and the number of tithing classified by race for which he was responsible

The tithing list provides some insight into the disposition at the time of the inhabitants in Cameron Parish, above Goose Creek. A tally of the tithing list reveals 138 names for head of household including 190 people and 71 slaves. The white people were classified according to their religious preference including 94 Quakers, 43 Papists (Catholics), 24 Presbyterians, 19 Anglicans, 5 Anabaptists, and 5 Sectarians. Probably, a "Papist" was anyone who took communion and believed even remotely in the doctrine of transubstantiation, including some in the Church of England. One of the names on the list of householders counted as a Quaker was named "Edward Thomson" with a note, "He and wife both Preachers".[41]

Chapter 2

Israel Thompson in his heart and soul was one of a "peculiar" people known as Quakers. His devotion to the Quaker denomination was a faith that came from the depth of his being. For most of his adult life he lived under the care of the Fairfax Monthly Meeting. The early members were mostly common stock folk, many of them American born, of mostly Anglo-Irish, English, Welsh, Anglo-Dutch, Dutch, German, Scot, and mixed background. The great majority of them had moved to the backwoods from antecedent Quaker settlements on the Atlantic Eastern Seaboard stretching from Southern Maryland through the Middle Atlantic Region to New England.

The members of the Fairfax Monthly Meeting met in meetings, usually once a week on "meeting day." The Fairfax Meetinghouse was a simple rectangular building with massive stonewalls and white painted doors and shutters.[42] It lay on a site originally in the line dividing the land of Mahlon Janney from the land of Francis Hague, nearby to where the later village of Waterford would come to be developed.[43] Friends entered the interior of the Meetinghouse by different doors for men and women and were expected to take seats in order of arrival, not by social rank or by pew. Their ritual of worship centered on the inner light and the movement of the spirit. Anyone could speak in meetings and it was commonplace for folk to rise up and preach or pray. But, sometimes no words were spoken as Quakers considered the condition or quality of being or keeping silent with reverence. After a time the worship would end and everyone departed the meeting in peace.

The deed record indicates that the Meetinghouse grounds served as well for a schoolhouse. Little information on the early school attended by Friends has been gleaned, but the evidence indicates that from the earliest days of the settlement provisions of sorts were made for education. The Quaker leaders held a practical education to be useful and recommended the same for all children, no matter whether rich or poor, male or female. The neighborhood schools were supposed to teach children to read and write by the age of twelve and to be trained in a useful occupation or trade. But, in practice, they were small privately funded sectarian schools of lower education.[44] The reading material in the country was largely confined to the Bible and Friends books.[45]

Depending on his station in life, Israel Thompson was a farmer or a planter, tanner & currier, and a miller or a merchant miller. The farmer or planter practiced the art of mixed-husbandry on a farm or plantation. The tanner was an artisan who tanned hides or pelts and skins into leather whereas the currier was an artisan that finished or dressed the leather for an end user. The miller was a manufacturer of flour, whereas the merchant miller was a manufacturer and merchandiser of flour.

There was great difficulty making a living in the country as an artisan for lack of business as a consequence of poverty or a general deficiency in the means of providing material needs or comforts, cheaper sources of competing labor services, competition from British goods, and lack of infrastructure. However, Israel Thompson seems to have operated a considerable business as a tanner & currier. They were separate crafts in England but often combined in one house or in the same man in colonial America, such as in Israel Thompson & Company. His final estate would include a set of two fleshing knives and two curry knives, and another set of two fleshing and one curry knife. Apparently, he did work in his own account and on shares. He both employed and apprenticed tanners and curriers, and shoemakers. It's likely that he worked in association with other leatherworkers such as the shoemaker or cordwainer, saddler, breeches-maker, apron-maker, harness-maker, hater, book binder, and the glover or glove-maker.

The slow and laborious processes of tanning and currying were an untidy business occasioned by unpleasant odors thus requiring a detached dedicated craft site or tanyard. A tanyard required ready access to a perpetual supply of running water. A tanyard required ready access to natural resources such as lime, oak bark and sumac leaves. A tanyard required a bark-mill or building space for shredding and storage. A tanyard required a series of vats for scrubbing, rinsing, and soaking of skins and hides or pelts. A tanyard required a dry and durable building for the processing and storage of goods in trade. Practically all the tanner's work was direct manual labor almost unrelieved by any mechanical help and was considered particularly hard and exhausting work. At the time of his decease, according to his final estate papers, Israel Thompson maintained a tanyard and curry shop with the appurtenances including an iron skimmer, iron hooks, tanbark.[46]

The works of the tanner and currier were absolutely indispensable in the pre-industrial world as leather was much more widely used than in our time. Israel Thompson's final inventory of leatherwear goods which sold at his crying sale included a combination of more than 575 items comprising his stock in trade. His possessions would include the goods of the tanner such as 18 sheep and hog skins, 2 horse hides & 21 sheep skins, 8 horse hides, 2 skins, 25 hip skins, ½ of 6 hip skins, 109 calfskins, and 46 dry hides. His possessions also included the dressed goods of the currier such as 3 sides leather, 144 sides leather upper, ½ of 162 sides leather upper, 148 harness sides, 5 lots of sole-leather weighing 294 lbs., and sundry scraps of leather. Also, Israel Thompson deceased owned finished leather-ware goods including at least five pair of relatively expensive shoes, which sold for between seven shilling and eight-and-a-half shillings each at his crying sale, buckets, three horse collars, three curb bridles, three saddles, one saddle and bridle, and harness set for a wagon and four horses.[47]

Israel Thompson had made a solemn and formal commitment to the causes and laws underlying reality as perceived by the Society of Friends, which he endeavored to apply himself towards through the Fairfax Monthly Meeting. In 1754, in good form, he formally obtained a certificate with Aquila Massey to travel to the West River Monthly Meeting in Anne Arundel County, Maryland; it appears that, in order to engage Ann Richardson in marriage.[48] He was devoted enough to the cause to deliver testimonies against Friends as he did in 1758, against Elizabet (sic) Wils and Sarah Mekenney.[49] Also in 1758, he and John Hough visited the Falls Monthly Meeting, Bucks County, Pennsylvania, on an official matter concerning Samuel Mead.[50] Israel Thompson even served as an overseer of the Fairfax Monthly Meeting as he was excused from the position in 1761, in favor of Moses Cadwalader.[51] Beginning around 1770 with a group of other Friends including Francis Hague, Jonathan Myers, and Jos. Janney, he made a commitment to assisting an occasional meeting at David Williams's, above the Great Gap in Short Hill Mountain.[52] Israel Thompson was a devoted Quaker with a network of friends and family who were affiliated with the Fairfax Monthly Meeting, Goose Creek Monthly Meeting, and the Hopewell Monthly Meeting in the vicinity of Winchester, Frederick County, Virginia.

Courtship among Friends was a solemn affair, and was pursued in a most decorous and circumspect manner, Albert Cooke Myers wrote. Before declaring his affections, the young man first required the consent of the young woman's parents. One important preliminary to marriage was to obtain the consent of the monthly meeting(s). To this end the parties appeared before two monthly meetings and declared their intentions, which was followed by an inquiry to find if the couple was "clear of all entanglements".[53] The Quakers maintained a very strict and disciplined set of customs for members to adhere to at times of marriage(s) including no fewer than sixteen sequential steps meant to include the bride and the groom, monthly meeting(s), and the extended community of the Society of Friends. Quakers insisted marriage should be neither for the sake of gain or lust, but should be grounded in a love between true believers.[54]

A great event among Friends was a wedding. The matrimonial union of Israel Thompson and Ann Richardson was an important event, which was planned and executed with painstaking attention to numerous parts or details. In the minutes of a Quaker Meeting held April 2, 1754, was recorded the marriage of Israel Thompson of Fairfax County, Virginia, to Ann Richardson of Frederick County, Maryland, at the Sandy Spring Meetinghouse, Frederick County, Maryland. Apparently, she had previously been affiliated with the West River Meeting, Anne Arundel County, Maryland, in all probability, through her late husband, William Richardson.[55]

Ann Richardson was a woman of apparently respectable connections, irreproachable character, and affluent fortune. She was the widow of William Richardson. She was a lady with two children entitled by law or according to the terms of the deceased's last will and testament to inherit an interest in his estate including probably human chattel. She brought two children with her into her union with Israel Thompson, a son and daughter, Joseph Richardson (b. 1744) and Ann Richardson (b. 1747). According to Elise Greenup Jourdan the said Ann Richardson, was lately Anne Harris of West River Meeting, possibly.[56] And, according to Grace L. Tracey and John P. Dern, Ann Richardson was previously Anne Davis of Monocacy Meeting, Frederick County, Maryland, perhaps.[57]

The subject Sandy Spring Meetinghouse was located in modern day Brookeville in Montgomery County, Maryland. William Henry Farquhar wrote that the earliest reference to the "Meeting at Sandy Spring" was published on July 27, 1753. The first members composing the Meeting appear to have principally belonged to families with the names of Brook or Brooke, Thomas, Snowden, Richardson and others.[58] Indicative of the time and the place the wedding was formally witnessed by eight people with the sir name of Richardson, seven people with the last name of Brook or Brooke, seven named Thomas, three identified by the name of Holland, two with the Massey name, two called Mathews, two with the appellation of Duval, and fourteen other differently named witnesses including one Thomas Davis, Junior, and one Edward Thompson, but none named such as Harris in the group.[59]

Israel Thompson was a bachelor of more modest means than his well to do bride. He was the son of Edward and Mary (Barrett) Thompson, at the time of Cameron Parish and Fairfax County, Colony of Virginia. His father, as noted, was identified as a weaver by trade. Also, his parents were "both preachers", apparently.[60] The Thompson family members were Anglo-Irish or so called Irish Quakers, that is to say, ethnic English converts to Quakerism in Ireland. It is interesting to note that many of these Irish Quakers had been officers and soldiers in Oliver Cromwell's "New Model" and had settled down on the land they had conquered under Lord Lieutenant, Henry Cromwell, son of Oliver.[61]

The founder of the Quaker Church in Ireland under George Fox was William Edmundson of Westmorland (1627-1712), himself once a sergeant in Cromwell's forces. Albert Cook Myers wrote that he had been influenced by the Puritan movement in England before he came to settle in Ireland and became convinced of the ways of the Quaker Church. In 1653 he and his brother and sister began the first organized Quaker Meeting in Ireland, in Lurgan, County Armagh, in modern day Northern Ireland. Also, Edmundson was a storekeeper and one of several Quaker merchants credited with introducing an ethical system of merchandising goods known as the single price system later imitated by Friends in America, perhaps, even by Israel Thompson, himself a merchant.[62]

Meanwhile, the turn of events in Ireland eventually brought a large number of folk to migrate overseas including many Irish Quakers who moved to the Delaware River Valley, such as the above referred to Edward Thompson. In 1712 he was formally received under the care of the Chester Monthly Meeting, Chester County (Delaware County), producing a certificate from Lurgan Monthly Meeting, County Armagh, Ireland, and a more recent one from the Newark MM or Kennett MM, New Castle County (Delaware County), Pennsylvania.[63] About one year later the said Edward Thompson, son of Henry and Prudence Thompson, identified as a weaver living at the time in Upper Providence Township, Chester County (Delaware County), was betrothed and married to Mary Barrett, daughter of Giles and Mary Barrett of Ridley Township.[64]

Back to Israel Thompson and his spouse Ann or "Nancey" Thompson, as she was nicknamed;[65] on a document dated March 21, 1755, and shortly after they took each other in marriage, his wife, lately Ann Richardson, Administrator to William Richardson late of Frederick County, Maryland, in the company of Israel Thompson, solemnly and sincerely affirmed and declared an accounting of the deceased's Estate with the Prerogative Office of the Frederick County Court. Her assets by way of his estate amounted to the hefty sum of 421 pounds and 14 shillings and 11 ½ pence against liabilities of only 61 pounds and 17 shillings and 11 pence. To that degree at least Ann afforded them the means to take advantage of the opportunities that awaited them in the backwoods, and as such she was an underwriter for Israel's varied and many commercial undertakings.[66] Israel Thompson moved back to Northern Virginia with his wife and her children in 1756.[67]

About a month before that occasion, on February 19, 1755, at a Court held for Fairfax County, Virginia, George William Fairfax Esquire acknowledged making an indenture of lease for lives to Israel Thompson, which was admitted to the record. It is not presently clear where that land was as there is no surviving deed record of the same.[68] But, there was such an entry made for the transaction on page 20 in the missing portion of Fairfax County Deed Book D. There is a possibility it was in the same place where his later home plantation was described as being, which he would go on to fully control via indentures of lease and release made in 1759. George William Fairfax was the West Indies born son and heir to William Fairfax Esquire of Belvoir in Fairfax County.

Northern Virginia's economic prosperity depended on the agricultural production of myriad small proprietors such as Israel Thompson on the vast lands that spread out beyond the port of Alexandria. The locals had not been complete strangers to farming and trade; since the beginning of the Century they had engaged in coastal trade and exported varied quantities of tobacco. But, frustrations were compounded because a medley of circumstances that worked against uniform prosperity, including uneven harvests, fluctuating prices and markets abroad. The dangers of backwoods frontier life and the difficulty of acquiring rights to desirable landholdings close to roads and rivers resulted in a shortage of marketable goods for export.

The would-be grain and flour wholesalers lamented that internal improvements had preceded slowly thereby proving a disincentive to agricultural production. The merchants' country agents encouraged rural agricultural producers to orient more production towards exportable goods such as grain and flour, but periodic scarcities, sparse settlement, a dearth of agricultural skills, and absorption by consumers of most available food products ensured a slow start for grain and flour exporting. The unevenness of internal agricultural development and the growing demand in the West Indies for food and timber created a tension that merchants and exporters tried to resolve. They moved to quicken the pace of settlement and to motivate large landholders to turn over more of their soil. Exporters tried to shape port policies that would both encourage more production for export and discriminate against conflicting economic interests.

Chapter 3

Most of the tracts or lots of land that Israel Thompson would go on to acquire over his lifetime including that one tract comprising his home plantation, were based on rights acquired through indentures for lands that once belonged to William Fairfax Esquire, on his "Kittockton Tract." William Fairfax had served as the Agent of the Northern Neck Proprietary in the service of his cousin and old time friend, Thomas, Lord Fairfax and Baron Cameron. Nevertheless, these lands were his private holdings taken up in the open market from speculators, in association with John Colvill of Fairfax County.[69] John Colvill controlled vast acreage in old Fairfax County, Virginia (Loudoun County), as well as in Frederick County, Maryland.[70]

It has been surmised that William Fairfax Esquire had as his goal and objective to develop his given lands into two entailed manorial estates for the support of his heirs, one of them styled as Piedmont Manor of 17,296 acres and the other styled as Shannondale Manor of 19,170 acres.[71] Whereas that may have been his goal and objective all the same, the earliest use of those names on deeds was not until the early 1770's, about fifteen years after his death, and when the lands were under the control of his son, George William Fairfax.[72] The house of William Fairfax Esquire had done a masterful job of accumulating a vast amount of premium quality real estate in Northern Virginia but there wasn't to be enough income developed from the same to support it. His heirs would ever be scrambling to liquidate real estate for money to live on as well as to service liabilities.

William Fairfax Esquire was a transitional figure. He worked with Amos Janney of Fairfax County who served as his surveyor of record to establish on his lands on the Greater Catoctin Creek, a permanent community of freeholders. As early as 1743 he sold two indentures of lease for lives for land on the North Fork of Catoctin Creek. One of them for 100 acres of land was made to George Griffith of Fairfax County including the said George Griffith and his sons Benjamin Griffith and George Griffith.[73] The said Griffith may have assigned the lease lot to Samuel Mead in 1745.[74] The other one for 100 acres of land was made to Jonathan Richardson of Fairfax County including the said Jonathan Richardson and Elizabeth Richardson his wife and Joseph Richardson his son.[75]

The next year, William Fairfax sold four more indentures of lease for lives for land on the Greater Catoctin Creek. Two of the lots were on the Beaverdam Branch of Catoctin Creek. One of them for 150 acres of land was made to Samuel Gregg of Fairfax County including the said Samuel Gregg and Elizabeth Gregg his wife and Thomas Gregg his son.[76] The other one for 150 acres was made to John Hough, blacksmith, of Fairfax County including the said John Hough and Sarah Hough his wife and Joseph Hough his son.[77] The other two lots were on the South Fork of Catoctin Creek. One of the indentures for 165 acres was made to John Bishop, carpenter, including the said John Bishop and Elizabeth Bishop his wife and Samuel Bishop his son.[78] The other one for 165 acres was made to William Janney including the said William Janney and Elizabeth Janney his wife and Mahlon Janney his son.[79] The next year, William Janney assigned his indenture of lease to Robert Yates.[80] These lots were a toehold for Friends in the Loudoun Valley, which would encourage further migration into the region of the Greater Catoctin Creek.

By 1755 George William Fairfax Esquire was in charge of and operating as the proprietor over a lot of his late father's estate including his "Kittockton Tract". Just as well, George William Fairfax Esquire was a transitional figure at a disadvantage from the beginning, undone by his perpetual need for ready money. He commenced to trade indentures of lease and or release with or without additional lives, for premium lands on or about the Catoctin Creek and Dutchmans Creek.[81] He worked with John Hough of Fairfax County (Loudoun County), who served as his surveyor of record, to expand in number the community of freeholders. In general, his prices were low but his terms were tedious and nearly obsolete. Although he managed to enhance his income, even so, it was offset by contra charges for surveying, legal bills, administrative expenses, supplies, as well as for land taxes.

On December 1, 1756, Israel Thompson acquired a lot of land containing 148 acres of land by indentures of lease and release from Abel Janney of Fairfax County in consideration of £ 40 current money of Virginia.[82] He would name this land holding "Cold Spring".[83] The land was located amidst a scattering of folk settled on or about an old intersection of roads or paths under the Short Hill Mountain, near the later village of Morrisonville. One of the old roadways was referred to in 1767-1768, as Abel Janney's Road ("Abel Jeneys Road").[84] It meandered in an easterly-westerly manner to and from Abel Janney's old tract up and down the forks of the Beaverdam Branch of Catoctin Creek to the South Fork of Catoctin Creek (Route 693). The other roadway in the intersection went in a northerly-southerly manner from "Pain's Ferry" or Payne's Ferry on the Potomac River up and down the Dutchmans Branch in a course that went across Abel Janney's tract (Route 690).

The backwoods were filling fast with settlers, not all of them by choice. By the beginning of the second half of the 18th Century, one third of the Colony's total population of slaves resided in one of civil jurisdictions straddling the Piedmont Region such as in western Fairfax County (Loudoun County). During the following generation, the slave population in the Region would increase in number by three fold.[85] In fact, a small community of mixed African American and American Indian people would come to emerge in the Piedmont Region, no doubt also mixed with European people. Much as the miniscule number of free people of color in the Region, they lived precariously in a condition somewhere between slavery and freedom.

The slave's status before the law was such that he or she was in involuntary servitude to a master for life. Furthermore, the local courts had jurisdiction to hear cases concerning slaves, even capital cases. Slaves were capitalized working assets used to enhance productivity. They were liquid based on an age factor. A cruel aspect of the condition of slavery was the arbitrariness of life. It was a very fluid here today and gone tomorrow world as most slaves were used and abused, traded, transported, confiscated, kidnapped, punished, and executed.

The slaves of the Piedmont Region were, generally, a youthful population of folk with great diversity among their number. Virtually all the slaves were either Africans or Creoles. Some of them were American born with American born parents and a kinship network including sometimes even free people. About one third of their number was made up of recent arrivals from the West Indies, Africa, and Bermuda. A large number of the slaves were Christians, reconciled in some way to liberation in the world to come, possibly. There was a miniscule population of free people of color.

As a consequence of pressures brought to bear by increases in the permanent population of western Fairfax County, the new county jurisdiction of Loudoun County was duly created in 1757. Loudoun County was conceived during the French and Indian War and thus was named after one John Campbell, Earl of Loudoun and one of the sixteen peers of Scotland, and Captain General and Governor in Chief of his Majesty's forces in North America. At the time, about half of Loudoun County was made up of the Blue Ridge Uplands lying to the west of the foothills of the Catoctin Mountain. The more level eastern portion of the County was originally settled by British folk from, mostly, Virginia and Maryland. The western portion including those lands on and about the Branches of Catoctin Creek was settled by varied folk from, mostly, Greater Pennsylvania.

The boundary lines of Loudoun County then went from the mouth of Difficult Run and meandered in a southerly direction up the running waters of the same to its head. Then, the boundary line went in a straight southerly course to the line of Prince William County. From that point, the line went westerly as formed by the Bull Run of Occoquan River to Bull Run Mountain. The line then extended from Bull Run Mountain in a direct southwesterly course to the top of the Blue Ridge at Ashby's Gap. The boundary line then went in a northerly direction along the summit of the Blue Ridge to the Potomac River below Harper's Ferry (Robert Harper's Ferry. The boundary line then went easterly down the Potomac River to the beginning. Most of the waters of

Loudoun County flow into the Potomac River except a small portion that drains into Bull Run. The western shore of the Potomac River separated this county from Frederick County, Maryland.

After the jurisdiction of Loudoun County came into its administrative being, most of the ground encompassing the region of the Greater Catoctin Creek remained available for acquisition in consideration of ready money. The bulk of the land holdings still belonged to absentee owners as Catesby Cocke deceased by Aneous Campbell; Catesby Cocke to John Mercer and sons; John Tayloe deceased to John Tayloe to James McIlhaney; William Fairfax deceased to George William Fairfax; John Colvill deceased to Thomas Colvill to Charles Earl of Tankerville; William Fairfax to William Henry Fairfax deceased to Bryant Fairfax.

On June 12, 1760, John Patterson advertised in the Maryland Gazette that he had land for rent, the property of Charles Earl of Tankerville, lying on Potomac River and Catoctin Creek, in Loudoun County, Virginia. Those interested were advised to apply to Patterson at William Kirk's on Kittockton Creek or Andrew Adams, merchant, in Leesburg.[86] There were some land holdings available in the Loudoun Valley from end users who theretofore had acquired the same from the Proprietor or speculators, such as Amos Janney, Abel Janney, George Gregg, Richard Wood, John Mead, Joseph Hollingsworth, and others.

At the time, George William Fairfax Esquire of Fairfax County and John Hough of Loudoun County continued to aggressively expand trade in indentures for land[87]. But, shortly afterwards, George William Fairfax Esquire would drastically reduce his personal involvement in the operations of the land office as he planned a return visit to England. His real estate business suffered under the weight of high administrative expenses and confiscator taxes and or penalty. By the spring of 1761, his subject real estate holdings were in the hands of his attorney-in-fact, John Carlyle of Carlyle & Dalton, Alexandria. John Hough would continue to promote the lands and to act as the transactional surveyor of record. It was reported in the Maryland Gazette dated July 17, 1760, that the ship Wilson under Capt. Judion Coolidge, master, had left the Patuxent River the week before for London carrying George William Fairfax, Esq. and family.[88]

The empirical evidence suggests that Israel Thompson was a highly organized and an enormously resourceful man. Moreover he was a cautious and prudent merchant with sharp business acumen. He was an industrious man whose spirit was reinforced by a Protestant devotional ideal of serving God with one's best talent. Israel Thompson was on the verge of becoming a relatively powerful and influential man of means, based on a formidable agricultural base complimented with artisanship and merchandising. Israel Thompson applied himself to the business of acquiring real property in the backcountry from speculators, mostly in the area of the Greater Catoctin Creek. He sought to develop such land as an end user for the sake of increasing his current income or dividends and realizing future capital gains. In turn, he would reinvest his surplus income or wealth into real property. As a plantation owner he exhibited entrepreneurial behavior by constantly expanding his land holdings and adjusting the size of his workforce including the enslaved, indentured servants, free laborers and journeymen, to maximize his wealth.

Israel Thompson's education was suited to the business of the country. Nevertheless, he indulged himself in reading and writing as is evidenced by his library and final papers including personal notes, as well as by his habit of meticulous bookkeeping. His personal library had but few books, however, they were carefully selected and well read, whether religious or civil matters. Also, he left some furniture that was well suited for study and bookkeeping in the form of a valuable walnut desk and bookcase valued at 240 shillings(£ 12: 0: 0), and another desk, and a portable desk. Additionally, his final estate included 5 quire of paper.[89]

As for the contents of his library, the most valuable book among Israel Thompson's final personal possessions was a Three Volume Dictionary of Arts and Sciences, which was sold at his crying sale to Dr. John Nicklin of Waterford for five pounds. He owned a book called *Cook's Voyages,* about the great English mariner and explorer of the Pacific Ocean, Captain James Cook

(d. 1779). He left behind what is considered to be the chief epic in the English language, *Paradise Lost*, by poet John Milton (1667). He left a work by Alexander Pope, the English poet and satirist (1688-1744), also, another by Joseph Addison, the English essayist and poet (1672-1719). Yet another book he left was called, *The Farmer's Wife or The Complete Country Housewife*. Additionally, he owned one book each about bookkeeping, measurements, English grammar, as well as an old law book, dictionary and a Latin testament.[90]

Still other publications in the possession of the late Israel Thompson were other works centered on religion and his denomination in particular including, *Life of Edmund*, apparently, about the founder of the Quaker Church in Ireland, William Edmundson. Also, he owned Robert Barclay's book on the doctrines of the Quaker Church entitled, *Apology for the True Christian Divinity* (1678). He owned a book published in 1717 by the Dutch Quaker historian, William Sewel, entitled, *The History of the Rise, Increase and Progress of the Christian People called Quakers*. He owned a book entitled *Life of John Richardson*, recounting his life's work including sojourns to Virginia (1663-1726), apparently. He owned a publication entitled *Young's Night Thoughts* and another called *Purer Translation of the Bible*. Lastly, he left a family Bible, a small Bible, and sundry pamphlets.[91]

With at least two lots in the country already in his possession, Israel Thompson would next come to acquire a lot in town. Shortly after the creation of Loudoun County he moved to purchase a lot in George Town or Leesburg as it would shortly thereafter come to be known as being. The transaction was completed in 1758 by feoffment, that is to say, a grant of land as a fee. Israel Thompson had acquired a half-acre lot of land from Nicholas Minor in consideration of three pounds current money of Virginia, including all that lot numbered three situated in George Town and bounded by Royal Street and Loudoun Street.[92] But, by the time John Hough's plat entitled "Plan of Leesburg" was published in 1759, the same numbered lot was identified as John Ashby's.[93]

The town of Leesburg (Leesburgh) or "Lee's burg" was at the time more of a plan than a reality, but it was a perfectly logical concept considering that it was conceived at the intersection of the Alexandria Road (Route 7) and the Carolina Road (Route 15). The site of the town on the Tuscarora Creek was in a sparsely settled glade on or about Nicholas Minor's Ordinary, in a vast country abounding in trees. But, it was in such a place that it drew ferry traffic going north and south over the Potomac River and folk traveling easterly or westerly through the Catoctin Mountain. Leesburg was developed to serve as a marketplace and as the seat for the Court of the County of Loudoun.

On December 10, 1759, George William Fairfax Esq. by indentures of lease and release did bargain and sell to Israel Thompson all that lot of land he would refer to as his home plantation, in consideration of the sum of £123:12: 0 current money of Virginia. It consisted of 641acres of land on the North Fork of Catoctin Creek and was bounded as by a survey thereof made by John Hough. Israel Thompson's land was on the east side of John Tayloe's line of his Short Hill Tract. It was below Frederick Cooper's lot of land, which was on the South Fork of the Beaverdam Branch of Catoctin Creek. It was on the west side of a lot formerly surveyed for George Griffith. It was above Edward Thompson's additional lot of land. The boundary description delineated the presence of what was styled as the main road, which served in it self as a southern boundary marker for his plantation (Vestal's Gap Road). The agreement was signed or marked by George William Fairfax Esquire, Israel Thompson, Benjamin Sebastian, Lee Massey, and John Hough.[94]

A portion of Israel Thompson's home plantation tract was already improved by 1759, as he had paid a premium for the given property. The boundary description makes the implication that Israel Thompson and or Edward Thompson was already established in that place as there was a reference made in the present tense to "Thompson's Meadow". Also, the boundary description made a reference to a neighboring survey made for George Griffith, which was likely the previously referred to 1743 indenture of lease from William Fairfax to George Griffith (George Griffeth).[95]

One of the most valuable aspects of Israel Thompson's given land holding was the presence thereon of the main road or old Vestal's Gap Road, which closely approximates modern day Charles Town Pike or Route 9. The road was a reliable way for folk to go back and forth through the Blue Ridge and over the Shenandoah River from points to the east and west. The roadway served to make his home plantation readily accessible and convenient to travelers. In 1761, George Washington recommended 'Israel Thompson's' as a place where Parson Charles Green might break his journey to 'the Bath' (Berkeley Springs, WV).[96]

It is interesting to note that Vestal's Gap Road and the nearby Snickers's Gap Road were considered so important that by 1786 the State Government had interposed and passed a law for keeping the roads in repair from Snickers's and Vestal's Gap to Alexandria, and for erecting turnpikes thereon. The old Vestal's Gap Road was then new and improved and renamed the Key's Gap Turnpike (Route 9) and the Snickers's Gap Road, similarly, became an improved turnpike road (Route 7)[97]. They were modeled and developed after English turnpikes and furnished with tollgates. At the time, George Gilpin and Charles Little, Commissioners, were authorized to open the two turnpike roads.

Labor resources were scarce. Over a long life, Israel Thompson engaged in slavery as a master of slaves and finally as a manumitter. Once a slave arrived at his place of domicile or home plantation, his or her personhood would have been subsumed under a general principle. They were placed in a more comprehensive category under the plantation and used for the sake of profit. Israel Thompson's plantations were worked by slaves supervised by overseers or foremen, both black and white, probably. A quarter was provided with appurtenances and some combination of domestic goods. The quarters could be a part of or adjacent to or quite separate and distinct from the tract on which the landowner lived.[98] The presence of some of his slaves was recorded in the records of tithing, property taxes, deeds, registers, wills, codicils, and administrative accounts. They were sometimes identified by a given name and or a designation of some kind.

A structure known as a quartering house would have been devoted for the accommodation of servants on Israel Thompson's home plantation.[99] It was an outbuilding that provided both functional and social separation between servants and those they served. The quartering house or houses sheltered a combination of servants and or laborers. They were often architecturally indistinguishable from the dwelling houses of freeholders. Typically, they were single story gable end buildings with one or two rooms and an unfinished interior. The presence of some of Israel Thompson's domestic servants was recorded in the records of tithing, final papers. They were identified by a given name and a designation of some kind, possibly.

In all likelihood some of Israel Thompson's slave laborers belonged to Mrs. Ann Thompson, personally, and were merely controlled by her said husband. The former Ann Richardson had come into a substantial inheritance including human chattel, probably. It was not uncommon where she was from in Maryland, for a widow woman to receive as part of her "thirds" of personal property an interest in human chattel. It was considered a form of security, thereby providing a widow with a means of support. Apparently, Ann retained an interest in her slave or slaves until the time her son by her late husband, William Richardson, attained an age of majority. Thenceforth in the year 1774, her son, Joseph Richardson of Loudoun County a farmer, did bargain and sell to his stepfather Israel Thompson, one slave "a Negroe Man called Peter", in consideration of the enormous sum of 103 pounds and 13 shillings current money of Virginia.[100]

The undulating or hilly landscape on or about Israel Thompson's home plantation allowed for a considerable fall in the North Fork of Catoctin Creek, giving rise to the possibilities of waterpower to be harnessed in a millseat location on a certain bottom of the North Fork of Catoctin Creek. Upon a petition by Israel Thompson and by the order of County Court in 1762, Israel Thompson was granted leave to build on his home plantation, a "Griss Mill on Kittocton Creek", that is to say, a gristmill on the North Fork of Catoctin Creek. It was ordered that the sheriff summon a jury of twelve freeholders of the vicinage to view and examine his lands and neighboring properties as well, which should be impacted by the proposed mill. The jury was charged with several duties including estimating externalities or damages to neighboring properties.[101]

A gristmill was a type of water-mill whose machinery was powered by a waterwheel for the grinding of grain. The gristmill contained two rotating millstones, ironworks, gears, bolting chest, bolting cloth, and other machinery connected to a source of waterpower.[102] The milling process involved both the cleaning and conditioning of wheat as well as separation of the husk from kernel. From an economic point of view, the amount added by the milling process to the value of the raw material was the measure of the margin to be made by the grinding of grain, either in shares to a farmer and miller or in full to the merchant miller.

The development of the mill's landscape site required access to labor resources and technical expertise in order to develop a working system of damming and channeling waters into water courses with dam and flood gates, and mill-race. Israel Thompson would have used a millwright to build and develop his site. A millwright was a mechanic skilled in the building and development and repair of mill works.[103] Milling was a complicated business representing a considerable investment of capital and technical expertise, a prospective market, and permission from local authorities to dam watercourses.[104]

This old photograph of the Wheatland Mill in Loudoun County, with Millard Fillmore Janney standing in the door, is printed through the courtesy of Asa Moore Janney of Lincoln, a nephew of the miller. As far as Asa Moore can tell, the photograph was taken sometime around 1915, but he believes the old building may have dated to the 18th Century. Water splashing from the wheel eventually weakened one wall until it fell down, says Asa Moore, and the Highway Department finished razing the building when the road north of Purcellville was widened. The road at that point was only wide enough for two buggies. Asa Moore also recalls that during the summer months when stream flow was low, especially during August, the mill could only be operated at night: "They'd let the water back up all day, and save up enough to run the mill for a few hours at night."

Israel Thompson would have sought improvements to the transportation infrastructure to access his plantation from all points. He served as a surveyor of the road from his mill to the Catoctin Creek.[105] In April of 1767, a publicly supported roadway was formally established from the road to "Pains Ferry" (Payne's Ferry) on the Potomac River in a northerly-southerly aspect, to and from Israel Thompson's millseat.[106] But, in the May term of 1771, the County Court rejected as unnecessary a proposal to publicly support a roadway, which would have run from Israel Thompson's millseat to a new mill of John Brown & others.[107]

In 1768, Israel Thompson would acquire assignment of a neighboring lot of 150 acres of leaseland from John Newland.[108] And, almost two years later he would purchase an indenture for another lot of land in close proximity to Newland's, from George Tingle in consideration of £ 22:0:0.[109] Those acquisitions may have been inspired by concerns over circulation as by 1772, there was appropriated public monies to support a then twenty year old roadway beginning at the end of the lane to Israel Thompson's mill and running in a southerly course in a line between Isaac Thompson and George Tingle and through a lot lately Thomas Townsend's, and keeping nearly the same course to an "old" ford in a meadow belonging to a lot then in possession of Craven Peyton, and crossing the Catoctin Creek (South Fork of Catoctin Creek). The roadway then went between the lands of John Davis and John Bishop continuing in a southerly course leading to Nathan Spencer's goose pond near the Leesburg to Snickers's Gap Road (Route 7). The newly officially recognized roadway also served to facilitate travel and transportation between the neighborhood about the Fairfax Meetinghouse and the neighborhood about the Goose Creek Meetinghouse.[110]

100

Tingle to Thompson
Bill Sale

KNOW all men by these presents that I George Tingle of Loudoun County and Colony of Virginia for and in Consideration of the sum of Twenty Two pounds current money of Virginia to me in hand paid by Israel Thompson of the County and Colony aforesaid the Receipt whereof I do hereby Acknowledge Have Bargained Sold and Delivered by these presents do bargain sell and Deliver unto the said Israel Thompson his Heirs and assigns my Right, Claim and Interest in and to the Lot of Lease land whereon I now Dwelleth with the Houses and Improvements thereon also one Gray Horse without any brand visible about Ten years old also 1 Cow marked with a Crop on the Left Ear and a Slit in the Right Ear To have and to hold the said Lot and Appurtenancies thereunto belonging also the said Gray Horse Cow &c unto the said Israel Thompson his Heirs and assigns forever. And I the said George Tingle doth hereby Warrant and Defend the said Lot, Horse Cow &c to the said Israel Thompson and to his Heirs and assigns forever against all and every other person and persons whatsoever In Witness whereof I have hereunto set my hand and seal this Eleventh day of December in the year one thousand Seven Hundred and Seventy 1770

The Condition of the above Bargain and Sale is such that if the above Named George Tingle shall well and Truly pay or cause to be paid unto the above named Israel Thompson his Heirs &c the above mentioned sum of Twenty Two pounds Current money of Virginia with Legal Interest from the Date hereof and that on or before the Tenth day of December next which shall be in the year 1771 without fraud or farther Delay that then the above Obligation or bargain and Sale shall be void and of None Effect else to Stand and remain in full force and virtue in Law

Sealed and Delivered } George Tingle (LS)
in the presence of }
David Wilson

At a Court held for Loudoun County June the 10th 1771
This Bill of Sale was Acknowledged by George Tingle party thereto and Ordered to be Recorded

Test. Cha.s Binns Clerk

Meanwhile, Mahlon Janney of Loudoun County was already the master of an improved millseat located in the vicinity of a sectarian neighborhood on or about the Fairfax Meetinghouse (Waterford). The earliest published reference to Mahlon Janney's mill in the deed records was in 1762.[111]

Mahon Janney would expand his land holdings in the vicinity with the addition of a twelve acre parcel of land acquired through a real estate transaction with Francis Hague and Jane his wife in 1762.[113] The boundary description of the lot made a specific reference to the mouth of the tailrace of Mahon Janney's mill on the South Fork of Catoctin Creek, and binding therewith the millrace to the division line between said Janney and Francis Hague's land.[114] Also, Mahlon Janney would append one hundred and fifty-five acres more of land to his contiguous land holdings through a real estate transaction with John Hough in 1770,[115] on land which Hough had lately acquired through John West from John Colvill.[116]

Again, the said millseat location was specifically described in a couple of later boundary descriptions for an early Loudoun County deed. In 1773 a certain deed from Francis Hague, yeoman, to Thomas Hague described the boundaries for two adjacent parcels of land. The first one was described as beginning near the road corner to Mahlon Janney's mill lot and extending thence with the millrace to the beginning, containing twelve acres of land. The boundaries of another lot was described as beginning at a white oak standing near the sawmill corner to Mahlon Janney's mill lot, before extending about the millrace to a gum bush on Mahlon Janney's line, thence with said line to a gum tree standing near the ford, before crossing the South Fork of Catoctin Creek and up the tailrace to the beginning, containing 5¾ acres of land.[118]

In the locality of the millseat on the South Fork of Catoctin Creek was a mill lot and a sawmill, apparently, that being Mahlon Janney's mill. The growth in the neighborhood spurred development and by the early 1790's, the deed records describe a little town or a village which had come to evolve commonly known as Waterford.[120] The site was about three and one-half miles northeast of Israel Thompson's home plantation, on the other end of the road from Israel Thompson's mill to Mahlon Janney's mill (Old Wheatland Road or Rt. 698).[121]

Yardley Taylor advanced the notion published in 1853, based on tradition, that during the early years of the settlement of this country, the timber was inferior in size and quality to what he was accustomed to nearly one hundred year later. He maintained that good woodland in the early years was a scarce resource, already. The cause was believed to be, that previously the forest had been burned down by the design of hunters, probably.[122] There are numerous references in the early Loudoun County land books to a "poison field", apparently, an oblique reference to a burned landscape. That would explain the apparent prevalence of sawmills and the evident demand for timber.

A place described as a mill in and of itself is hard to classify, definitively. A mill could have been almost any machine that produced something by the repetition of a simple process. It could have been a gristmill or sawmill. Otherwise, it could have been a machine that releases the juice of fruits by pressing or grinding known as a cider-mill. It could have been a machine that grinds bark into tannin known as a bark-mill. It may have been any of various machines used for shaping, cutting, or dressing metal surfaces. It could have been a building or group of buildings equipped with machinery for processing materials such as textile fibers. A couple of early indentures of lease for lives from John Patterson attorney in fact for Charles Earl of Tankerville to Samuel Schooley for land on Broad Run (Milltown Creek), required them as the tenants to use the landlord's mill should he happen to build or cause to be built, "any water suit mill saw mill bolting mill or fulling mill", under the penalty of absolute forfeiture of lease.[124]

In addition to Israel Thompson's gristmill and Mahlon Janney's mill lot and sawmill, there were a few other commercial water powered mills operating at the time on the Branches of Catoctin Creek, at the time. About one mile and a half upstream from the mouth of Catoctin Creek on the Potomac River there was a mill under the control of William Kirk.[125] Within about a mile away from there was a gristmill belonging to Richard Roach, a blacksmith by trade.[126] George Gregg had a sawmill as well, on a secondary branch straddling the Catoctin Mountain.[127] Nearby to it were another mill and a store, which belonged to Farling Ball.[128] Additionally, John Hough possessed a mill dam somewhere near the mouth of either the Beaverdam Branch of Catoctin Creek or the North Fork of Catoctin Creek.[129] Off of the South Fork of Catoctin Creek there was another mill belonging to John Brown and others.[130] Far upstream on the North Fork of Catoctin Creek there was recorded "Buchers Mill" or John Butcher's mill, apparently, near the later village of Hillsborough or the Great Gap in the Short Hill.[131] Furthermore, there was at least a millseat on John Tayloe's Kittockton Land.[132] Lastly, in the vicinity of the Branches of Catoctin Creek there was John George's mill on the Dutchmans Run.[133] Also, there were nearby a host of other mills on the Goose Creek.

Perhaps the earliest improved mill seat on the Catoctin Creek had been originally on the property of Richard Brown, on or about the site of the later and contemporary William Kirk's mill, referred to above. But, the deed record indicates the earlier presence thereon of a Saml. Mayberry (Maxberry?).[134] Richard Brown was an early settler who had come to the region of the Greater Catoctin Creek to develop certain choice tracts of land acquired from the Proprietor's office, Thomas, Lord Fairfax. Upon the time of his premature death in 1745, he left to his third wife Mary (Norton) Brown, a portion of his land holdings together with the improvements including a house, millhouse, mill, millhouse, sawmill, brew-house, outhouses of all kinds and all the appurtenances to them.[135] A certain watermill would later become the property of their son, Mercer Brown, when he reached an age of majority.[136]

The Loudoun Valley was grassland producing edible grains such as wheat, oats, barley and corn. The cash crop grown in this country was wheat, which was generally manufactured into flour before being taken elsewhere to market. The permanent residents desired for themselves the utility provided by watermills so they organized commercial schemes to capitalize and to develop millseat locations. The sites were developed sometimes by a proprietor such as Israel Thompson, or in syndication by a group of investors such as John Brown and others. There was much economic activity manifest in the production of types of wheat flour, maize, and oatmeal. The mills were located either on a plantation or on a mill lot.

The Thompson Mill became the nucleus around which a small settlement clustered as his gristmill was a lucrative enterprise serving local farmers and traders known as a merchant mill. The merchant mill was a facility in the business of buying and storing wheat and manufacturing and merchandizing flour. The merchant miller bought wheat from farmers and manufactured flour on his own account, making a capital gain or loss on the sale of the goods. Wheat was and is and essential commodity. All other materials are of secondary importance to wheat and rye for making bread, for only those grains yield flours, which mixed with water forms a dough type capable of leavening.

As the owner of a gristmill, Israel Thompson would have probably employed an honest and diligent miller to operate his machinery. The miller attempted the manufacture of flour at an operation with machinery that used waterpower to create friction at the point of contact between two rolling millstones, to perform the grinding of grain. Flour is defined as fine, clean, sound product made by bolting wheat meal. The term is generic and covers a wide range of products. The miller provided types and grades of flour, each to a degree suitable for certain purposes.

Israel Thompson's oldest surviving son and one of the executors of his estate, Jonah Thompson, would take out on behalf of the estate, a mutual insurance policy for the gristmill and the miller's dwelling house in 1796, which he renewed in 1805, in his own name, covering against loss by fire the merchant mill and miller's dwelling house. The mill building was described therein as a building made of stone, two stories high, with a floor plan or footprint of 27 feet by 20 feet and a shingle roof. About fifty feet away from it was the miller's dwelling house with walls of stone and a roof of wood, with a footprint of 20 by 16 feet, in 1796. In 1805, the miller's dwelling house was described as a building with walls of stone and roof of wood, with a footprint of 17 by 13 feet. In 1796 the mill building was insured at $ 2,000 and the dwelling house at $ 500, against an aggregate replacement cost of $ 3,000.[137] In 1805 the merchant mill building was insured at $ 3,000 and the dwelling house at $ 500, against an aggregate replacement value of $ 4,000.[138] The mill's headrace may have been more than a mile long.[139] From Israel Thompson's final papers we know that at the time of his death, the mill was furnished with a bed and blanket.[140] The old Thompson Mill was razed in 1937 under the authority of the State Highway Department to make way for improvements to a nearby intersection of roads (Route 9 and Route 287).

There is in the deed record a contemporary account of the makings of a merchant or grist mill and dwelling house, cooper's shop, and the assignment of a sawmill, which was on a lot about six miles away from the Thompson Mill on the Northwest Fork of Goose Creek.[141] One Thomas Shepherd controlled a mill lot which he was going to improve and rent to William Nielson, for twenty years. It required Thomas Shepherd before a date certain, September 1, 1772, "(to) fitt up and complete in a good workmanlike manner another pair of grinding stones three feet nine inches the diameter, double geared and properly and completely finished for use by the said time." What's more, "(to) provide, finish of, complete and fitt up another Bolting cloath and Bolting chest suitable for merchant work which shall go and work by Water only, and shall also make fit up and complete by the said time Hoisting gears to and for said Mill in the usual and customary manner, and shall also finish and compleat a stone chimney to and for the use of the said Mill. Also, "(to) have the said mill house well and completely fitted in with clay, and also have the floors of the said mill house laid well and close with good seasoned plank." Furthermore, "fix up two good and sufficient girders in the said Mill below, and also two other good and sufficient girders above with pillars strong enough to support the floors of the house, and also will have another Door cut in a proper place in the said Mill and finished off in a workman like manner."

Thomas Shepherd was obligated by the same date to build in a workmanlike manner a framed house, "which shall be twenty eight feet by fourteen feet in the clear, well weather boarded and tight roofed as also a cellar under the said House seven feet high well and sufficiently wall'd up, and shall also make a Division of the floor above with good seasoned plank wrought up in the common form, and shall also build and erect a good and sufficient chimney of stone to one of the rooms and also run up a small stairs to the floor above, and also finish of Doors and glass windows to the said House according to William Nielson's Directions." It was further agreed that he shall build a cooper's shop with logs twelve feet square with a fireplace.

Thomas Shepherd was to finish the landscape as well. He was, "(to) make and finish of both the Dam and Race to the said Water Grist or Merchant Mill, tight, close and in good order, and have the flood Gate of the same in good and sufficient order and condition, and also have and make the Race to the merchant or Grist Mill five feet wide from the Dam to the said Mill." Additionally, Thomas Shepherd was obliged to assign the sawmill to William Nielson, which was then, "standing on the premises together with all her gears, wheels, saws and appurtenances thereunto belonging."

In the neighborhood of Israel Thompson's grist or the merchant mill there was a storehouse, which Israel Thompson was licensed to operate.[142] Typically, country storekeepers were the only convenient retailer within a radius of a few miles. They provided critical financial services for the local economy by sometimes extending credit on account and or accepting payment in kind while in the process of conducting trade on items such as salt, spices, textile goods, hardware goods, general household goods, food and liquor. Convenient credit terms were made available to increase profit margins while serving to attract customers and to hold accounts. Rural retailers who were themselves local farmers became indispensable purveyors of goods to homes, centralizers of small farm surpluses that were subsequently sent to Alexandria for sale or export, and often the rural community's bankers.

Israel Thompson was the master as well of a sawmill plant, either on or off of the North Fork of Catoctin Creek. It was a structure where lumber was machine-cut into finished goods. There was a certain voucher of one David Johnston's in Israel Thompson's final papers, where he made a reference to the "sawmill dam", thereby establishing it to have been a watermill. Such a sawmill would have contained machinery consisting of a carriage with a long blade attached to a frame that moved in reciprocating motion when turned by gears attached to a waterwheel.[143]

There were other vouchers running from 1788 to 1792 that document the operations of the sawmill plant under the direction of Joseph Thompson for Israel Thompson. The entries on the voucher represent a sample of the sort of work they were turning out. They regularly manufactured one-inch thick boards of wood. They produced a small piece of timber used in frame construction called scantling. They made thin strips of wood as a supporting structure for plaster called lath. They made timber beams for pitched roofs called rafters. They made timber beams for ceilings called joists. They constructed lintel to make windows and doors. They sawed thick planks for a wagon, and so on. Israel Thompson's sawmill was an establishment for the sawing of lumber into timber products.[144]

Israel Thompson maintained an account with Robert Yates who was a wheelwright or carpenter, apparently. He manufactured finished goods on Israel Thompson's behalf in addition to doing other odd jobs as there were documented voucher charges of his against Israel Thompson's estate, running from 1791 to 1794. He was a versatile artisan who manufactured various moving parts for vehicles including a bolster, shafts, axletrees, wagon-tongues, and nuts. He charged Israel Thompson's Estate for riming a wheel and putting in two spokes, and for mending a wagon wheel, mending a sleigh, and putting in new cogs in the rack. He was a building contractor who charged Israel for making a four-light sash window and a manteltree. He laid a floor on one occasion and laid plank on another. He mended a forebay it would seem, for a Pennsylvania style barn. Also, he'd charged Israel Thompson for manufacturing practical objects such as a shovel-plow and cradle or cradling scythe.[145]

Additionally, Robert Yates involved himself in the tanyard business as he charged Israel Thompson for the making and minding of "tann Fates", in other words, a solution for soaking hide or skin. He had sold Israel Thompson a hide weighing forty-four pounds and another calf skin weighing eight and three quarter pounds. Apparently, he farmed as well as there was a charge for ten bushels of wheat. Otherwise, he charged Israel for time spent working at his store, mill, and at his west-gate.[146]

On a larger scale the development of Israel Thompson's home plantation including the Thompson Mill was driven by macroeconomic forces bending the commerce of the Potomac River Valley towards wheat. The dynamic growth in demand for wheat in the West Indies, Great Britain, and Continental Europe raised wheat and flour prices, which pushed husbandmen into markets that stretched from the farm to the miller who bolted the wheat, and then from the miller to a network of import-export merchants in the port town of Alexandria. Much of the grain came from lands that were better suited for the cultivation of wheat than for tobacco. The trade in wheat and flour increased in volume year after year until by 1766 they had superseded tobacco as Alexandria's most important exports.[147]

Exporters welcomed the shift toward grain and flour exporting to coastal markets and Caribbean ports in the next decades. External demand for the Colony's provisions fueled their confidence, as did the prospects of shipping clothing, foodstuffs, work animals, implements, staves, beeswax, pork, beef, butter, candles, and tanned hides in exchange for coin, sugar, slaves, and staples. Once merchants established linkages to correspondents who could offer slaves in return for exports, they acquired a steady stream of seasoned labor as partial payment for cargoes. A greater emphasis on West Indian markets would not only benefit town merchants but also the agricultural producers.

It was the ambition of some producers to cultivate larger portions of their field in exportable commodities. Given good soil and weather, fourteen or sixteen acres might yield one hundred and sixty to one hundred and eighty bushels of wheat a year, about ninety of which were necessary to help feed a family, servants, and slaves of ten. Some of the remainder might be used in the web of local labor and commodities exchanges over the off season, while the residual might be available for export. Indeed, hundreds of families in Northern Virginia produced thousands of bushels of wheat by the 1760's. The staple commodity of western Loudoun County was wheat and flour which was sent to all parts of the West Indies.

Wheat was a particularly important crop in the Piedmont Region of Virginia. The exacting adaptation of wheat to a given soil was accomplished over generations of time through a variety of strains of spring and winter wheat. Generally, consumers preferred using wheat flour to meal and willingly paid a premium for its more agreeable flavor. At the time wheat yielded from 5 to 12 bushels per acre.[148] Once the grain ripened it had to be cut quickly at the risk of spoilage in the field so labor resources were of critical importance. The significance of the crop colored the thinking of human society and its activities and centers of production such as Israel Thompson's home plantation and the Thompson Mill would acquire characteristic names like Wheatland.

The Thompson mill on Israel Thompson's home plantation was a merchant mill and Israel Thompson was a merchant miller and planter or farmer (husbandman). The farmer would sell their grain to the mill owner at set prices, expecting the merchant miller to bolt it and market flour as his own commodity, often by collaborating with Alexandria exporters to keep up the quality of barreled flour and to regularize the flow of exports into the port. In fact, some town merchants were connected to merchant millers by birth or marriage, and established a well-integrated business for securing supplies of grain, controlling the grinding and barreling of flour, and arranging for its transport and sale in distant places.

In addition to wheat, Israel Thompson also would have planted and cultivated crops of corn, barley, oats, buckwheat, rye, flax, hemp, and some tobacco. The chief grain crop was Indian corn or maize as it was highly adaptable and a hardy plant that was resistant to the diseases that affected wheat. Also, garden vegetables would have been planted for food including cabbages, turnips, asparagus, cauliflower, peas, onions, carrots, beets, spinach, leeks, endive, sweet potatoes and some herbs such as parsley and dill. Additionally, planted for food were potatoes, watermelon and pumpkins, beans and other squashes too. Acreage would also have been devoted to orchards of apple and peach trees for consumption of fruit or for cider and brandy. Lastly, a residual share of the lands was usually set aside as a forest reserve for the use of future generations.

Israel Thompson's final estate contained a number of different tools used for the clearing of land and for farming and gardening. He owned 9 axes and 1 iron wedge to remove trees from the surface of the earth and to split them, 5 plows including 2 shovel-plows and 2 bar-share plows, 1 harrow with eleven teeth, 1 grubbing hoe, 2 weeding hoes, 1 spade, 1 shovel, 1 wheat-fan, 1 cradling scythe, 1 hay-fork, 1 dung-fork, 1 crank pitchfork, 1 wheelbarrow, 4 trowels, 9 bags, 1 hedge knife, and other tools of agriculture. Also, Israel owned two empty hogsheads and numerous barrels as well as a cooper's adz. Tenant farmers would have also worked his lands as well, with their own tools.

Chapter 4

One of the items in Israel Thompson's final papers was an original letter penned by Israel Thompson, son of Israel and Ann (9/9/1755-12/1/1766), to his grandfather and aunt, Edward Thompson and Prudence (Thompson) Woodward, dated on March 30, 1766. Apparently, Israel had kept it in remembrance to the love and affection he felt towards his firstborn as well as towards his father, and sister. The letter is an interesting study in many ways including his son's use of the language of the Society of Friends.

"*March the thirty 1766, Dear Encient (sic) Grandfather, I take this opportunity by Aunt Prudence to let thee know by a line that we are all in prity good health and we have got another grandson for thee so old that I have learned to write and spell such as I here presenteth thee with (,) and made my first letters two weeks after (.) My brother(,) Samuel Thompson(,) made his first appearance in this inconstant world which may perhaps appear as if it was almost two long for thee to stay a way(,) an my father and mother(.) And I myself do wish that thou would visit us. I am thy Dear Grandson (,) Israel Thompson.*"[149]

Young Israel Thompson's use of *thee* and *thou* as the standard second-person pronoun had been customary among Quakers of the Delaware River Valley and the tradition was continued in the Loudoun Valley. It's interesting to note that even though he'd only recently learned how to write and spell, nevertheless, he was sophisticated enough to make an allusion to the uncertainty of the temporal world. His pointed commentary was made in perspective to the recent birth of his little brother, Samuel Thompson. But, the manners and customs of Quakers would not remain entirely static in Virginia. As time passed, the speech ways of Quakers came to wear away against the constant friction with the more commonplace dialects of Northern Virginia.

Ann or "Nancey" Thompson, Israel Thompson's wife, departed the natural world on November 12, 1772, after six weeks of sickness. Israel wrote that during her last three weeks of life, she endured a fever and a cough and she suffered from pain as she screamed so violently that she could scarcely get any rest. He noted that she retained her good senses and was almost insistent in prayer, not only for her own sake but on behalf of her children, especially her first two, Joseph and Ann Richardson. Five children were born to the union of Ann and Israel Thompson including Israel (b. 9/9/1755: d. 12/1/1766), Jonah (b. 3/14/1758: d. 1/21/1834), Mary (b. 3/21/1761: d. 3/28/1761), Edward (b. 3/18/1762: d. 3/25/1762), and Samuel (b. 1/8/1766: d. circa 1796). Moreover, they had adopted a child cousin and orphan girl named Ann Sheane (Shinn, Shene).[150]

By even the standards of the age the rate of mortality in the Thompson household was high. According to David Hackett Fischer, the Quaker attitude towards death might be described as optimistic fatalism, in other words, they regarded the event of death with confidant expectation as the climax of life and thus to be embraced.[151] Quakers often dreamed about death and published their dreams in journals as is evidenced by Israel's possession of a publication entitled, *Young's Night Thoughts*. In his own hand, in *Births and deaths of my children with some remarks*, Israel Thompson recalled an elaborate death fantasy of his son's, Jonah Thompson, featuring his late brother, Israel Thompson, which in the usual manner of such dreams included an initial feeling of revulsion towards death turned into a glorification of the same. Israel Thompson wrote that man should not repine the occurrence of death, that is to say, to be discontented or in low spirits; rather, it should be considered as a providential event.[152]

Israel Thompson would live as a single man for a period of five years seven months and twenty-three days, as he put it in *Births and deaths of my children with some remarks*.[153] On July 2, 1778, Israel Thompson and Sarah Hague, the daughter of Francis and Jane Hague, took each other in marriage. The wedding took place under the care of the Fairfax Monthly Meeting. The event was formally witnesses by six people with the sir name of Hague, five were named Janney, four were named Schooley, three were named Hough, three were named Howell, one was named Mathews, one was named Williams, one was named Baker, as well as Israel and the late Ann's oldest surviving son, Jonah Thompson, who was then nineteen years old, and their adopted daughter, Ann Sheane. The witnesses to the wedding event included some of the leading members associated with the Fairfax Monthly Meeting.[154]

Before his second marriage occurred, Israel Thompson had negotiated with the father of the bride to be, Francis Hague, for a marriage contract which bound Israel Thompson's estate should he happen to predecease Sarah, to indemnify her with a £600 settlement.[155] The courts recognized such settlements between prospective partners much as what we refer to in our time as a prenuptial agreement.[156] Such settlements allowed married women full or partial managerial control over their property. Israel's second matrimonial union with Sarah (Hague) Thompson would result in the birth of six offspring. They were in order of their birth, Ann or "Nancy" (b. 6/16/1779: d. circa 1811), Elizabeth or "Betsey" (b. 9/28/1780), Israel (b. 4/1/1782: d. 6/24/1783), Israel H. (b. 1/9/1784: d. circa 1806), and the twins, Sarah W. or "Sally" (b. 3/5/1786: d. circa 1807) and Pleasant (b. 3/5/1786). It's interesting to note in review that Israel Thompson through two marriages named three sons seemingly after himself, Israel.[157]

On September 1, 1779, Israel and the late Ann Thompson's adopted daughter, Ann Sheane, and Samuel Canby, took each other in marriage under the care of the Fairfax Monthly Meeting. There were seven Thompson family members who formally witnessed the wedding including Israel Thompson and sons, Jonah Thompson and Samuel Thompson. Also, his brother was there, Isaac Thompson, with his children, seemingly, Isaac Thompson Jr., Joseph Thompson, and Sarah Thompson Jr. Among the witnesses were nine people named Hough, six people named Hague, six people named Janney, three people named Wildman, two people named Myers, and thirteen others.

Before the French and Indian War there were very few wagons of any kind light enough for horses to draw. To match with the unevenness of the surface of the earth both oxen and a small hardy breed of horses raised and trained exclusively for the saddle called pacers were in steady use. With the steady improvement of the roads there came simultaneously the need for wagons and harness horses for teaming. By 1768 Israel Thompson had come to acquire one wagon with hind gears and one bay horse neither branded nor docked called "Buck", and one roan mare branded on or near the buttocks with the letter "H", in consideration of the sum of £ 20:19:1.[158]

It was a governmental interest that roads be established and maintained leading to mills. During the second half of the 18th Century, the old roads were improved and new roads were established, which evolved into a transportation network as the spokes of a wheel around Israel Thompson's home plantation. People of all types valued the utility provided by an efficient system of transportation and they paid for it in the form of levies and personal service. Israel Thompson's home plantation would become a trading post of a sort on the old Vestal's Gap Road, later known as the Key's Gap Turnpike Road (Keyes Gap Road).

Israel Thompson had the capacity through the conveyance of goods by wagon to both deliver and to receive in return, a relatively high volume of goods. The flour that he mostly dealt in was the ideal portable mercantile good as it was light, dense, and easily packaged. At the time of the settlement of Israel Thompson deceased, his single most valuable personal property item was a lot comprising a mounted wagon with four horses and harness, which was purchased at his crying sale for £ 110:10: 0 by Col. Thomas Respass. Also, he had an old wagon which sold for 81 shillings and another wagon with only three wheels which sold for 71 shillings, and a cart which sold for 101 shillings. Additionally, his estate possessed three sets of gears, old wagon wheels, one and one half set of wagon boxes, other boxes, trunks, and ten casks.[159]

The trade in goods reached near and far from Israel Thompson's post in the Blue Ridge Uplands. In fact, it stretched all the way from the ports on the Atlantic Coastal Seaboard all the way to the Ohio River Valley. In the 1775-1780 Minute Book of the Virginia Court held for Yohogania County (Washington, PA) was recorded the business affairs related to the County's supply of salt. It was noted at the time that the salt was lodged with one "Israel Thompson of Louden County" and it was "Ordered that Benj. Kuykendal Esq. be authorized to have the Publick Salt now lying at Israel Thompsons in Lowden County brought up on the same principals".[160]

Engaging in a high volume of commercial trade had the potential to lead to differences and ultimately to litigation of some kind. In 1788 the administrators of the late Jacob Hite brought action against Israel Thompson in a Chancery Suit filed in Loudoun County. This matter concerned differences in the accounting for an old bill of exchange running from 1769 to 1770 totaling the hefty sum of nearly 340 pounds. Apparently, Israel Thompson was grinding wheat into flour and then delivering wagon loads of flour to Alexandria in consideration of finished goods in return, including 477 gallons of Barbados rum, 88 gallons of New England rum, 4 barrels of tar, 3 barrels of oil, 15 gallons of cordial liqueur, 1 fagot of steel, one dozen of Boston's best scythes, 2 other scythes, 1 hogshead of molasses, 1 hogshead of muscovado sugar, one dozen boxes of sugar, two dozen pails, and 3 more pails with covers, 3 piggins, 7 barrels of rye, 28 bushels of bran, and new shoes. As it turned out there was a finding for the plaintiff in this case in the amount of six pounds and fourteen shillings current money damages.[161]

On his landed estate Israel Thompson would have put up fences and built gates to enclose his lands to protect livestock and define boundary lines. The swine were normally allowed to run freely and forage for themselves. Israel Thompson would have cultivated meadows with different varieties of English grasses and clovers for the pasturage of livestock. The presence of livestock offered nearly every kind of utility as they were used in countless ways. Animals were put to work and used for traveling and transportation, plowing, hauling, nourishment, insulation and so on. They allowed for the consumption of meat and the intake of dairy products including milk, butter and cheese, which were kept in a springhouse to forestall spoilage. Animals of various kinds provided hides, skins, pelts, bone, wool and feathers for insulation from the cold and specialty purposes. At the time of his decease, Israel Thompson's estate was appraised to include 36 sheep; 14 ewes and lambs; at least 43 swine including 33 pigs and 4 sows, 1 sow & young pigs, 4 shoats, and 1 fat boar; 21 bovine including 10 calves and 5 cows, 4 heifers, 1 steer, and 1 bull; 16 equine including 6 colts and a one-half share interest in a stud horse called "High Flyer"; and 35 geese.[162]

It should be noted that livestock and the other items included in the appraisal of his personal property are not a perfect match with the items which sold at Israel Thompson's estate crying sale. It appears that his inventory suffered some shrinkage along the way, especially from his list of livestock. The single most valuable animal was a stud horse named "High Flyer" valued at fifty pounds in which he owned a half interest. The account sales reveal that Ferdinando Fairfax purchased at the crying sale, one equine and four bovine including 1 bay mare @ £ 12: 7: 0, 1 cow & calf @ £ 8:10: 0, 1 cow at £ 8: 0: 0, and a young bull @ £ 7:15: 0. Among the other equine was a bay mare named "Trimsharp" sold for eighteen pounds, while another bay mare sold for only three pounds, and a certain black mare sold for twelve pounds. There were five colts listed in the account sales which sold for between nine pounds and sixteen pounds for each. Among the other bovine there were six other lots of cow & calf which sold for between six pounds/twelve shillings and seven pounds/eight shillings for each lot. There were three cows which sold at an amount of money between five pounds/eleven shillings and eight pounds for each lot. Also, there were two heifers, one which sold at 65 shillings (£ 3: 5: 0), and the other at four pounds/eight shillings. There were two lots of two calves, each which sold for seventy-three shillings. There was a young bull which sold for seven pounds/fifteen shillings and, also, a red steer which sold for ninety-one shillings.

Additionally in the mix of account sales there were three lots of six sheep, which sold for between forty-three shillings and eighty shillings for each lot. There were two lots of six ewes & lambs, which sold for forty-nine and ninety-two shillings respectively. One hog sold for thirty shilling and a lot of two hogs sold for twenty-four shillings. A lot of one sow and three pigs sold for one pound/seven shillings, whereas another lot of one sow and four shoats sold for one pound/seventeen shillings. A separate lot including a sow and pigs sold for twenty-five shillings. And, there were some young shoats too, which sold at an unknown amount.

There is an old record in the minutes of a County Court Order Book dated in 1779, wherein James McIlhaney returned a certificate as a witness for Israel Thompson whereby he made a formal claim of legal custody over stray groups of livestock he had taken up. One lot was described as ten barrows and one sow, almost all of them a little sandy with black spots and marked with a large half penny in the right ear, supposed to be about two years old, and valued at six pounds and six shillings and six pence for the whole in gold or silver by weight or if in bills at the current rate of exchange. And, another lot containing two barrows and three sows, one of which had nine small pigs, which were described as of a light blue color and marked with a hole in the left ear and a small bit out of the under side of the right ear, and valued at one pound and eight shillings and nine pence for the whole as above. Also, two white ewes marked with a crop off the right ear and a swallow-fork in the left ear and valued at sixteen shillings for the whole as above.[163]

There would have been few idle hands on Israel Thompson's home plantation as home industry thrived. Some of the many concerns of a country business included gardening, marketing, making straw-works, combing, carding, spinning, knitting, sewing and needlework. Instruction and encouragement were provided beginning in youth so household members could be put to work spinning wool and flax, sewing, knitting and needlework. The planter and his servants and slaves raised wool and flax in the outdoors and his wife and children as well as the old and infirm labored to spin it into thread and yarn in the indoors. The art of spinning was a practical and dependable occupation, which afforded many folk a ready and honorable means to earn a living.

On Israel Thompson's home plantation the culture of flax was encouraged. Flax is a widely cultivated plant species with seeds which yield linseed oil, and slender stems from which a fine, light colored textile fiber is obtained. After the flax plants had been pulled and spread the product was put through a long and laborious process before the flax was ready for the spinner's wheel.

The manufacturing equipment for flax included little wheels or spinning wheels for spinning the flax thread for homespun linen, and a separate device called a clock-reel for counting the exact number of strands in a knot that ticked when the requisite number had been wound. These skeins of thread then had to be bleached. The spinning and weaving of flax was a perpetual means of providing cloth for domestic use and to earn an income from weavers with ready money for piecework. Israel's final estate included a clock-reel, two little wheels, two hatchels, and 4 lbs. of flax.[164]

Likewise, encouragement was given to the raising of sheep and the culture of domestic wool manufacture on Israel Thompson's home plantation. The wool industry easily furnished home occupation to many in the household converting the dense and soft hair forming the coat of sheep into a textile fabric for use as a yarn for knitting or as a woven material or broadcloth. The process of manufacture was tedious work that took many weeks and months from the time the fleece was shorn from a sheep. Then commenced the work of the spinsters, which was a highly skilled labor requiring great flexibility and alertness of mind. The capital equipment required for wool production included the big or great wheel for spinning and a host of ancillary furnishings including the reel and wool-card, niddy-noddy, spindles and so on. Israel Thompson's final estate included a large flock of sheep and an additional "long wheel" spinning wheel for making woolen yarn, one card, combs and files, and a mill spindle.[165]

As time would pass Israel Thompson accumulated income from his operations and his balance sheet came to show a surplus of equity, which enabled him to speculate in real estate. He engaged himself in acquiring several patents in his name for lands on the waters of the Monongahela River, some of it taken in a partnership with Joseph Smith. Also, Israel Thompson owned rights to a vast acreage of land in the District of Kentucky in association with Isaac Hite Junior, Leven Powell, and Burr Powell. Additionally, Israel Thompson was an investor in General George Washington's Potowmack Canal scheme of navigation as he subscribed to one share of its stock.[166] The enterprise was chartered in 1785 to build a canal which would bring goods from the Shenandoah Valley and the Potomac River Valley to the ports of the Tidewater Region. His son, Jonah Thompson would later come to inherit the share of stock, which was valued at the time at £ 160.[167]

It is interesting to note that General George Washington stopped at Israel Thompson's home plantation on September 2, 1784, during his journey to the Ohio River Valley in the interest of promoting a commercial union between the Great Lakes Region and the Potomac River Valley Region. General Washington noted in his diary that he and his party had arrived in Leesburg by 11:00 a.m. and dined before proceeding to Israel Thompson's for lodging.[168] There is no record that Israel Thompson's place of domicile was ever a licensed tavern per se as some have surmised; rather, it was merely a relatively comfortable backwoods trading post on an important wagon road where one could lodge in the course of conducting business or traveling.

General George Washington would have known that Israel Thompson was a patriot and appreciated the service he gave to his country during the American Revolution. The extent of his involvement is unclear but it is known that he took an oath of allegiance to the United States which cost him his good standing with the Society of Friends. As a consequence of that act he was disowned by his church. It had happened to him before as well, on another occasion for paying "priest's fines" or tithes.[169] It's possible that Israel Thompson's home plantation was utilized by the militia before marching into service during the Revolutionary War under Capt. James Rateken, possibly, based on a reading of entries made for 1781 in the record of Cameron Parish Tithing.[170] After the War, Israel Thompson filed a claim for damages he had suffered as a consequence of the support he lent to the war effort including a charge for personal property taken for the militia marching into actual service and never recovered.[171]

The oldest published reference known to the author of the nearby neighborhood of "Waterford", specifically, as such, comes from an advertisement in The Virginia Journal and Alexandria

Advertiser. It was a public notice to attract attention to a reward offered for the return of two runaway apprentice lads from James Moore and John Coffee, dated Waterford, Loudoun County, January 1, 1787.[172] The site was the residence of Thomas Moore (Senior), an Irish Quaker, who had come to America and settled first in Pennsylvania, afterwards removed to Loudoun County, Virginia, where he built a residence and called the place "Waterford", after his native home.[173]

The land on or about Waterford would come to be promoted by real estate developers including Joseph Janney and at least three of Thomas Moore's (Senior) children, Thomas Moore (Junior), James Moore, and Asa Moore, as a village or small town named Waterford on the South Fork of Catoctin Creek. Houses were to be built in small clusters, which would become became the nucleus of a rural neighborhood. The spatial organization of Waterford quite self consciously facilitated the regimen of "watchfulness" to which Quakers committed themselves. The countryside would remain open whereas Waterford would be a secure and regulated environment. The plan was to combine physical autonomy with a spiritual community in the immediate vicinity of the Fairfax Monthly Meeting of the Society of Friends.

The Waterford site was well suited to accommodate growth. There was an ample supply of accessible soft water and the soil was considered first rate for the production of grain. Moreover, there was enough of a current in the South Fork of Catoctin Creek and other secondary bodies of running water in the immediate vicinity to power water suit mills and other light industrial concerns. On March 24, 1789, the following advertisement appeared in the Virginia Journal and Alexandria Advertiser: *"Rolling screens, and all kinds of Fan Riddles, Shaking Screens, & c. Made and Sold by the Subscriber on the shortest notice; who having served a regular apprenticeship to the Wire weaving business, with one of the most noted workmen in the United States, flatters himself that those who please to favor him with their orders, will find them as well executed as they could have been in Philadelphia, and at a lower price that they can be delivered in Alexandria from thence. William Paxson, Waterford, Loudoun County."*[174]

Although Israel Thompson was a devout Quaker in fact, word, and deed, nevertheless, it is reasonable to conclude that he held conflicting feelings or thoughts about his denomination. In a time of evangelism, superstition and irrational religion, his mind was relatively free and unfettered, and it was the rational tone of his thoughts that enabled him to prosper. In fact, in 1792 he asked for the permission of the Fairfax Monthly Meeting in order to sue at law a fellow Quaker, James Dillon, for payment of a note receivable. Also, the records of the Anglican Church's Shelburne Parish Vestry show Israel Thompson to have been a regular contributor per levy to the same quantified in pounds of tobacco. The high rate of payments he made was a reflection of the law and his relative wealth, as well as of his close attention to public service and his devotion to the churchwardens, among them friends such as Leven Powell, Francis Peyton, Joshua Gore and others.[175]

The fact that a man of eminence and material wealth such as General George Washington would have happened to have stayed at Israel Thompson's home plantation informs us by association that he must have found the place including the buildings, structures, and objects thereon, to have been at the least, safe, convenient, and accommodating. Israel and Sarah Thompson would have welcomed him with warmth and generosity, and at the same time to have been submissive, courteous and yielding to his judgment. There was on Israel Thompson's home plantation usually plenty of food and ready access to clean water. When it was cold there would have been warm fires burning and being attended to in the interior of the buildings. Israel Thompson deceased's estate would own a hearth brush, 4 pair of andirons, 4 trammels, 2 shovel and tongs, 1 tongs, and one bellows.

There is empirical evidence to suggest that Israel Thompson's place was a welcome respite for friends or travelers. The most valuable furniture on his home plantation based on both an appraisal of his final personal estate as well as the sale of the subject items, were his beds and bedsteads. Israel Thompson deceased owned 6 sacking bottom bedsteads and furniture which sold between fourteen and sixteen pounds for each. Also, he owned 7 feather beds and furniture which sold between nine pounds ten shillings and fifteen shillings for each. Additionally, he possessed one sacking bottom bedstead which sold for 30 shillings, two bedsteads and boards which sold for 10 and 12 shillings respectively, one low pair of bedsteads which sold for 12 shillings, and several under-beds.[177]

One of the books in Israel Thompson's library at the time of his death was, *The Farmer's Wife or The Complete Country Housewife*, which according to the publisher included instructions on how to live the happy country life. The country housewife of the Period was in charge of a wide range of indoor and outdoor duties considered useful in accommodating family members to surroundings or an environment. It was not uncommon for women and girls to be in charge of breeding and managing turkeys, geese, ducks, pigeons and fowls. Also, they worked on fattening hogs, pickling of pork, cutting of bacon and making sausages. They learned methods of making ciders and brandy and pickling various kinds of fruits. They attended to the dairy and learned ways of making butter, cream and cottage cheese. It was not uncommon for members of the female sex to learn instructions how to brew beer and ale. The attention of women and girls was also directed towards the management of bees and the uses of honey.

The kitchen or kitchens on Israel Thompson's home plantation were buildings or structures that were separated from the mansion house or living quarters as a guard against the risk of fire. The evidence suggests they were modern and very well equipped for the service of family and guests. Israel Thompson deceased owned a six-plate stove and pipes which sold for £ 3: 6: 0 as well as another six-plate stove that sold for 31 shillings, 2 bake iron, 3 dutch-ovens, and 1 dutch-oven and fat pot. The kitchen contained 2 kettles, 4 brass kettles, 1 iron kettle, 2 tea kettles, 3 tea pots, 2 tin coffee pots, 1 coffee mill, 2 pots, 11 iron pots, 2 frying pans, 1 copper stew pan, 1 tin colander, 1 dough trough, 1 cream jug, 1 churn, 1 large tub, 12 cider tubs, 3 funnels, 1 ½-gallon bottles, 1 keg, 2 bread trays, and 1 rat trap. Apparently, the Thompson family members and hands were ready and prepared to serve many folk simultaneously as his estate would include 3 decanters, 2 large tumblers, 1 pewter tankard, 16 plates, 23 pewter plates, 4 dishes, 4 pewter dishes, 1 dish and plates, a set of queen's china, 7 cups and 1 mug, 3 tea canisters, 1 canister, a set of coasters, 1 lot of jugs, and two japanned waiters. The interior space was organized with a pot rack, pot hooks, knife box, spice box, salts, candle box, and a cutting knife with box. Israel Thompson had kept his valuable sugar in a stylish japanned sugar cabinet and served it in a sugar-glass. Also, he had 3 snuff bottles and 5 snuffers to indulge in the inhalation of pulverized tobacco. At the time of his death, Israel Thompson's estate was provisioned with bran and shorts, 16 lbs. of rice, 200 weight sugars, 8 bushels of lime, 5 bushels of corn, 12 bushels of buckwheat, beeswax, salt, and two bushels of dried apples.[178]

Additionally, there was a host of household goods made of silver. Israel Thompson owned 6 tablespoons and 6 teaspoons marked "IST", apparently, for Israel Thompson. He owned 6 tablespoons and 6 teaspoons marked "ST", apparently, for Samuel Thompson. He owned 2 tablespoons marked "WR", apparently, for William Richardson. There were 6 more silver teaspoons, 2 silver tablespoons, silver soup ladle, and silver tea tongs.[179]

In his final papers Israel Thompson referred to his place of residency at the time as his mansion house[180]. A mansion house was a dwelling house or the primary residence of the landowner. The term was rarely used to distinguish a building of large size and good appearance.[181] His mansion house and other houses were generously furnished, apparently. In addition to the before mentioned desks and beds and furniture, Israel Thompson's estate owned the following pieces of furniture in descending order of their value according to sale price. The most valuable furniture item he had owned was an 18-day clock and case worth £ 15: 0: 0 (300 shillings). Otherwise, he had owned a set of drawers which sold @ 120 shillings, floor carpet @ 110 shillings, set of drawers @ 95 shillings, set of drawers @ 93 shillings, set of drawers @ 86 shillings/6 pence, table and cloth @ 60 shillings, walnut table @ 42 shillings, table and cover @ 41 shillings, table and cover @ 40 shillings/6 pence, 1 looking glass @ 36 shillings, 6 chairs and 1 armed chair @ 36 shillings, 1 dining table @ 31 shillings, 1 looking glass @ 31 shillings, 1 table @ 31 shillings, 1 oval tea table @ 30 shillings[182].

Also, Israel Thompson's estate was in possession of 1 table and 3 chairs @ 24 shillings, pair of stillards (?) @ 22 shillings, 1 looking glass @ 20 shillings, 1 large trunk @ 20 shillings, and 1 set of window curtains @ 20 shillings, 1 table @ 16 shillings/7 pence, 1 looking glass @ 12 shillings/6 pence, 4 chairs @ 12 shillings/3 pence, 1 large chair @ 12 shillings, 1 small trunk @ 12 shillings, 1 chest @ 12 shillings, 1 pair candlesticks @ 10 shillings, 1 arm chair @ 7 shillings, 1 looking glass @ 5 shillings, 1 box @ 3 shillings/4 pence, 1 box @ 1 shilling/6 pence, and 1 candlestick @ 1 shilling. He had spare hardware in the form of a chest lock which sold for £ 1: 9: 6, 1 chest lock @ 1 shilling/3 pence, and mountings for a desk.[183]

The usually oversimplified conception of a Quaker was a pacifist who went plain in the world. Israel Thompson's final papers are suggestive of the likelihood that he fancied to a degree going about in a higher style. He maintained an account from 1775 to 1795 with one Stephen Donaldson, apparently, a silversmith, which is very telling. The account should be considered with some caution however, as far as it may apply to Israel Thompson personally, as he may have been procuring the subject goods for clients. Israel Thompson regularly ordered silver goods such as sets of silver shoe buckles including some decorated with fluting, and sets of silver knee buckles as well. He ordered silver thimbles for sewing. During the time of the Revolutionary War he ordered two large size sword buckles and silos. Additionally, Israel Thompson had ordered a set of gold buttons, and other sets of semiprecious stone buttons. His apparel came to include a "great coat", which sold at his estate's crying sale for 15 shillings. He had owned at least five pair of expensive shoes, perhaps merchandize, which sold for between seven shillings and eight and a half shillings at his crying sale.[184] Additionally, Israel Thompson had owned an old smooth (bore) gun which sold at his estate's crying sale for 14 shillings/6 pence. His son, Samuel Thompson, had owned a gun, powder horn, and shot pouch, valued at one pounds/four shillings.[185]

Israel Thompson's final inventory of personal goods came to include an inordinately high volume of textile goods of many varieties comprising, apparently, much of his stock in trade at his licensed country dry-goods store. These garments included linen, striped linen, wool, cotton, velvet, sagathy, black velvet, nankeen, calico, florentine, jennet, silk, corded dimity, moreen, velvet, fustian, striped cloth, chintz, crape, ticking, kerseymere, mock kerseymere, wild boar, muslin, muslinet, tatternet, calamanco, durant, camlet, shaloon, mohair, fearnaught, corduroy, satinet, broadcloth, blue broadcloth, plaid broadcloth, green baize, blue half-thicks, buckram, everlasting, duffle, cambric. There were a large number of finished goods as well such as sheets, fine cotton sheets, homemade linen sheets, pillow cases, stockings, thread stockings, worsted stockings, hose, threaded hose, worsted hose, handkerchiefs, shawl handkerchiefs, checkered handkerchiefs, silk handkerchiefs, black silk handkerchiefs, gauze handkerchiefs, napkins, bed quilts, blue quilts, counterpanes, coverlets, blankets, duffel blankets, table cloths, coverlids, blue & white coverlids, saddlecloth, gloves, buttons, sundry buttons, metal buttons by the dozen, and 14 scissors.[186]

Quakers thought in terms of "redeeming the time", that is to say; they tried to purge time of sin and corruption. They recorded the passing of the months and days by purging every vestige of what they regarded as pagan corruption. Generally, the traditional names of months and days were abolished as "unscriptural".[187] Friends took a long view of their temporal condition and considered time to be much too important to be squandered in haste or waste. Hence, they sought precision in the management of their time. Apparently, Israel Thompson was obsessed with the notion of time. He had precisely calculated the time between his wives as a "single man" at five years seven months and twenty-three days and measured other aspects of his life with extraordinary exactness.[188] The most valuable piece of furniture he owned at the time of his death was a clock & case valued at fifteen pounds value. Also, he owned a day clock of modest value and a silver watch, which he left to his son, Israel H.[189] His second wife, Sarah Thompson, would own a gold watch valued at $ 65.00 in 1811.[190]

Israel Thompson was knowledgeable about building and construction, as well. He was an honest man with broad practical experience and training, who was distinguished in the hierarchy of his community at large and well suited to take on a large project supervising a diverse crew of journeymen, apprentices, and laborers. He served on behalf of the County Court in 1787 as a Commissioner along with Leven Powell, James M'shony, and John Littlejohn, in awarding a heavily advertised contract for an undertaker to take on the building of a new stone gaol in Leesburg.[191] Israel Thompson's final estate contained a large and varied number of tools including many especially suited for building and development including 2 mason trowels, 3 planes, 3 augers, 9 ½-inch augers, 1 lot of augers, 1 lot of awl blades, 2 files, 2 crowbars, 2 screwdrivers, 2 measuring reels, 5 ladders, 1 saw, 1 crosscut saw, 1 froe, 1 chisel, 1 gauge, 1 pumice stone, 1 grindstone, various size nails, and screws. Additionally, Israel Thompson deceased possessed blacksmith tools including 1smith's anvil, 1smith's vise, eleven pair of iron strap hinges, 1 hammer, 2 iron poles, 1 bar of steel, and a lot of old iron.[192]

The earliest permanent buildings and structures on Israel Thompson's home plantation were single cell and double cell structures built of squared logs that were dovetailed at the corners. The openings between the logs were filled in or "chinked". The roof was made of boards covered with shingles. A stone chimney and fireplace were built into the end of a one cell house, and into both ends of a two cell house. Although no such log buildings on his old home plantation have survived time, nonetheless, there are at least two such log cabins on John Wolford Road (Route 694) in the immediate vicinity including one of two cells, on adjacent lots neighboring the old home plantation.[193]

During the next generation of permanent building and development on Israel Thompson's home plantation, both single and multiple cell structures were built of dressed stone and rubble. Again, a stone chimney and fireplace was built into one end of a single cell building or were built into both ends of a double cell building. At least one chimney in a house would be of a larger size for cooking as well as heating. The buildings and structures or improvements were constructed for use rather than display with heavy fieldstone walls, shingle roof, and simple wood trim all combined in a plain style making efficient use of space and material. Although only one stone springhouse structure and relics of other buildings and structures on Israel Thompson's old home plantation have survived time, nonetheless, there are such stone buildings and structures in the neighborhood.[194] Those early buildings and structures resemble in style and construction the early prototypical buildings and structures of the Delaware River Valley.[195]

Before his demise in 1795, Israel Thompson had recently built for himself a replacement dwelling house or mansion house on his home plantation. In his time and place, Israel Thompson's latest mansion house was a little out of character from his neighbors' places of domicile as his mansion house was constructed out of brick, two and one half stories high on a stone foundation, with a gable roof. The interior of his house was fitted with what his appraisers referred to as a garret,[196] which was finished space designed and created for living and working immediately beneath the roof.[197] The floor plan or footprint of the foundation was 27 by 20 feet. There was attached to one gable end of the mansion house, a one-story brick kitchen with a footprint of 10 by 9 feet. Approximately one hundred and fifty feet away from the mansion house, was an impressive two story stone barn, apparently, a Pennsylvania style structure built into a bank with a forebay. This was a relatively large building used for storing grain, hay, and other farm products, and for sheltering livestock.[198] And, just fifteen feet way from the barn was a cowhouse. The cowhouse was a structure where cattle were sheltered.[199]

We may know the above about some of the improvements on Israel Thompson's home plantation from his final papers and from old insurance declarations that were made on some of the buildings and structures thereon. In 1796, Israel Thompson's estate insured the subject four buildings including the mansion house, kitchen, barn, and cowhouse, for $ 3,800 against a replacement cost of $ 3,800. At the time, Samuel Thompson was listed as the principal occupant.[200] In 1805, Jonah Thompson insured the subject four buildings in his own name for $ 4,000 against a replacement cost of $ 4,500. At the time, either a William Payton or Peyton was listed as the principal occupant.[201]

The supply of Labor was scarce and expensive during the Colonial Period and more so in the back woods. Vast landholdings were only of marginal value without the complementary human resources required to make them both habitable and potentially profitable. Nevertheless, there is empirical evidence to suggest that Israel Thompson did not go wanting. He utilized a potentially combustible combination of adults and children of both genders in subservient service to him as laborers and servants, and others in involuntary service to him as slave laborers. Over and above them he would have employed skilled workers on a contractual basis such as a journeyman and apprentice blacksmith, cooper, wheelwright, carpenter, miller, and tanner and so on.

The information and data in the Loudoun County Court Order Books reveals that Israel Thompson utilized the labor of apprentices, poor children, and bastards, in order to increase productivity. Children were indentured to a master until they reached an age of majority, males at the age of 21 and females at the age of 18. In some cases they were assigned to a master from another, such as in 1772 when Israel Thompson acquired the usage of Samuel Homan according to the terms of a former indenture.[202] In 1980, Israel Thompson took in an apprentice named Morgan Hoge to be a tanner.[203] A year later he took in John Saxton, about fifteen years old, to be a tanner and shoemaker.[204] And, in 1990 he took in a fourteen year old girl named Elizabeth Cammell (sic).[205] Two years later, apparently, Elizabeth Campbell was assigned to Samuel Gregg per agreement with Israel Thompson.[206] It seems that Jonah Thompson used the same labor resource in order to assist in manning the Potowmack (Company) in 1798, apparently.[207]

We may make inferences concerning the quantity and quality of Israel Thomson's labor resources based on the surviving records of tithing and records of personal property taxes paid, as well as from his final papers. A tithing was the act of levying a charge for the support of the parish vestry and was required for all resident white men over 16 years of age and all enslaved men and women over 16 years of age. Most of these records are available for examination from 1760 to 1769 in Cameron Parish, and from 1771 to 1781 in Shelburne Parish. Afterwards, instead, a statutory contribution for the support of the County Government was required based on one's inventory of personal assets.

The earliest records for tithing in 1760 reveals Israel Thompson himself and another resident white male, Nathan Burns, and three slaves in his possession, Peter, Sarah, and Minta, for a total of five tithes. The next year in addition to Israel Thompson there were two resident white males, Robert Bell and James McKemie, and the same three named slaves for a total of six tithes. By 1764, he was up to eight tithes including the same three named slaves. The entries for 1765 reveals Israel Thompson's plantation with five other white male residents and four slaves, Peter, Minta, John and Abraham, for a total of ten tithes. The volume of resident workers and slaves on his home plantation continued to increase until 1774, when it peaked at fifteen tithes including three slaves, Peter, Abraham, and Phillis. The advent of the Revolutionary War probably dampened business as by 1776; Israel Thompson was down to paying 10 tithes including two for slaves, Peter and Phillis. In 1778 Israel Thompson paid ten tithes including two representing his slaves, Abraham and Phillis. In 1780, he paid five tithes including one for his then adult son, Jonah Thompson, and none for slaves. The latest tithing entry in 1781 shows Israel Thompson covered payments for four tithes including one for his given son, and none for slaves.

The labor trend may be picked up again beginning in 1782 based on the Loudoun County personal property tax rolls, which required payment of a levy based on certain definitions for a white male resident worker, slaves, horses, cattle, 4-wheel stage coach, and for a stud horse.

Apparently, after the Revolutionary War business picked up again as the number of laborers increased and slaves reappeared on Israel Thompson's rolls. In 1782, the number of resident white males charged to Israel Thompson was three plus he was charged for 15 horses and 28 cattle for a total of 46 charges. The number of resident white males charged to Israel Thompson would increase in number up to 12 by 1788, and continued at a steady rate with 11 in 1792, and 9 in 1793. Likewise, the additional charges to Israel Thompson for livestock increased in number to 52 by 1784, and continued at a steady rate for the rest of his life. In 1788, Israel Thompson was charged a personal property tax levy for 27 horses plus a "4 wheel stage".[208]

It is interesting to note that there was a separate entry in 1782 for Israel Thompson's oldest living adult son, Jonah Thompson, then dwelling on Israel Thompson's home plantation. Jonah Thompson was charged a levy payment for himself plus three more for slaves, and two more for horses for a total of six charges. The next year, he was assessed a levy for possession of four slaves and three horses for a total of eight charges. The latest entry for Jonah Thompson in Loudoun County before he would permanently move to Alexandria was in 1787, and included charges against him for four slaves.[209] In fact, Jonah Thompson had come to acquire human chattel through his marriage to the former Margaret Peyton of Alexandria, Virginia.[210]

An early influence in the anti-slavery movement in the United States may be traced back to a pamphlet by John Woolman published in 1754, entitled *Consideration on Keeping Negroes: Recommended to the Professors of Christianity in Every Denomination*. The author was a Quaker spiritual leader who devoted much of his life's work to agitating against slavery. John went to a number of Quaker Meetings in Virginia to speak on the subject and even attended the Virginia Yearly Meeting for 1757, at Western Branch Meetinghouse. It's conceivable that the movement came to influence Israel Thompson in view of the fact that he manumitted some of his slaves as early as about 1770.[211] However, at the time of his death he was still in possession of two slaves, Will and Hannah.[212]

Israel Thompson's children may have been sympathetic to the movement for the termination of slavery and the slave trade, perhaps, susceptible to multiple interpretations. A daughter of his, Ann "Nancy" (Thompson) Griffith, died by 1811 while in possession of as she stated it in her last will and testament, "my Black Girl Beck Risby a slave".[213] In 1792, Jonah Thompson of Alexandria, District of Columbia, made a deed of manumission in Fairfax County of a slave named Sib, age 28.[214] About a year and a half later he made a similar deed of manumission in Fairfax County of a slave named Daniel, age 25.[215] On June 15, 1803, Jonah Thompson made a visit to the Courthouse in Leesburg, Loudoun County, to swear out an affidavit to the effect that certain children of his father's former slaves had been free born and were thereby rightfully due a numbered certificate of free Negro.[216] Likewise, Jonah's wife, Margaret Thompson, swore out at least four such affidavits during the second quarter of the 19th Century on behalf of freeborn people of color. However, she continued to own human chattel throughout her lifetime as she still possessed at least four slaves at the time of her death, by 1841.[217]

Israel Thompson's business was deal making and up to the end of his life he was immersed in merchandizing and trading in landed property including all inherent natural resources and improvements established thereon. Being that he was well connected, generally, and a leader amongst Friends, particularly, he found himself from time to time in advantageous situations. One of those resulted from the death of Joseph Yates in 1761. At the time, Yates held two lots of premium quality land on both banks of the South Fork of Catoctin Creek comprising a plantation named "Get". One lot was already surveyed of 165 acres of land whereas the other lot was not yet surveyed. The 165 acres lot of land had previously been assigned in 1745 to Joseph Yates of Fairfax County by William Janney of the same place, it being certain land the said Janney had leased under a lease for lives provision from William Fairfax, in 1744.[218] It was Joseph Yates's will that his surveyed lot be assigned to son Robert at age of majority, and his other lot that was not yet surveyed was to be assigned to other son Benjamin Yates, when he reached age of majority. Israel Thompson was named by the deceased as his executor along with his widow Alice Yates in the settling of the Joseph Yates estate.[219]

As time would come to pass Robert Yates grew to adulthood and took possession of his late father's plantation named "Get." It appears that he would come to be regularly employed as an artisan by Israel Thompson as is documented in his final papers, seemingly. In 1793 Robert Yates assigned his indenture of lease for the lot of land containing 165 acres of land to the then old and infirm Israel Thompson in consideration of the sum of £ 200 to him in hand.[220] According to the description of the same landed property in Israel Thompson's last will and testament, he received just as well a right or claim to the neighboring lot which had not yet been surveyed, as he specifically cited his possession of both of them.[221]

In his final years of life Israel Thompson was sick with a malady or maladies that would not be cured. There are vouchers in Israel Thompson's final papers for an account he maintained with Doctor James Heaton with a long list of entries running from January 27, 1791 to January 20, 1795. He served in attendance to Israel Thompson and his extended family and regularly carried on various services chargeable to Israel for everything from administering medicines to performing inoculations to other events of attendance, nocturnal attendance, and chirurgery (surgery). He charged 16 shillings for a "chyrurgical operation & attendance" on behalf of Jesse Woodward in 1791. During a busy spell in late November and early December of 1793, he attended to Elizabeth or "Betsy" who suffered from pox and inoculated the family against the same.[222]

Another doctor of medicine in Israel Thompson's service was Doctor James Channel. His voucher detailed charges from April 10, 1794 to January 7, 1795, for a series of regular visitations, special visitations per messenger, and visitations per request at 18 miles distance. He administered medicines to Israel Thompson including cathartic medicine, which was a purgative; vials of elixir, which was believed to have generalized curative or restorative powers; tincture thebaine, which is an alkaloid obtained from opium; vials of liquid laudanum, which is a tincture of opium. Today, thebaine is classified as a poison. The habitual use of laudanum or opium induces strong addiction and excessive use is fatal.[223]

Israel Thompson's final papers included vouchers from at least two other doctors of medicine. One of them was Doctor Edward Tiffin who charged his final estate for sundry medicines and events of attendance during the year 1794. The other voucher was a charge for medicines among various goods from Doctor John Nicklin of Waterford, dated 1794.[224] Additionally, Israel Thompson's final estate included nine gallons of a kind of spiced mead or medicinal alcoholic beverage made from fermented honey and water called metheglin.[225]

Israel Thompson died by January 27, 1795, for on that day his survivors put four shillings down with Henry Burkitt to making a walnut coffin with a lid valued at two pounds.[226] On February 9, 1795, the last will and testament and codicil of Israel Thompson deceased was proven by Mahlon Janney, Benjamin Purdum, and John Redmond (Redman), and ordered to be recorded. The executors named therein were William Hough, Jonah Thompson, Samuel Thompson, and Israel H. Thompson, but the later did not at the time qualify because he was a minor. It was ordered by the Court that John Nicklin, John McIlhaney, Benjamin Purdum, Asa Moore, and Charles Bennett Senior, or any three of them, do value and appraise in current money the personal estate of Israel Thompson deceased and make a return of the same to the Court.[227]

The pattern of asset distribution from Israel Thompson's estate followed Quaker inheritance customs, more or less.[228] According to the custom, widows usually received their "thirds" of the personal property, that is to say, one of three equal parts. The residual personalty was divided equally among the children, "share and share alike". Generally, income producing real estate assets were divided equally among brothers as primogeniture was uncommon. Quakers often included charitable bequests in their last will and testament. Israel Thompson's estate would make payment of a subscription for building a schoolhouse,[229] and another payment of a subscription for building a bridge over "Kittocton",[230] and a payment towards the Fairfax Monthly Meeting.[231]

The execution of a will by a testator was thought by Quakers to be an important social event, which required the participation of near relatives and friends. Israel Thompson's last will and testament was literally a deathbed proof or tribute as it was dated only about two weeks before his demise. His will was that his real property including his home plantation of nearly seven hundred acres of land including his mill, tanyard, and mansion house, and three adjacent lots; Cold Spring Plantation and two adjacent lots; the plantation willed to Israel by his father Edward Thompson at the death of his sister Prudence Woodward near Goose Creek Meetinghouse (Lincoln); one lot on Catoctin Mountain; two adjacent lots of land on the South Fork of Catoctin Creek (Get Plantation), all to be liquidated by his executors. Furthermore, his personal estate consisting of household goods and furniture, storehouse goods, utensils of husbandry, carriages and livestock, all of it to be sold by his executors.[232]

It was Israel Thompson's will that the monies arising from the sales be used firstly to pay his outstanding obligations including the indemnification of his widow, Sarah (Hague) Thompson. He complied with the terms and conditions of his marriage contract and willed the sum of six hundred pounds current money to be paid as soon as collected to his widow Sarah, agreeable to the marriage contract annexed to his will by a codicil. Over and above that he provided her with the sum of twenty pounds yearly and every year as long as she should continue his widow. Additionally, he left her a mare with a saddle and bridle, one feather bed and furniture, one case of drawers, one large walnut table and tablecloth, six plates, three dishes, three basins, one tea stand, six painted chairs and one arm chair, one looking glass, and a life estate in a clock & case, afterwards, which afterwards was to go to their son Israel H. Thompson.[233]

Israel Thompson would provide for his surviving children from his first marriage, to Ann. He left Jonah two silver spoons marked "WR" and a fifth part interest in the residual value of his estate. Additionally, he gave him one share of stock in the Potowmack Navigation Co. Likewise, he left Samuel an equal fifth part of his estate and a feather bed and furniture, and one silver spoon with the same mark as above. He noted that he should like them to keep the spoons in remembrance of their late mother, the late Ann Thompson. There were two more spoons of the same metal and with the same mark that hade been either lost or stolen, and if they were ever to be found it was Israel's will that they be given to Joseph Richardson, his first wife's son. What's more, Israel Thompson willed to Samuel Thompson six silver teaspoons and six silver tablespoons marked with his initials.[234]

Israel Thompson would provide for his surviving children from his second marriage, to Sarah Hague Thompson. He left Israel H. Thompson an equal fifth part of his residual estate and a feather bed and furniture, as well as a set of six silver tablespoons and six silver teaspoons marked "IST", to be delivered to him on his twenty-first birthday. Besides, he left him his silver watch to be delivered to him on his eighteenth birthday. He left his four daughters, Nancy, Betsy, Sally, and Pleasant, an equal fifth part of his residual estate to be divided equally between them, and a feather bed and furniture for each of them upon reaching their eighteenth birthday. It was the late Israel Thompson's will that his youngest son, Israel H. Thompson, be a boarder at one of the Friends best schools until age twenty, and that his daughters be sufficiently learned not only at school but also at needlework to fit them for business, the expenses to be paid out of their inheritances.[235]

Otherwise, Israel Thompson left portions of his western lands on the waters of the Monongahela River and in the District of Kentucky as follows. He left to each of three daughters, Betsy, Sally, and Pleasant, 750 acres of land in Kentucky. Apparently, his daughter Nancy already possessed 1,000 acres in her name subject to assignment. Additionally, he gave 100 acres of land to Thomas Hague, and the undefined residual acreage was to go to his surviving sons, Jonah, Samuel, and Israel H. Thompson.[236]

Annexed to his last will and testament there was a codicil. It was Israel Thompson's will as he put it, that the black girl residing in his family named Hannah be freed on 11/1/1797. Likewise it was his will as he put it, that the mulatto boy named William (Will) be freed upon turning 21 years of age. Additionally, he gave to his widow the house and lot of ground in Waterford where John Nicklin then lived, and two lots of ground nearly opposite on which Stephen Wilson possessed an indenture of lease (ground rent). Israel Thompson willed to his son Israel H. Thompson that the money arising from the sale of his Catoctin Mountain woodland lot to Thomas Edwards was to be assigned to him when he should arrive at the age of twenty-one years together with the interest. Another portion of the codicil concerned the before referred to marriage contract entered into between Israel Thompson and Sarah Hague dated May 20, 1778, and witnessed by Israel Thompson's adopted daughter, Ann Sheane.[237]

Excluding Israel Thompson's special bequeaths, the remainder of his personal property was sold between March 24, 1795 and December 11, 1795 for the sum of £ 1,302:11:11½ current money of Virginia. It should be noted that one of the many lots that sold at his crying sale was described as, "1 Negro Boy called Will", and the buyer was Jonah Thompson in consideration of £ 10: 0: 0, current money.[238] There was an account entry made for the sale of the remaining time of involuntary service of Hannah's to Tho$^s\cdot$ Pursell (Purcell) in consideration of £ 1: 4: 0.[239] At a court held for Loudoun County on December 14, 1804, an inventory and the record of sales of the personal estate of Israel Thompson deceased was returned and ordered recorded.[240]

Apparently, the sale of the late Israel Thompson's above mentioned Catoctin Mountain woodland lot to Thomas Edwards fell through as it did not come to fruition. Instead, the subject one hundred and fifty acre lot of land was sold by Israel Thompson's surviving executors in 1807 to Hugh Douglas of Loudoun County in consideration of £ 155: 0:0.[241] The land had originally been purchased by Israel Thompson from Joseph McGeath, John McGeath, and Wm. McGeath, according to a deed bearing date February 2 and 3, 1791.[242]

Chapter 5

By the time of his father's death, Jonah Thompson was already an accomplished man. He was probably grave in character, sober, with a quality of seriousness about him. He was quick and accurate of judgment, as he had showed enough potential during his youth to merit a higher education and or an apprenticeship in Philadelphia. He had moved there in 1775 under the care of the Philadelphia Monthly Meeting. He probably served as an apprentice in a counting house. He would return to Virginia in late 1781.[243] But, the Fairfax Monthly Meeting would not formally accept him back as he had taken the test or an oath of allegiance to the United States during the Revolutionary War, and he had married out of unity to Margaret Peyton, a member of the Protestant Episcopal Church (Anglican Church).[244]

Margaret Peyton was the daughter of Colonel Francis Peyton of Peyton's Grove, on the western limits of King Street (1100-1200 blocks), Alexandria.[245] Margaret and Jonah had probably known each other for many years considering that Francis Peyton had been at the least well acquainted with Israel Thompson, or he was probably even friendly with him. The Peyton family owned lands and had business interests in Loudoun County including an ordinary named the Red Lion in Leesburg, which had belonged to Margaret's brother, Craven Peyton.[246] In her own right, Margaret Peyton had owned a valuable piece of Loudoun County real estate at the foot of Bull Run Mountain and in the vicinity of the intersection of the Carolina Road and the Little River Turnpike containing 266 acres, which had been devised to her by her uncle, Thomas West.[247]

It seems apparent that Jonah Thompson had acquired from his father a certain keenness of insight of things business or the buying and selling of commodities or services. He kept books meticulously accurate in details. But, he was very different from his father and especially different from his grandfather, in that he was decidedly of a quality or character of being more conventional. He was sophisticated enough to have learned to modify his manners and customs through contact with fashionable society. Apparently, he was a social climber who strove for acceptance in high society.[248] Jonah Thompson would rent a pew in his name in the gallery of the Christ (Episcopal) Church, Fairfax Parish, Alexandria.[249]

Jonah Thompson was a busy man as at the very time of the settling of his late father's estate, he was contemporaneously serving his first of two separate terms as the Mayor of the Town of Alexandria (1796-1797).[250] What's more, with a group of others he was in the midst of establishing the Bank of Alexandria. In 1792, a group of Alexandrians had petitioned the Virginia Assembly to charter the Bank of Alexandria, "not only to increase the commerce of this place and, of course, of this State, but to preserve that share of it which it at present possesses."[251] The charter was granted and the bank opened in 1793, and Jonah Thompson was one of those to receive stock subscriptions and sat on the board of directors. In fact, he would even come to serve as President of the Bank of Alexandria.[252] Additionally, he served nearly simultaneously as an agent or representative of the Mutual Assurance Society, a fire insurance company.

Jonah Thompson was a solid citizen. He was a member of the mercantile class of Alexandria. Essentially, Jonah Thompson was a merchant and property manager. His occupation was the wholesale purchase and retail sale of goods for profit. His other business enterprise was managing a portfolio of real estate. He was a person from whom a tenant leased land, buildings, or dwelling units. He would be in and out of an array of business partnerships including Thompson & Peyton, McPherson & Thompson, Thompson & Veitch, Adam Lynn & Jonah Thompson, Philip Poyer & Jonah Thompson, Jonah Thompson & Son, Tucker & Thompson, and C.& J.P. Thompson.

When in Alexandria, Jonah and Margaret Thompson lived in the so called "Thompson House" or "The Married Houses" at 211 N. Fairfax Street.[253] The building or buildings were on a prime lot of land north of Cameron Street to Queen Street and between the Potomac River and Fairfax Street. Jonah Thompson had purchased the improved real estate with David Finley in 1793 from William and Catherine Bird in consideration of £ 1,500 current money. When Finley died shortly thereafter Jonah Thompson bought out his heir for £ 500:12: 0 current money of Virginia. Jonah Thompson undertook further improvements until two large houses were standing back-to-back thereon. They were built separately in a neoclassical style boasting arched stone entrances and an open gallery along the south facade, with a design attributed to Benjamin Latrobe. Jonah Thompson had a dry goods and hardware store that was located nearby at 122 N. Fairfax Street. And, the Bank of Alexandria was close by as well at N. Fairfax Street and Cameron Street (305 Cameron Street).

Tragedy would strike the Thompson family again in 1796 as Samuel Thompson died by June 13, aged 30 years old. His death must have been rather sudden as there were no vouchers in his final papers for medical expenses. Although he was an heir to a relative fortune, nonetheless, in his own right he was a single man with a practical education of more or less modest material means. At the time of his death he possessed an indenture of lease for a strategically located lot of land on and about a settlement at the Great Gap in the Short Hill (Hillsborough, Hillsboro).[254] His most valuable personal property possession was a one-half interest in a stud horse named "High Flyer," valued at fifty pounds.[255] It's possible he was the same "Samuel Thompson" who was recorded by the Fairfax Monthly Meeting, according to William Wade Hinshaw, of drinking to excess and after long care failing to reform thus being disowned in 1793.[256] He died having made no legal will thus leaving his fifth interest in his late father's estate and other effects to siblings.

Around the same time, Israel's Thompson's executors arranged for the sale in the open market of Israel Thompson's former home plantation through John Redman, soliciting bids from all comers.[257] As it would turn out the highest bidder awarded the contract on the home plantation was Jonah Thompson of Alexandria. The transactions were dated June 27 and 28, 1796, and included the original 641 acres tract plus an annexed parcel of land containing about 14 acres in consideration of the sum of £ 4,130:0:0 current money of Virginia.[258] The old home plantation and all the appurtenances thereon then became Jonah Thompson's real property.

About a month later dated July 29, 1796 the late Israel Thompson's more remote plantation named "Cold Spring" at the foot of the Short Hill Mountain containing 148 acres of land, was bargained and sold by his executors to Theopulus Harris of the Town of Alexandria, in consideration of the sum of £ 480 current money.[259] About a year later, dated on July 29, 1797, the deceased's indenture of lease for lives for an adjacent lot of land containing 100 acres on the Shannondale Tract of George William Fairfax was assigned by the late Israel Thompson's executors to Isaac Miller of loudoun County in consideration of the sum of 100 pounds lawful money of Virginia.[260] Israel Thompson had originally taken up the indenture of lease in 1787 from George Nicholas, the attorney on fact for George William Fairfax.[261] Additionally, the deceased owned a small lot of 26 acres joining thereto, which he had lately bought of Joseph Janney.[262]

Also, Israel Thompson's executors did come to assign the before referred to two adjacent lots of lease-land (Get Plantation) formerly occupied by Joseph Yates and later by Robert Yates on the South Fork of Catoctin Creek, to Sanford Ramey, in consideration of £ 300 current money. There is an unambiguous summation of the deal reflected in Israel Thompson deceased's administrative accounts.[263] Sanford Ramey later purchased the underlying landed property amounting to 300 acres of land from Ferdinando Fairfax on a fee simple basis, that is to say, an unqualified ownership and power of disposition.[264] He would establish still further improvements on the plantation which would ultimately take on the name of "Rosemont."

As for the three lots of leased land adjacent to the old home plantation, they were disposed of in the following manner. On August 8, 1797, Israel Thompson's executors assigned one of them to Jonathan Lodge of Loudoun County in consideration of 200 pounds lawful money.[265] It was a lot of land of 178 acres located about the same place where the former Edward Thompson's "additional lott" had been located.[266] Israel Thompson had originally taken up the indenture of lease in 1787 from George Nicholas, the attorney in fact to George William Fairfax.[267]

The other two lease-lots were two contiguous parcels, which had formerly been the in the possession of Thomas Hutton of Loudoun County, circa 1765. They were on or about where the previously referred to former lot once surveyed for George Griffith had been located.[268] The two lots dovetailed together on the North Fork of Catoctin Creek thus providing each with lawful access to the water. Thomas Hutton's messuage included 134 acres of land and his additional lot included 81 acres of land for a total of 215 acres of land. Thomas Hutton had assigned the additional lot to Israel Thompson in 1785.[269] About seven years later he assigned his messuage to Israel Thompson.[270] Thomas Hutton had previously attempted to assign it to Thomas Davis in 1785, unsuccessfully.[271] Israel Thompson's executors would assign the former Thomas Hutton's messuage to Wm. Wirtz (William Virts) in 1797 in consideration of about £ 170:5:16 current money.[272] And, the former Thomas Hutton's additional lot was assigned in 1796 to Garlock Stickler in consideration of £138:19:5, current money.[273] A messuage was a contemporary expression in Middle English from Norman French meaning a freeholder's dwelling house with its outbuildings and adjoining land; a right in consideration of ground rent.

Israel Thompson's executors made a deal of bargain and sale dated 9/11/1797 for Edward Thompson's former plantation near Goose Creek Meetinghouse to Stephen Wilson of Loudoun County in consideration of £ 240 current money of Virginia.[274] The said deal was related to a separate transaction made between Stephen Wilson and Sarah Thompson dated the same day for an indenture of lease on three lots situated in the village of Waterford, and known in a division thereof made by Joseph Janney as lots numbered 9, 10 & 11.[275] The deal was a land swap and included a cash premium as well.[276] Stephen Wilson had previously assigned the indenture of lease for the pieces of ground to Israel Thompson in consideration of thirty pounds current money of Virginia. But, Israel Thompson had died without ever having received a conveyance of the same.[277] Consequently, Stephen Wilson assigned the same to Israel Thompson's widow, Sarah Thompson. Two years later Stephen Wilson would bargain and sell to Sarah Thompson all that lot or messuage of land in the village of Waterford where she then lived, in consideration of the sum of £ 110 current money.[278]

Jonah Thompson had been an absentee owner of his late father's home plantation. On January 31, 1798, he would offer his late father's former tanyard for rent through an advertisement in an Alexandria newspaper. It was described as a tanyard with curry shop and a bark & millhouse that was efficient for working with up to 600 hides and skins, and a convenient dwelling house and shoemaker's shop, located within ten miles from Leesburg on the turnpike road leading from Alexandria to Key's Ferry (Keyes Ferry). In a good neighborhood for the sale of leather and the procuring of tan bark. For terms the ad read, inquire of John Kleinhoff on the place or to the subscriber living in Alexandria, Jonah Thompson, Thompson Mill, Loudoun County.[279]

In the early winter of 1804, Jonah and Margaret Thompson of the Town and County of Alexandria in the District of Columbia mortgaged the home plantation to Alexander Sutherland of Loudoun County in consideration of the sum of 8,000 pounds lawful money of Virginia. The event resulted in a new survey of the lands together with all houses, outbuildings, ways, waters, water courses, mills, distilleries and tanyards whatsoever, which amounted to 775 acres two roods and eighteen poles of land, and a small lot annexed thereto, containing 14 acres two roods and thirty six poles. Apparently, the total included some messuage lands or tenancies. The boundary description in the deed of mortgage is interesting as it informs the reader that the mill dam served as a contemporary means to cross over or bridge the North Fork of Catoctin Creek.[280]

It was the late Israel Thompson's will that his executors arrange for his youngest son Israel H. to be sent to one of the Friends best schools for a good education. Also, that his daughters were to be schooled in needlework to make them fit for business. The same was accomplished through an institution of learning named the Westtown Boarding School. At the time, it was a new school including a meetinghouse and dormitory facilities situated on an old farm near Westtown, Chester County, Pennsylvania. John Dickinson and other Quakers chiefly from around the Philadelphia area had established the school, which opened in May of 1799. The said Israel H. Thompson was one of the first twenty students to have ever attended the Westtown Boarding School, under the care at the time of the Concord Monthly Meeting.[281] Also, at least one and probably two of his sisters attended the school as well, Pleasant Thompson, and Sarah (Sally) Thompson.[282]

TO RENT,

A TAN YARD, with curry shop, bark mill house, and a number of vats, sufficient for the working in upwards of five hundred hides and skins—also a convenient dwelling house and shoemaker's shop, situate in Loudoun county, within ten miles of Leesburg, on the turnpike road leading from Alexandria to Key's ferry, in a good neighbourhood for the sale of leather, and the procuring of tan bark.

Possession may be had early in next summer, and as part of the vats are unoccupied by the present tenant, liberty will be granted to the person renting the premises to go to work immediately. For terms enquire of John R. Nickoff on the place, or to the subscriber living in Alexandria.

JONAH THOMPSON.

Thompson Mill,
Loudoun county, Jan. 31.

At the time, the young Israel H. Thompson's guardian was Asa Moore of Waterford who maintained such an account for the record.[283] There was a charge made for transporting him to school in Chester County and expenses that amounted to the sum of ten pounds and seven shillings and eight and one-half pence. There was another charge made to paying John Price for tuition at twelve pounds. Additionally, there was a charge made for boarding and sundry clothing as well as pocket money that totaled fourteen pounds and five shillings and eleven pence. Lastly, a final charge was made at six pounds for board and schooling. It's interesting to note that within about one month of his enrollment at the Westtown Boarding School, Israel H. Thompson was disowned by the Concord Monthly Meeting, Society of Friends, and June 3, 1799.[284]

Israel H. Thompson would return to his native Loudoun County. In 1804, Israel H. Thompson and Ann H. Hough took each other in marriage under the care of the Fairfax Monthly Meeting. Ann was the daughter of the prosperous William and Eleanor Hite Hough of Waterford. The young Israel H. Thompson already had a substantial estate including personal property, receivables, real property, and rights to land. He owned a two-acre lot with a dwelling house in Leesburg. It was located near the Leesburg town spring and adjacent to John Hough's lot, Francis Hague's currying shop, Jacob Towner's tanyard lot, and William Peyton's lot. Apparently, he had previously lived there for about three years, during the time between his late father's death in 1795 and when he went to boarding school in 1799.[285]

Good luck was not to be with the young couple. Although they were fortunate enough to have had a daughter born to them named Sally Eleanor Thompson, nevertheless, by early 1807 both of her parents were dead. Israel H. Thompson survived his wife for a relatively short period of time and made his last will and testament leaving his net estate to his daughter and his surviving sisters. He named his father in law to act as Sally Eleanor Thompson's guardian.[286]

Two other of the late Israel and Sarah Thompson's surviving children died prematurely as well. One of them was Sarah or "Sally" W. Thompson of the Town of Waterford who died shortly after she made her last will and testament dated 7/6/1807. She made the legal instrument while at the time, "being in a weak habit of body but through divine favor of sound disposing mind and memory." Sally left her personal estate to her mother and devised her land rights to her three surviving sisters, Nancy Griffith, Betsy Hamilton, and Pleasant Vandeventer, and to her niece, Sally Eleanor Thompson. Apparently, Doctor Heaton treated her before her demise.[287]

The other one of their children to have died prematurely was the before mentioned Nancy Griffith of Waterford, who died by June 10, 1811. At the time of her death she was a widow and mother of two infant children, Israel Thompson Griffith, and Sarah Pleasant Griffith. As was mentioned previously her final estate came to include human chattel in the form of an African-American female slave. Also, she was in possession of some personal goods and land rights.[288]

Late in the year 1810 or early 1811, the late Israel Thompson's widow, Sarah Thompson, died. It had been about thirty-three years since her wedding day and she had since lived to see her husband and three of their children die and, possibly, a fourth one gravely ill. Sarah Thompson predeceased her daughter Nancy by about six months of time. Her estate was charged per account by Doctor (Isaac) Hough as well as by Doctor John Vandeventer for services rendered. Sarah Thompson had been a well to do lady with a substantial personal estate. At the time of her death she owned stock in Jonah Thompson's Bank of Alexandria and dividends receivable valued at $ 928.00. Her assets included notes receivable principally from Moore & Phillips and Isaac Steer worth well over one thousand dollars and her liabilities were proportionately few. Sarah Thompson deceased left her net estate to her children and her granddaughter, Sally Eleanor Thompson.[289]

During the time of the War of 1812, Jonah Thompson entered into two different financial transactions, which liquidated his late father's old home plantation and pretty much put an end to his real estate interests in his native Loudoun County. Dated on March 30, 1813, Jonah

Thompson and Margaret his wife of Alexandria of the one part did bargain and sell to George Janney and Daniel Eaches of Loudoun County of the other part, a certain tract or parcel of land in Loudoun County, formerly the property of Israel Thompson, containing 767 acres 2 roods and 1 pole together with all improvements in consideration of forty silver dollars per acre or $ 30,700 per schedule. On the same day, three parties struck a deal in the form of an indenture tripartite including George Janney and Susannah his wife and Daniel Eaches of the first part, Thomas Swann of Alexandria and District of Columbia of the second part, and Jonah Thompson of Alexandria and District of Columbia of the third part. The three-party transaction served to effectively secure the debt through a temporary and conditional pledge of the real estate to Thomas Swann.[290]

The United States post office named Wheatland, which had been open since 1802, was closed in 1816. During that period of time Robert Heard had served as the postmaster. About twenty years later the Wheatland post office was reopened under the direction of Samuel Nixon, postmaster. The post office would continue in operation under a series of postmasters through the time of the Civil War. At the time of the Civil War on October 29, 1862, Wheatland was described by a New York Times correspondent as a little secessionist hamlet of half dozen or more houses including a flourishing mill and store.[291]

Jonah Thompson was a man of seemingly enormous energy with the power to pull or put people together and things in an orderly, functional structured whole. In addition to his parochial business concerns he was a capitalist shipping merchant with international ties and trade interests throughout the Atlantic Ocean. The base of Jonah Thompson's commercial operations was Thompson's Wharf in the port town of Alexandria. The wharf stretched into relatively deep water in the Potomac River and had warehouse facilities for the storage of goods and merchandize. Ships would regularly sail in and out of the harbor within eyesight of the open arcade along the front of Jonah Thompson's house and then down the River and through the Chesapeake Bay to the Atlantic Ocean, so to conduct domestic and international trade with merchants in the United States, West Indies, Latin America, Bermuda, Western and Southern Europe, Africa, Canada and so on. There was a time as well when Jonah Thompson was in the lucrative but highly risky marine insurance business.[292]

Jonah Thompson was civic minded in the best sense of the expression, as pertaining to the incorporated Town of Alexandria and County of the same name.[293] He was a gentleman who in his later years was bestowed the title of esquire after the man's name as a courtesy in appreciation of his public service. He served two separate terms as the mayor of Alexandria (1796-1797:1806-1808). On a number of occasions he served a term of office as justice of the peace. He was an alderman elected to the council of Alexandria. He served as a trustee for the poor house. He served on the vigilance committee so to influence the exercise of police powers as applicable. He worked as an officer on behalf of at least two municipal fire companies. Also, Jonah Thompson served in a committee for the retrocession of Alexandria County back into the Commonwealth of Virginia, which was a successful effort.

During the War of 1812 in the context of Jonah Thompson's professional association with the Bank of Alexandria, he served on behalf of the entity in a consortium of regional banks that furnished the Federal Government with an emergency loan of $ 200,000 in order to more effectively prosecute the war. The next year he served in a special committee so to apprise the President of the United States as to the defenseless condition of Alexandria as an appeal for consideration. Shortly after the invasion of Washington, D.C., the town of Alexandria was occupied by British forces from August 29 to September 4, 1814, which required the powers that be, theoretically, including Jonah Thompson, to pay a ransom to their captors in order to spare the town further suffering. Be as it may, nonetheless, there was looting of flour, tobacco and cotton.

It was Jonah Thompson's practice as well to involve him self in regional matters of importance as they concerned Northern Virginia. He was both an equity holder in and served as an officer of the company managing George Washington's Potomac River canal scheme. He worked towards promoting and developing the Alexandria Canal. He was treasurer of the Little River Turnpike Co. and, also, served as a collector of subscriptions on behalf of the Middle Turnpike Co.

The framed painting (oil on canvas, artist unknown, 27½ inches x 21 inches) pictured below was wrongly described as being an image of Jonah Thompson of Alexandria in the publication, Our Town at Gadsby's Tavern 1749 – 1865: Likenesses of This Place & Its People Taken from Life by Artists Known and Unknown, Alexandria, Virginia, The Alexandria Association, 1956 (pp. 57-58). According to its owner, Taylor Burke Jr., Alexandria, instead, it's probably an image of Samuel Thompson of Alexandria, son of Jonah and Margaret Thompson circa 1815.

Additionally, Jonah Thompson would serve as the director of the Alexandria & Washington Turnpike Co. He was a stockholder in the Georgetown Bridge Co. And, he was involved in the development of the Long Bridge over the Potomac River, which was styled at the time to be the longest bridge in the world.[294]

On a more personal note, Jonah Thompson worked on behalf of young people and was given to social pleasures. He worked to promote education on behalf of the Alexandria Academy, serving as trustee and as an additional teacher. Jonah Thompson was a patron of the theater in Alexandria. He served as a manager of dancing assemblies at City Hotel. Jonah Thompson was a member of the Masonic Lodge. Also, he served in the vestry for the congregation of members of the Christ (Episcopal) Church, Alexandria.

Then there were three: Jonah Thompson, Pleasant (Thompson) Vandeventer, and Elizabeth or Betsy (Thompson) Hamilton. The author could not find any conclusive evidence as to the final disposition of Pleasant (Thompson) Vandeventer, or Betsy (Thompson) Hamilton. On January 25, 1834, The Daily National Intelligencer of Washington, D.C. reported the recent death of Jonah Thompson referring to him as "one of the most respected citizens & formerly one of the most active merchants of the city."[295] His wife, Margaret (Peyton) Thompson died in 1841.

In the graveyard of the Christ Episcopal Cemetery, Alexandria, Virginia, is found lot No. 45 for members of the Thompson family.[296] The inscription on the grave marker and memorial to Jonah Thompson reads, *Sacred to the memory of Jonah Thompson who departed this life on the 21st of January, 1834 in the 77th year of his age.* The inscription on the grave marker and memorial to Margaret Thompson reads, *Sacred to the memory of Margaret Thompson who departed this life on the 18th of September, 1841 in the 80th year of her age.* At least three of their children were buried in the cemetery lot with them including Craven Peyton Thompson and his wife, Samuel Thompson and his wife, and Margaret Thompson. Apparently, a relation named John Thompson was buried in the plot with them. The other children known to have been born to Jonah and Margaret Thompson were Israel P. Thompson, William Edward Thompson, J. P. Thompson, Mary Ann Thompson Popham, Ann H. Thompson Morgan, Eugenia Thompson Morgan, and Julia Thompson Burke.

Appendix I

R4 V37

I the undersigned Jonah Thompson residing at Alexandria in the county of Alexandria do hereby declare for Assurance in the Mutual Assurance Society against Fire on Buildings of the State of Virginia.

My four Buildings on my Plantation now occupied by Alex Peyton situated between the Lands of James Arellno Sr and those of Jonathan Lodge Sr. in the county of Loudoun...

The Dwelling House	at 2200	Twenty two hundred Dolls
The Kitchen	at 300	Three hundred do
The Barn	at 1000	One thousand do
The Cow House	at 500	Five hundred do

$4000

Say Four Thousand Dolls. in all.

...this 16th day of October 1805.

P. C. Marble, Special Agent.   Jonah Thompson

WE the undersigned, being each other Freeholders, declare and affirm, that we have examined the above-mentioned Buildings of Jonah Thompson and that we are of opinion that they would cost in cash Four Thousand Five Hundred Dollars to build the same, and that now (after the deduction of five hundred Dollars) they are actually worth Four Thousand Dollars...

James Roach
David Anderson   Loudoun

P. C. Marble

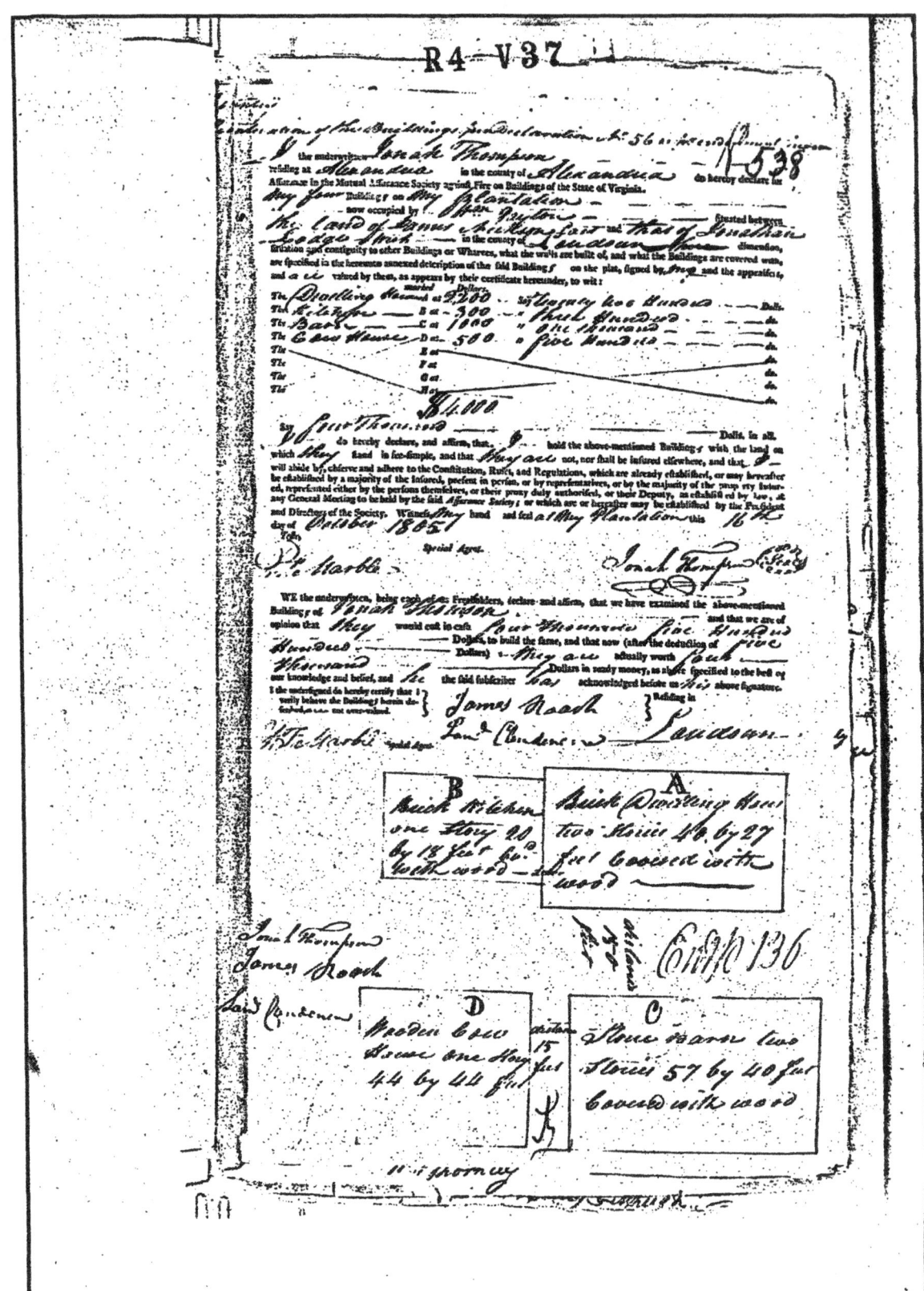

B — Brick Kitchen one Story 20 by 18 feet covered with wood

A — Brick Dwelling House two Stories 44 by 27 feet covered with wood

Jonah Thompson
James Roach
David Anderson

D — Wooden Cow House one Story 44 by 44 feet (distance 15 feet)

C — Stone Barn two Stories 57 by 40 feet covered with wood

R4 V37

I the underwritten **Jonah Thompson** residing at **Alexandria** in the county of **Alexandria** do hereby declare for Assurance in the Mutual Assurance Society against Fire on Buildings of the State of Virginia.

My two Building s on **My Plantation** now occupied by **William Payton** situated between **My land of Samuel Nickson** and **That of Jonathan Lodge Street** in the county of **Loudoun**...

are valued by them, as appears by their certificate hereunder, to wit:

	marked Dollars
The Merchant Mill	A at 3,000 — say Three Thousand — Dolls.
The Dwelling house	B at 500 — Five Hundred — do.
The	C at
The	D at
The	E at
The	F at
The	G at
The	H at

$3,500

Say **Three Thousand five Hundred** Dolls. in all.

...this **16th** day of **October 1805**

Fifis Marble, Special Agent

Jonah Thompson

WE the underwritten, being each of us Freeholders, declare and affirm, that we have examined the above-mentioned Building s of **Jonah Thompson** and that we are of opinion that **they** would cost in cash **Four Thousand** Dollars, to build the same, and that now (after the deduction of **five Hundred** Dollars) **they are** actually worth **Three Thousand five Hundred** Dollars in ready money...

James Roach
Saml Clendenen
Residing in **Loudoun**

Fifis Marble, Special Agent

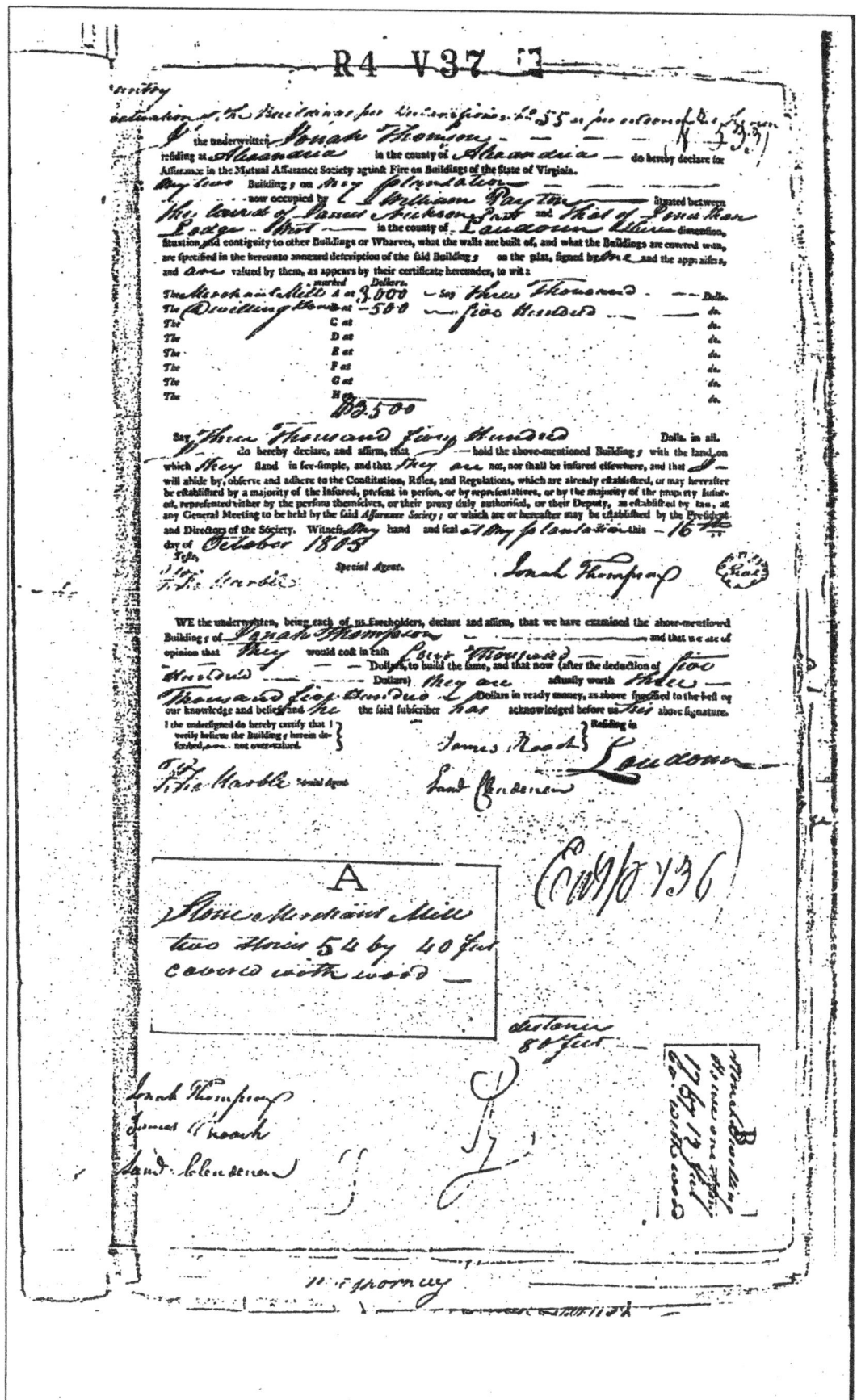

A
Stone Merchant Mill
two stories 54 by 40 feet
covered with wood

distance
80 feet

B
Stone Building
two stories
18 by 18 feet
covered with wood

Jonah Thompson
James Roach
Saml Clendenen

Appendix II

Israel Thompson's Last Will and Testament

Be it remembered that this tenth day of January in the year of our Lord one thousand seven Hundred and ninety five I **Israel Thompson** of Loudoun County & state of Virginia, being in Health as usual but calling to mind the uncertainty of Transitory life Do make this my last will and Testament Touching the disposal of what temporal Estate I have Hereby revoking & disannulling all former Wills by me made and this only to be taken for my last will and Testament and none Other. Imprimis I will that all my just debts be fully paid & Satisfied by my Executors hereafter Named. Item my will is that my Land, Plantation Mill, Tanyard mansion House whereon I now dwell Containing near Seven Hundred Acres of Land also one other Tract of Land & Plantation at foot of Short hill called cold spring containing one Hundred & forty one Acres Together with a small Tract I lately bought of **Joseph Janney** joining thereto & Containing twenty six acres of Land, also a Lott of Lease Land joining said twenty six Acres & laying on side of short Hill. Likewise a Tract of Land & Plantation laying near Goose Creek meeting House joining the Lands of **Nathan Spencer** and Containing one hundred and fifty Acres Willed to me by my Father at the death of my Sister **Prudence Woodward**, also one Hundred acres of wood land which I bought of the **McGeach**^{s} Laying on the Kittocktan mountain joining the Land of **William McGeach** & **Joseph Coldwell** & three Lotts of Lease Land laying and joining my first mentioned land also two Lotts of Lease Land formerly belonging to **Robert Yates** Situate on both sides Kittocktan Creek & c. Be all sold by my Ext^s for the best price that can be got Giving Credit for such part of the purchase money as will not be immediately wanted But may lay on Interest until wanted for my Young Childrens part or parts thereof also all my personal Estate Consisting of Household goods & furniture Store Goods wares & merchandize Utensils of Husbandry horses Carriages Cattle Sheep & Swine on twelve months Credit the sale to be as soon after my decease as may be Convenient (Except Such Articles as shall be hereafter particularly Devised) and the money arising from Such Sale or sales to gather with all my outstanding debts & Cash to be distributed in manner hereafter directed my just Debts being First paid It is my will that the sum of Six Hundred pounds Current money be paid to my Wife **Sarah** (agreeable to a marriage Contract made Agreed to, & signed before marriage which is hereunto Annexed) as soon as it can be Collected in cash or in Good Bonds (barest interest) with Sufficient Security & also The additional Sum of Twenty pounds yearly & every year (as long as she shall Continue my Widow & no longer) to assist Her in bringing up & Supporting my young I give the mare she usually Rides (t)he saddle & Bridle one feather bed & Furniture one Case of Drawers one large walnut Table & Table Cloath Six plates, three dishes & three Basons best pewter one teastand Six high backed Chairs painted red & one arm Chair also one looking glass of the Second Size I have also my Clock & Case during her life & after death said Clock to go to my Son **Israel**, & to my Son **Jonah** I give two Silver Spoons marked WR Likewise I bequeath to him my said son **Jonah** one Equal Fifth part of the balance or remainder of the sales of my said Estate and to my son **Samuel** I give one Equal fifth part of my said Estate also one Goose feather Bed & Furniture likewise one Silver Spoon same mark of those willed to his Brother **Jonah** which I desire them to keep in remembrance of their Mother. There was two more Spoons of Same metal & mark which are either stolen or lost. If they are ever found or got again My Will is that they shall be given to **Joseph Richardson** my first wife's Son. I give also to my Son **Samuel** Six Silver Table & six Ditto Tea spoons marked with the initial letters of his name, and to my Son **Israel** I give also one Equal fifth part of my said Estate, one Feather Bed & Furniture, Six Silver Table & Six Ditto tea Spoons marked IST also my Silver Watch & to my four Daughters (to wit) **Nancey Betzey Sally & Pleasant** I give the remaining part of my said Estate to be Equally divided Between them share and Share alike, and to each of them I give one Feather Bed & furniture & furniture to be delivered to them as they arrive at the Age of Eighteen years, & my son **Israel** to receive the Silver Watch in his Eighteen Year the other Articles when he is twenty one Years of Age But if either of my said Children (viz.) **Nancey Betzey Israel Sally** or **Pleasant** shall depart this life before they arrive To full Age or have Lawful Issue that the Share or Shares of the deceased shall be Equally divided Between the Survivors Share & Shares alike & it is my will that my son **Israel** Shall be kept at one of friends best schools until He shall arrive to the Age of Twenty Years & that my said Daughters be Sufficiently Learned not only at school But also Needlework to fit them for Business the expense to be paid out of the Interest of their Legacies, & be'g possessed of Several Tracts of Land on the waters of the Monongahalia river part of Which was taken up in partnership with **Joseph Smith** now as the Pattents are all in my Name, I do Will that my Exr^s or any two of them shall Convey to him his heirs or his representative one Equal half of all said Lands that He has not already to me & having Several tract of Land Laying within the district of Kentuckey, part of which are Pattented, part Surveyed & part p'haps only located which lands are to be Divided Between me & **Isaac Hite Junr** who located them agreeable to a Contract between him & **Leven Powell** on my behalf & in order to have said Contract complied with Have appointed **Burr Powell** my attorney in fact to convey to said **Isaac Hite** his part or Share of said Lands, & Having said Power of Attorney Authorised Said **Burr Powell** to also convey to said **Isaac Hite** his part of one 1000 Acres of Land Located by him & Pattened For & in the Name of my Daughter **Nancey** a Minor now, now if my said Daughter **Nancey** when she arrives to Lawfull age, or her legal representative, shall refuse to Ratify & Confirm said Conveyance made by said **Burr Powell** to said **Isaac Hite** his Heirs or Assigns when thereupon legally called upon & Required to Confirm the Same that then & on refusal She shall forfet & loose her part of my Estate willed to her as above and having promised to give **Thomas Hague** one Hundred Acres of my land on the Western Waters I do hereby Direct my Exr^s to Convey to said **Thomas Hague** one Hundred Acres of said Lands which is to be laid off that it shall not injure or lessen the value of the remainder of the Tract, and it is my will that all my said lands shall be lett or rented until my son Israel shall arrive to full Age, to such people as will Agree to make such improvements thereon as maybe Agreed upon by my Exr^s & the tenants of shall pay the Land Tax, and when my Son Israel shall arrive to said Age It is my Will that all my said Lands shall be disposed of in following manner (Viz.) that my three Daughters **Betzey, Sally** & **Pleasant** shall have Seven Hundred & fifty acres Conveyed to each of them their Heirs or Legal representatives of any part of my Kentuckey Lands that they shall chuse, the residue of my said western Lands I give & Bequeath unto my Sons **Jonah Samuel** and **Israel** and to their Heirs & Assigns forever and having Subscribed for one Share of the Potomack Navogation & paid every dividend heretofore Called for, I will that my Son **Jonah** Shall have my said Share with the issues & profits thereof Conveyed to him & to his heirs & assigns forever, Lastly I constitute and appoint my Sons **Jonah Samuel & Israel Thompson** also my friend **William Hough** my Executors to this my Last Will & Testament hereby revoking & disannuling all former Will or Wills by me made, & this only to be taken for my last will & Testament & none other & that they my said Executors or any two of them make Deeds of Conveyance for any Lands I have sold or Directed to be sold by my said Exr^s as if I were present.

Signed Sealed, Publish'd and
Declared to be my last Will & Testament   **Israel Thompson** (Seal)
In the Presence of
Mahlon Janney
Benjamin Purdum
John Redman

Be it remembered that I, **Israel Thompson** make this my first Codisel to my Will this 11th day of the first month 1795. Item-It is my Will that the Black Girl Residing in my Family Named **Hannah** be free on the first day of the Eleventh month that may be in the year one thousand seven

Hundred & Ninety Seven. It is likewise my Will that a Molatto Boy Named **William** be free when he arrives at the Age of Twenty one Years. Imprimise I give unto my Dear Wife **Sarah** as further Provition to what I have Already Bequathed The House and Lott of Ground In Waterford where **John Nicklin** now lives to her & her Heirs & assigned forever also two Lotts of Ground Nearly Opposite the before mentioned Lott which said Lott which said Lotts **Stephen Wilson** obtained a Lease for, under a Certain ground rent which said Lotts I give to my Wife during the tenure of said Lease to her Heirs and Assigns. Imprimis I give to my Son **Israel** the money arising from the Sail of a Lott of Ground I sold to **Thomas Edwards** provided he Comply with the Contract, in the time he has engaged to do it in & if said **Edwards** Should not Comply therewith & Neglect the payment for two Years after the limited time my Will is that it be sold by my Executors for the best price that can be had, & the monies arising from said Sail to be given to my said Son **Israel** when he Shall arrive at the Age of twenty one Years together with the Interest arising thereon and Lastly it is my & I do hereby Authorise my before Named Executors to make Deeds of Conveyance for any Lands I have heretofore sold or that is Directed to be Sold by my Executors in as full & ample a manner as if I were Personally present.

Signed Sealed Publish & Declared to be the
First Codisel in my last will In the presence of   **Israel Thompson** (Seal)
Mahlon Janney
Benjamin Purdum
John Redman

To whome it may Concern. Whereas a Contract of Marriage is proposed Between **Israel Thompson** & me the Subscriber **Sarah Hague** both of Loudoun County Virginia. And as it hath often so happened that great disputes have arisen between Stepmothers and Children after the decease of their fathers, Therefore willing to guard against Such Disputes & their unhappy Events I do hereby Promise that in case we the said Parties Shall hereafter be joined Together in Marriage that I will (Agreeable to this Contract made Between us) accepts of the Sum of Six Hundred Pounds Current money Virginia that is if the said **Israel Thompson** Shall be removed by Death before me, & by these Presents doth oblige my self in such Case to quit Claim to all the Estate Lands & Tenements that Shall or may belong to the said **Israel Thompson** & all & every part & parcel thereof both real & personal. Except the above mentioned Sum of Six Hundred pound, & what other Sum or Sums of money, thing or things that he may see Cause to will or Bequeath unto me. In Witness whereof I have hereunto to sett my hand & affixed my Seal this Twentieth day of May in the Year of our Lord one thousand Seven Hundred & Seventy Eight 1778.
    Witness Present   **Sarah Hague** (Seal)
    Ann Sheane

At a Court held for Loudoun County February the 9th 1795, This Will and Codicil annexed by the affirmations of the Subscribers Witness thereto & Ordered to be recorded & on motion of **William Hough Jonah Thompson & Samuel Thompson** three of the executors therein named who were Qualified as the Law directs Certificate is Granted them for Obtaining a probat thereof in due form giving Security whereupon **Wm Hough & Jonah Thompson** with **Josias Clapham & James McIlhany** their Securities entered unto & acknowledged their Bond in the Penalty of fifteen thousand pounds & **Samuel Thompson** with **James McIlhany Stacy Taylor & James Heaton** his Securities entered into and Acknowledged their Bonds in the Penalty of fifteen thousand Pounds Conditioned as the law Directs Liberty is reserved the other Executor to Qualify when he Shall think fit.   Teste
        Chas. Binns Cl.Cour.

(Loudoun County Will Book E, pp. 87-92)

Appendix III

Births and deaths of my children with some remarks

Israel Thompson & Ann his wife took each other in marriage the second day of the fourth month in the year 1754 in Frederick County in Mary-land, and came over in to Virginia to dwell the same month.

Israel Thompson son of Israel and Ann Thompson was born the ninth month called September in the year 1755 being the third day of the week about one of the clock in the morning.

Jonah Thompson son of Israel & Ann Thompson was born the fourteenth of the 3rd month called March in the year 1758 being the third day of the week at one of the clock in the morning.

In the year 1761 on the 21st day of the third month called March being the seventh day of the week about 12 a clock at noon was born unto us a daughter of a fair & comely aspect which had she lived we did purpose to have called Mary in remembrance of her grandmother, but it please the Lord that she died the 28 day of same month on the same day of the week and near about the hour that she came into the world.

The 18th of the 3 month called March in the year 1762 it being the fifth day of the week about ten a clock at night was born unto us a son which we called Edward after his grandfather but it please the Lord that he died the next fifth day after a little while before day.

Samuel Thompson son of Israel and Ann Thompson was born the eight day of the month called January in the year one thousand seven hundred and sixty six being the fourth day of the week.

On the first day of the month called December in the year 1766, departed this life my dearly beloved son Israel after 17 days sickness aged 12 years two months and 21 days. It is now almost five years since his decease and yet his memory is so fresh upon my mind that I can neither write nor think of him without feeling the most heart rendering grief, which the tie of natural affection prevents my shaking off (at the sensible in myself it must be wrong) and as for the encouragement of children to be dutiful to their parents I must in truth let me say in truth of this my dear & deceased child that from the day he was capable of speaking to the day he lost his speech in his last sickness he always & at all times showed a tender regard and in his words and actions most affectionately did express all the duty & love that could be expected or wished for, from a child to his parents, and when Meeting day came, it was his early care to get himself ready, and whilst there & in meeting he was remarkable for his solid sober & exemplary behavior, so that we had the greatest hope & expectations of his being a sober sensible & religious man, if it had pleased the Lord to have spared him to dwell here among us. But he was too ripe for Heaven, to stay her on & in this troublesome & uncertain world. Therefore we ought in all reverence to submit to the will of the Lord and say with (?) & Job of old, the Lord giveth & the Lord taketh away and blessed be the name of the Lord. And one thing which in some measure helped to please and settle my distressed mind was a dream which my son Jonah his brother had about two years after his brother's decease which I have freedom to mention. Notwithstanding it is generally and I believe justly observed & allowed that dreams for the most part are not to be regarded for several reasons judiciously set forth b some able hands & yet I must be of the mind that the Lord of heaven has & does at times reveal secrets as it were to babes & sick lings which seemed to be verified in the above mentioned dream and it was after this manner as near as I can remember from the relation he gave me in the morning as soon as he awaked he told me that he thought in his sleep that he had been at meeting and in his way home he met with his brother and being exceedingly glad to see him after his being absent so long (not thinking in his sleep that his brother was dead) says unto him Brother Issey where hast thou been this long time, to which he made no answer. He the pressed him earnestly to tell him saying that if he would only tell him the first letters of his name with whom he had been that he would be satisfied, whereupon his brother turned towards him & looking steadfastly upon him with a sober and solid countenance says unto him in a distinct manner these letters **Almighty** and turned away without saying any more, which my son Jonah told me he did not understand who it was until he awakened ~~who it was~~ and that then he knew very well.

On the 10th of this instant Nov.r 1772 departed this life my dear & loving wife about 2 o. clock in the morning after about six weeks sickness, upwards of three weeks of the ~~last of~~ (?) sickness she was afflicted with a cough & screams so violently that she would scarcely take any rest night or day yet in all that time she was favored with her senses and was almost insistent in prayer not only on her own account but for her children especially for he two first viz. Joseph & Ann, son and daughter of William Richardson her former husband often giving excellent advice to her friends & near relatives to keep them (?) (?) from the same (?) other worlds glory.

And on the second day of the 7 mo.h called July in the year of our Lord one thousand seven hundred & seventy eight I took to wife Sarah Hague daughter of Francis and Jane Hague after having lived five years seven months& 23 days a single life – and have had issued by her as followeth viz. Nancy our first daughter was born the 16th day of the month called June in the year 1779 about 2 o. clock in the morning. Betsey ours second daughter was born the 28th day of the month called Septem.r in the year 1780, at one in morning. And on the first day of the month called April in the year1782 was born unto us a son of a amicable countenance and very promising aspect. About four o. the clock in the morning which we called Israel Thompson as it seemed to be the choice and desire of a number of our friends & relations, who lived and was favored with health not having had one days sickness until about three weeks ago when he was seized with attacks which was supposed to be occasioned by the cutting of teeth as it did not prevent him from running about and eating as usual until the 24th of June 1783 when his disorder seemed to increase upon him by making a motion to vomit, from which time he failed visibly every day. Notwithstanding every means we could think useful was administered to him and sometimes appeared as if there was some little hopes of his recovery, but everything we did for him, proved to be as it were of no value at last for on the 29th of same month being first day of the week about two o. the clock in the afternoon he yielded up his natural life & breath and is we have great reason to hope & expect gone to rest in the mansions of bliss with him who first give him his life, breath and being. Oh that we may never repine, but in all things submit to the will and disposing hand of the almighty great creator, and disposer of all human events. On the 9th of January in the year 1784 was born about 3 o. clock in the morning, a son which we called Israel. And on the 5th Of March in the year 1786 about 2 of the clock in the morning two daughters the first called Sally the last called Pleasant.

(Vouchers for charges v. the estate of Israel Thompson, Loudoun County Will Book F, Loudoun County Circuit Court, Archives, Leesburg, Virginia)

Appendix IV

Account sales of the personal estate of Israel Thompson deceased commenced on the 24th March 1795

Andrew Copeland- 1 per linen 10 ¼ yards @ 3 shillings/1pence; 1 per sheets @ 10 shillings = £ 2: 1: 7½

Everit Oxley -1 per black velvet 2 3/8 yards @ 6 shillings; 1 kettle @ 17 shillings; 1 bed quilt @ 20 shillings; 1 feather bed & furniture @ £ 10:12: 6; 1 counterpane @ 16 shillings; 1 bed quilt @ 14 shillings/1 pence = £ 14:13:10

William Wright- 6 printed handkerchiefs @ 2 shillings/1 pence; 1 iron pole @ 4 shillings/1pence; 1 large chair @ 12 shillings; 6 sheep @ 43 shillings = £ 3:11: 7

Thomas Carr- 9 handkerchiefs (entered in the cash sales rec.^{d} per **Jonah Thompson**) @ £ 0:10: 6

Josiah Wood- 7 checkered handkerchiefs @ 1 shilling/3 pence; 2 sets razors & cases @ 9 shillings; 9 pair worsted stockings @ 2 shillings/9 pence; 2 yards nankeen 1 ½ yards check @ 8 shillings/9 pence; 8 pair scissors @ 8 shillings; 4 ½ dozen metal buttons @ ?; awl blades, gloves, & buttons @ 8 shillings/1 pence; 4 7/8 yards calico @ 4 shillings/6 pence; 4 yards cloth @ 20 shillings; 9 pair scissors @ 5 shillings = £ 8:17: 1

Timothy Taylor- 1 curb bridle @ 6 shillings; old gears @ 28 shillings; 1 pair sheets @ 22 shillings; 1 long wheel @ 13 shillings; 1 watering pot @ 3 shillings/ 9 pence; 11¾ yards jennet @ 3 shillings/4 pence   = £ 5:11:11

Joshua Hatcher- 1 curb bridle @ 6 shillings/10 pence; sundries @ 24 shillings; 5 ¼ yards florentine @ 5 shillings/11 pence = £ 3: 1:11

Edward Rinker- 1 set razors & case @ 4 shillings/6 pence

Samuel Perry- 2 1/8 yards corded dimity @ 4 shillings/3 pence; 1 iron pot @ 4 shillings/6 pence; 1 feather bed & furniture @ 190 shillings; 1 pair pillow cases @ 5 shillings; included in **H. Douglas** bond   = £ 10: 8: 0½

Ferdinando Fairfax- 1 bay mare @ £ 12: 7: 0; 1 young bull @ £ 7:15: 0; 1 cow & calf @ £ 8:10: 0; 1 cow @ £ 8: 0: 0 = £ 36:12: 0

Mahlon Janney- 1 black mare @ £ 12:10: 0; 1 desk @ 22 shillings = £ 13:12: 0

Josiah Clapham- 1 bay mare @ £ 15: 0: 0

Benjamin Holland- 1 bay mare @ £ 3: 0: 0

John Cummings- 1 set drawers @ 93 shillings; 1 bucket @ 4 shillings = £ 4:17: 0

Col. Thomas Respass- 1 wagon & 4 horses with harness @ £ 110:10: 0

Samuel Nichols- 1 young colt @ £ 16; 1 hip skin @ 7 shillings/9 pence = £ 16: 7: 9

John Statlar- 1 black colt @ £ 10: 6: 0

Stephen Wilson- 1 large sorrel colt @ £ 9: 0: 0; 1 per sheets @ 22 shillings; 1 per pillow cases @ 5 shillings/1 pence; 10 pair stockings @ 4 shillings/1 pence; 1 candle stand @ 3 shillings/6 pence; 3 chairs @ 4 shillings/3 pence; 1 churn @ 5 shillings/6 pence; 18 ¾ yards moreen @ 2 shillings/9 pence = £ 15:11:10¾

Patterson Wright- 1 black colt @ 117 shillings; 1 young heifer 65 shillings; 2 calves @ 73 shillings; 2 ditto @ 64 shillings = £ 15:19: 0

Sarah Thompson- 1 cow & calf @ 132 shillings; 1 ditto @ 130 shillings; 1 brass kettle @ 24 shillings/1 pence; 1 calf skin @ 8 shillings/6 pence; 2 hogs @ 24 shillings; 5 hinting handkerchiefs @ 5 shillings/6 pence = £ 17: 6: 1

James Lyons- 1 cow @ £ 5:11: 0

John McCarty- 1 cow & calf @ £ 6:16: 6

Nicholas Sanders- one cow & calf @ £ 7: 8: 0

Richard Taylor- 1 cow & calf @ £ 6:12: 0

John Davis- 1 cow @ £ 6:18: 0
Duncan McLean- 1 red steer @ 91 shillings, 1 calf skin @ 7 shillings/16 pence = £ 4:18: 6

To amount brought over £ 346: 6: 0

William Wilmouth- 1 young heifer @ £ 4: 8: 0
William Russell- 1 per linen 25 yards @ 2 shillings/9 pence; 28 sides harness @ 14 shillings = £ 23: 0: 9
Thomas Chapman- 1 dutch oven @ 9 shillings/6 pence; 1 iron pot @ 4 shillings/1pence; 1 chest @ 12 shillings; 1 spade @ 7 shillings; 2 skins @ 10 shillings = £ 2: 2: 7
Samuel Wilson- 1 iron pot @ 5 shillings
George Shoemaker son in law to **Mr. France-**
1 Kettle @ 20 shillings; 1 set gears @ 24 shillings; 6 yards cloth @ 36 shillings = £ 4: 1: 0
Isaac Ball- 1 iron pot @ 6 shillings; 1 old iron @ 7 shillings/1 pence; 1 hoe & 2 picks 11 shillings; feather bed & furniture @ 181 shilling; bedstead & board @ 10 shillings; 1 set razor & case @ 4 shillings/6 pence; 10 yards fustian @ 2 shillings/6 pence; 1 lot jugs 7 shillings/6 pence; frying pan @ 4 shillings/6 pence; shovel & tongs @ 5 shillings = £ 13: 1: 6
David Johnson- 1 smooth gun @ 14 shillings/6 pence; 1 bed quilt 16 shillings; sundry tools @ 11 shillings; frying pan @ 5 shillings/7 pence; 3 3/8 yards striped cloth @ 9 shillings/6 pence = £ 2: 1: 6
Thomas Shieds- 1 iron pot @ 6 shillings
Reuben Doughty- 1 iron pot @ 3 shillings; old wagon @ 81 shillings; old iron @ 5 shillings = £ 4: 9: 0
William Hanks- 6 sheep @ 80 shillings; 1 iron pot @ 3 shillings/2 pence = £ 4: 3: 2
Ignatius Davis- 1 set wagon boxes @ 7 shillings; 1 coverlet @ 20 shillings; 1 Salmon's Grammar @ 12 shillings; 1 per sheets @ 20 shillings; 2 table cloths @ 18 shillings/6 pence; 1 per sheets @ 34 shillings; 1 per ditto @ 17 shillings = £ 6: 8: 6
Edward Hodge- 1 cart @ 101 shillings; 1 table @ 31 shillings; 44 yards chintz @ 3 shillings/ 4 pence; 5 3/8 yards calico @ 3 shillings/8 pence = £ 8: 7: 3
Farling Ball 1 six-plate pipe stove & pipe @ £ 3: 6: 0
Edward Cunnard- 1 six-plate stove 87 shillings; 12 3/8 crape @ 4 shillings; sundry books @ 8 shillings   = £ 7: 4: 6
Aaron Scatterday- 1 smith anvil of 196 lbs. @ 9 pence = £ 7: 7: 0
James White- 1 old plow @ 3 shillings; 3 axes @ 12 shillings; 1 plow share & old iron @ 5 shillings; ewes & lambs @ 92 shillings; 6 ditto @ 49 shillings; 3 5/8 yards cloth @ 20 shillings = £ 11:13: 6
Thomas Nichols- 1 shovel plow @ 8 shillings; 1 per sheets @ 15 shillings; 4 chairs @ 12 shillings/3 pence; horse-collar & box iron @ 7 shillings = £ 2: 2: 3
James White- 1 shovel plow @ 4 shillings/6 pence; 1 set gears @ 31shillings/6 pence; 1 bedstead & board @ 12 shillings; 13 henting handkerchiefs @ 1 shillings/1 pence = £ 2: 9: 7
Benjamin Canby- 46 dry hides 779 ½ lbs. @ 10 pence; ½ of 57 sides upper @ 7 shillings/8 pence; ½ of 29 do. @ 8 shillings/6 pence; ½ of 6 hip skins @ 10 shillings/7 pence; 11 calf skins @ 71 shillings/5 pence; 6 ditto @ 34 shillings/6 pence; 8 sides harness 52 lbs. @ 2 shillings/2 pence; 2 fleshing and 1 curry knife @ 22 shillings = £ 63: 2:11
James Moore- 22 hip skins 154 @ 10¼ pence; 19 calf skins 60 @ 13 ¼ pence; 40 sides harness @ 9 shillings/4 pence; 17 sides red do. @ 11 shillings; 60 sides upper @ 8 shillings/5 pence; 2 razors & cases 4 shillings/1 pence; 1 bedstead @ 5 shillings/4 pence; combs & files @ 4 shillings/11 pence = £ 63:17: 5¼
William Blakely- ½ of 57 sides upper @ 7 shillings/8 pence; ½ of 29 sides do. @ 8 shillings/6 pence; ½ of 6 hip skins @ 10 shillings/7 pence = £ 18:13: 6

Joseph Hough- 17 sides harness @ 9 shillings/11 pence = £ 7:15: 5
Samuel Calender- 51 sides sole leather @ 6 shillings; 27 sides upper @ 8 shillings = £ 26: 2: 0
Asa Moore- 37 sides harness @ 10 shillings/4 pence; 34 calf skins @ 6 shillings/7 pence; 18 sheep & hog skins @ 1 shilling/6 pence; 8 horse hides @ 6 shillings/5 pence; 2 horse & 21 sheep skins @ 23 shillings; 1 Paradise Lost @ 3 shillings; 1 lot sundries @ 2 shillings/6 pence = £ 35:13: 0
Robert Ware- 1 feather bed & furniture @ £ 12: 5: 0
George Armstrong- 1 feather bed & furniture @ £ 11: 5: 0

Amount brought up £ 693:14: 3

Joseph Roberts- 1 feather bed & furniture @ £ 15: 0: 0
David Lacy- 1 feather bed & furniture @ £ 14:10: 0; 2 hip skins @ 5 shillings/6 pence; one lot old cask @ 3 shillings/10 pence; 7 5/8 ticking 3 shillings/7 pence = £ 16: 6: 8
Doctor John Nicklin- 3 Vol. Dictionaries of Arts & Sciences @ £ 5: 0: 0
Thomas Smith- 1 bedstead @ 7 shillings; table & cover @ 41 shillings; 10 geese @ 2/ shillings = £ 3: 8: 0
Abraham Davis- Cook's Voyages @ 2 shillings/6 pence; 25 geese @ 2 shillings; 1 sow & 3 pigs @ 24 shillings/6 pence = £ 3:17: 0
George Gregg- 1 pair sheets @ 15 shillings; 1 pair ditto @ 20 shillings; 2 table cloths @ 15 shillings/1 pence; 1 bed quilt @ 17 shillings; 1 set drawers @ 95 shillings; sundries in a lot @ 22 shillings = £ 9: 4: 1
Ebenezer Wilson- 1 pair sheets @ 24 shillings; 7 1/8 yards calico @ 3 shillings/4 pence; 1 iron pot @ 5 shillings/6 pence = £ 2:13: 3
Isaac Vandeventer- 1 pair sheets @ 9 shillings
Doctor James Heaton- 2 table cloths @ 26 shillings; sundries @ 91 shillings/7 pence = £ 5:17: 7
Mahlon Taylor- 2 table cloths @ 25 shillings; 1 ditto @ 15 shillings/6 pence; 3 horse collars @ 18 shillings/6 pence = £ 2:19: 0
Richard Griffith- 1 per pillow cases @ 2 shillings; 1 rat trap @ 8 shillings/1 pence; 80 lbs sole leather @ 16 pence; 7 calf skins @ 48 shillings; 18 calf skins @ 10 shillings = £ 13: 5: 9
Capt. Hugh Douglass- 4 napkins @ 4 shillings/6 pence; X cut saw @ 41 shillings = £ 2: 5: 6
   Note: **Samuel Perry's** account is included **Douglass's** bond
William Carr- 1 coverlid @ 30 shillings/6 pence; 1 brass kettle @ 34 shillings = £ 2:14: 6
William Wildman- 1 beds quilt @ £ 1: 8: 3
William Hough- 1 floor carpet @ 110 shillings; 1 calf skin @ 8 shillings = £ 5:18: 0
Abner Osburne- 1 tea table @ 30 shillings/6 pence; 1 brass kettle @ 22 shillings; table belong to widow   = £ 2:12: 6
James Nixon- 1 dining table @ £ 1:11: 0
Samuel Thompson- one desk & bookcase @ £ 12: 0: 0; 1 wheat fan @ 76 shillings; 1 cutting box @ 15 shillings/6 pence; 1 calf skin @ 4 shillings/9 pence; 25 yards linen @ 2 shillings/4 pence= £ 19:14: 7
Anthony Wright- 2 empty hogsheads @ 13 shillings/1 pence; 1 barrel @ 7 shillings/1 pence; 1 table @ 16 shillings/7 pence; 1 keg @ 4 shillings/4 pence = £ 2: 0: 0
Thomas Davis- 1 looking glass @ 31 shillings/6 pence; 1 yard kerseymere @ 14 shillings; 1¼ yards cloth @ 4 shillings/6 pence = £ 2:10: 0
Nancy Thompson- 1 looking glass @ £ 1: 0: 0
Betsy Thompson- 1 looking glass @ 12 shillings/6 pence
Joseph Woodward- 1 per jannett 24 yards @ 3 shillings/2 pence = £ 3:16: 0

Benjamin Meredith- 5 pair stockings @ 4 shillings; 1 side harness 15 lbs. @ 20 pence = £ 2:15: 0

John Richardson- sundries @ 2 shillings/6 pence; 1 lot ditto @ 8 shillings/6 pence; 75 lbs. sole leather @ 17 pence; 1 calf skin @ 7 shillings = £ 6: 8: 6

Benjamin Murphey- 18 lbs. wool @ 1 shilling/6 pence; 1 lot tubs & barrels @ 5 shillings/6 pence = £ 1:12: 6

Joshua Wildman- 1 lot sundries @ 3 shillings

Benjamin Meade- 1 box @ 3 shillings/4 pence; 2 fleshing & 2 curry knives @ 24 shillings/5 pence; 25 yards wild boar @ 2 shillings/8 pence = £ 4:14: 4

Mathew Wetherly- 1 iron bound cask @ 8 shillings/6 pence; 1 barrel @ 5 shillings; 1 copper stew pan @ 18 shillings = £ 1:11: 6

Joseph Tribbe- 1 fat pot & dutch oven @ 3 shillings/6 pence; 1 iron kettle @ 15 shillings; 1 bucket @ 4 shillings = £ 1: 7: 6

Joseph Wood- one large tub @ 6 shillings; 35 lbs. sole leather @ 17 pence = £ 2:15: 7

Joseph Lambag- 1 bake-iron & two pots @ 2 shillings/6 pence

Joseph Wilson- 1 iron pot @ 4 shillings/3 pence; 2 pewter dishes @ 8 shillings; 1 pewter dish and basin @ 10 shillings; 1 shovel & tongs @ 7 shillings/4 pence = £ 1: 9: 7

To amount brought over £ 840: 8: 4

John Copeland- 2 cider tubs @ 5 shillings/2 pence

Bridain Oxley- one pewter dish @ 9 shillings/1 pence; 2 calf skins @ 12 shillings; 1 pair tongs @ 6 shillings = £ 1: 7: 0

James Roach- 77 lbs. sole leather @ 17 ½ pence; 1 hog @ 30 shillings; 1 looking glass @ 5 shillings; 28½ yards calamanco @ 2 shillings/6 pence = £ 14:18:10

Nathan Ball- 27 lbs. sole leather @ 17 ½ pence; 2 calf skins @ 15 shillings; 10 yards cloth @ 6 shillings   = £ 5:13: 4½

Samuel Gregg- 6 ewes & lambs @ £ 4:11: 0

William Fox- 6 sheep @ £ 2: 8: 0

William Shipman- 4 shoats @ £ 1:17: 0

Stephen Underwood- 1 sow & 4 shoats @ £ 1:14: 6

Darby Murphy- 6 shoats @ £ 1:17: 0

Lawrence Wrigley- 6 shoats @ 25 shillings; 2 ½ yards calico @ 2 shillings/1pence = £ 1:10: 3

John Redman- 1 sow & pigs & young shoats @ 50 shillings; 1 iron shovel @ 6 shillings/1pence = £ 2:16: 1

John West- 1 calf skin @ 4 shillings/9 pence

Jonah Thompson- 1 Negro boy Will @ £ 10: 0: 0

Stacy Taylor- 13 5/8 yards durant @ 2 shillings/4 pence; 2 kings & 4 gauze handkerchiefs @ 2 shillings/10 pence; 2 ½ yards calico @ 3 shillings = £ 2:16: 4

Charles Bennett- 5 ½ yards mock kerseymere @ 5 shillings/6 pence; 1 pair scissors 1 shilling = £ 1:11: 3, deduct 3 shillings for short measure = £ 1: 8: 3

Amos Hague- 8 ½ yards camlet @ 1 shilling/9 pence; 2 yards calico @ 4 shillings/1pence = £ 1: 2: 5¼

Isaac Larrow- 14 3/8 yards jennet @ 3 shillings/6 pence = £ 2:10: 3 ¾

Edward Morriss- 23 yards camlet @ 1 shilling/9 pence = £ 2: 0: 3

Richard Mathews- 2 sides harness 23 lbs. @ 20 pence; 2 duffel blankets 18 shillings = £ 2:16: 4

Benjamin Murphey- 1 horse Trim-sharp @ £ 18: 0: 0

Received by **Jonah Thompson** for sundry sales 18 ¾ yards linen @ 2 shillings/9 pence; 8¾ yards ditto @ 2 shillings/6 pence; 9 checkered handkerchiefs @ 1 shilling/1pence; 2 cotton romals @ 3 shillings; 1 curb bridle @ 8 shillings; 1 set razor @ 4 shillings/3 pence; 3 silk handkerchiefs @ 6 shillings/1 pence; 2 3/8 yards muslin @ 3 shillings/6 pence; grindstone @ 25 shillings; 1 iron pot @ 4 shillings/7 pence; screws ½, pumice stone, and 2 trowels @ 11 shillings/3 pence; old wagon wheels @ 15 shillings; 1 plow @ 20 shillings; 2 pick axes & dung fork @ 5 shillings; 11 harrow teeth @ 8 shillings; 1 lot augers & hedge knife @ 6 shillings/9 pence; 2 pair stillards @ 22 shillings; 1 tea stand @ 7 shillings; 1 coverlid @ 7 shillings/6 pence; 1 sacking bottom bedstead @ 30 shillings; 1 brass kettle @ 42 shillings; 3 calf skins @ 19 shillings/6 pence; 1 side leather @ 10 shillings/9 pence; 1 set drawers @ 86 shillings/6 pence; 1 table & cover @ 40 shillings/6 pence; 1 calf skin @ 8 shillings/4 pence; upper leather @ 9 shillings/9 pence; 1 saddle @ 21 shillings; 1 hammer @ 2 shillings; 1 arm chair @ 7 shillings; 1 spice box @ 3 shillings; 1 check reel @ 6 shilling; 1 box @ 1 shilling/6 pence; 2 hatchels @ 7 shillings/6 pence; 1 per cards @ 1 ahilling/3 pence; 1 per bellows @ 2 shillings; 1 lot sundries @ 3 shillings/8 pence; 1 desk & trunk @ 5 shillings; milk & preserve pots @ 5 shillings; 1 iron pot @ 8 shillings; 1 dutch oven @ 5 shillings/1 pence; 1½ dozen plates @ 9 shillings; 1 side leather @ 20 shillings; 2 yards cloth @ 48 shillings; 4 sides upper 14½ @ 2 shillings/2 pence; black @ 4 shillings; 1 side upper of 1 (?) @ 20 shillings/7 pence; 1 side upper @ 9 shillings/2 pence; 1 hay fork @ 1 shilling; ½ set wagon boxes @ 7 shillings/3 pence; 1 iron pot @ 4 shillings; sundries at private sale as per sales book @ £ 12: 1: 9 = £ 47:22: 7

Sales 30th April 1795

Cash for sundries received by **Samuel Thompson** (viz.) sundry scrap leather @ 2 shillings; 1 bar steel @ 11 shillings/3 pence; 5½ shaloon @ 1 shilling/6 pence; 1 side upper @ 12 shillings; 3¾ calico @ 2 shillings/2 pence; 3 henting handkerchiefs @ 2 shillings/3 pence; 2 half gallon bottles @ 2 shillings; 2 dozen buttons @ 3 shillings/8 pence; 1 dozen ditto @ 1 shilling/3 pence; 3 linen bags @ 7 shillings/6 pence; 1 7/8 yards calico @ 3 shillings; 2 pair thread stockings @ 7 shillings/2 pence; 2 tubs @ 2 shillings; 1 hogshead @ 4 shillings/2 pence; copper (?) @ 3 shillings; 3 pair stockings @ 9 shillings; 7 plain bills for **Jno. Hanes** @ 7 shillings; for sundries sold **John Gregg** @ 99 shillings = £ 11: 7:10

To amount brought up £ 978: 3:11½

Pompy Vitus- 9 gallons metheglin @ 2 shillings; ½ yard cloth @ 9 shillings = £ 1: 7: 0
Sarah Thompson- 7600 4^d nails @ 4 shillings/6 pence; 7 beeswax @ 1 shilling/6 pence; 16 lbs. rice @ 4 shillings; 1 hearth brush @ 1 shillings/9 pence; 20 yards calamanco @ 2 shillings; 600 cedar shingles @ 30 shillings; 200 lbs. hay @ 2 shillings/6 pence; 200 sugar @ 80 shillings; 8 bushels lime @ 3 shillings; 5 barrels corn @ 12 shillings; 12 bushels buckwheat @ 3 shillings; 10 yards fearnaught @ 2 shillings; dough trough @ 3 shillings = £ 21:15: 6
John Redman- 7600 4^d nails @ 4 shillings/6 pence; sundries for T. Shunk @ 36 shilling; cooper's adze @ 2 shillings/6 pence; lot sundries @ 46 shillings/4 pence = £ 5:19: 1
Amos Hague- 4 1/8 yards (?) @ 4 shillings/3 pence; 2 shawls @ 5 shillings/6 pence; 2 silk handkerchiefs @ 5 shillings; ¾ yards kerseymere @ 11 shillings/3 pence; 3 yards wild boar @ 7 shillings/3 pence; 1 quire paper @ 1 shilling = £ 2:18: 2
Andrew Copeland- 4½ yards (?) @ 2 shillings/3 pence; 4¼ yards calamanco @ 2 shillings; 3 henting handkerchiefs @ 6 shillings; 2 black silk handkerchiefs @ 3 shillings/4 pence; 7¼ yards shaloon @ 2 shillings/4 pence = £ 2: 7: 8
Michael Ruse 7½ yards wild boar @ 1 shilling/7 pence; 3 1/8 yards striped linen @ 2 shillings/1 pence; 4 black silk handkerchiefs @ 3 shillings/6 pence = £ 1:12: 1
John Clinter- 9½ yards Joan spinning at 2 shillings; 1 candle box @ 2 shillings; 3 7/8 yards shaloon @ 2 shillings; 5¼ yards calico @ 2 shillings/8 pence = £ 2: 2: 9

Thomas Marks- 1¼ yards shaloon @ 2 shillings/10 pence; 1 bottle snuff @ 1 shilling/6 pence; 5 ¾ yards Jane @ 4 shillings/2 pence = £ 1: 8: 4

Thomas Smith- 1 candle box 2 shillings; 3 pair thread hose @ 3 shillings/6 pence; 5 tubs @ 5 shillings/8 pence; 1 pair worsted hose @ 3 shillings; 1 calf skin @ 5 shillings; 450 lbs. hay @ 2 shillings/6 pence; 2 large tumblers @ 2 shillings; 1 pair shoes @ 8 shillings/6 pence = £ 2: 9:11

Walter Crouch- 4 5/8 yards calico @ 3 shillings/10 pence; 1 shawl handkerchief @ 4 shillings/7 pence   = £ 1: 2: 4

Joseph Roberts- 2 shawl handkerchiefs @ 3 shillings/8 pence; 13 yards corduroy @ 2 shillings/5 pence   = £ 1:18: 9

Jacob Wine- 4¼ yards calico @ 2 shillings/6 pence = £ 11: 8: 0

Nicholas Tucker- 7 3/8 Jane @ 3 shillings/5 pence; 14¾ yards of Jane @ 3 shillings/7 pence; 5¼ yards linen @ 1 shilling/9 pence = £ 4: 7: 7

David Johnson- 2 silk handkerchiefs @ 7 shillings; 2 pair hose @ 3 shillings; 5 yards wild boar @ 2 shillings = £ 1: 3: 0

Robert Yates- 3 pair worsted hose @ 9 shillings; 1 dozen gauze handkerchiefs @ 30 shillings   = £ 1:19: 0

Thomas D. Stevens- 4 henting handkerchiefs @ 2 shillings/3 pence; 4¾ yards cloth @ 3 shillings = £ 1: 3: 3

John Morriss- 5¾ yards wild boar @ 2 shillings/1 pence; 1 bottle snuff @ 2 shillings/10 pence; 2 yards Janes @ 2 shillings/10 pence; 1 ¾ yards cloth @ 16 shillings; 6¼ yards calico @ 4 shillings/1 pence   = £ 17:09: 6

Thomas Davis- 10 7/8 yards Durant @ 1 shilling/10pence; 10 yards Jane @ 3 shillings/1 pence; 6 yards Joan spinning @ 2 shillings/3 pence = £ 3: 5: 2

Edward McDonald- 11½ yards Jane @ 3 shillings/8 pence = £ 2: 2: 2

Samuel Clendenin- 6¾ yards moreen @ 2 shillings; 2 7/8 yards satinet @ 15 shillings = £ 1: 7: 9

Samuel Evans- 13¼ yards Janes @ 3 shillings/1pence = £ 2: 4:10

James White- 10 yards Janes @ 3 shillings/1 pence = £ 1:10:10

Joseph Sopher- 6½ Jones spinning @ 2 shillings/10 pence; 2 shawls @ 10 shillings; 3 pairs threaded hose @ 9 shillings; 2 handkerchiefs @ 2 shillings/ 3 pence = £ 2: 1:11

Osburne King- 25 yards Durant @ 2 shillings/3 pence; 2 pair threaded stocking @ 3 shillings/7 pence   = £ 3: 3: 5

John Williams- 20 yards Janes @ 3 shillings = £ 3: 0: 0

John Nicklin Junior- 3¼ yards calico @ 3 shillings/11 pence; 5 cask(s) @ 3 shillings; 3 yards vist shapes at 4 shillings/9 pence; 1¾ yards kerseymere @ 16 shillings = £ 2:16: 0

Charles Bennett- 1 pair candlesticks @ 10 shillings = £ 0:10: 0

William Harrison- 4 yards tatternet @ 6 shillings; 1 bag @ 2 shillings = £ 1: 6: 0

To amount brought over £ 1,059:11: 9½

Samuel Thompson- 2 7/8 yards satinet @ 15 shillings; 2 yards muslinet @ 9 shillings; 1½ lbs. tea @ 4 shillings/6 pence; 1 chest lock @ 4 shillings = £ 1: 9: 6

John Potts- 2 7/8 yards satinet @ 75 shillings; 9700 10^d nails @ 12 shillings = £ 6:11: 5

Richard Mathews- 9¾ yards blue cloth @ 5 shillings; 21 yards wild boar @ 2 shillings/2 pence; 3¼ yards green baize @ 2 shillings/6 pence; 1 lbs. tea @ 3 shillings/4 pence; 1 pair blankets @ 14 shillings; 1 chest lock @ 1 shilling/3 pence; 3 quire paper @ 3 shillings = £ 6: 5: 3

Cash received by **Samuel Thompson** for sundries (Viz.)
1 scythe @ 7 shillings/6 pence; 4 lbs. flax; bran & shorts @ 18 shillings; 75 lbs. midlens @ 10 shillings/6 pence; 1 pair shoe @ 7 shillings; 14 (?) @ 2 shillings; 1 bottle snuff @ 1 shilling/8 pence; 2 silk handkerchiefs @ 6 shillings/2 pence; sundry scraps of leather sold J. Brown @ 12 shillings; 7 lbs. cotton @ 12 shillings; 1 mill spindle @ 34 shillings/4 pence; 1 pair shoes @ 8

shillings; 3½ yards velvet @ 17 shillings/6 pence; 1 side leather @ 12 shillings; 1 dutch oven per **Anthony Cunnard-** @ 10 shillings = £ 9: 9: 8

Thomas Leslie- 5 yards sagathy @ 4 shillings/6 pence; 2 yards Durant @ 2 shillings/4 pence; 2 yards muslin at 6 shillings; 10 lbs. cotton @ 1 shilling/10 pence, **Leslie** contends that the above goods were freedom dues

Jonah Thompson- 1 pair shoes @ 8 shillings/6 pence; 1 tea pot @ 1 shilling/6 pence; one cream jug @ 9 shillings = £ 0:10: 9

Stephen Ball- 4 ¾ yards cloth @ 24 shillings; 2 handkerchiefs silk @ 1 shilling = £ 5:16: 0

Thomas Bakehouse- 2 yards cloth @ 24 shillings; silk @ 1 shilling = £ 2:11: 0

Sales December 11th, 1795

Benjamin Hufty- 1 saddle cloth @ 8 shillings; 5 pair worsted hose @ 2 shilling/6 pence = £ 1: 0: 6

James Currel- 20 yards blue half thicks @ 2 shillings/2 pence = £ 2: 3: 4

Isaac Shunk- 13½ yards cloth @ 3 shillings/6 pence = £ 2: 7: 3

George Shaffer- 3¼ yards @ 5 shillings/9 pence; 6 pair worsted stockings @ 10 shillings/6 pence = £ 1:10: 1

Josiah White- Junuer(?) 14 yards moreen @ 1 shilling/8 pence = £ 1: 3: 4

Thomas Smith- 8½ yards Durant @ 1 shilling/10 pence; 12 yards ditto @ 1 shilling/11 pence; 3 yards cloth @ 5 shillings/6 pence; one trunk @ 12 shillings; 2½ yards durant @ 2 shillings/3 pence; 1 great coat @ 15 shillings; mohair & buttons @ 1 shilling; ½ yard wild boar @ 1 shilling; 1½ tea @ 3 shillings/9 pence; scissors @ 3 shillings = £ 4:19: 3

Asa Moore- 3 pair hose @ 1 shilling/10 pence; 17¾ Durant @ 1 shilling/5 pence; sundry buttons @ 15 shillings = £ 2: 5: 8

William Osburne- 9 half inch augers @ 8 shillings; 2 files @ 2 shillings/7 pence; 3 horse casks @ 4 shillings/6 pence; 17½ yards wild boar @ 1 shilling/9½ pence; 7 razors @ 4 shillings/9 pence; 2 pair snuffers @ 1 shilling/6 pence = £ 2:12: 3

Richard Griffith- 11 pair hinges @ 7 shillings/6 pence; 16 7/8 yards durant @ 1 shilling/7 pence; 19 7/8 yards half thick @ 1 shilling/7 pence; 15 lbs. cotton @ 6 shillings; sundries @ 80 shillings/5 pence; 17 yards buckram @ 1 shilling/4 pence = £ 8: 5: 2

cash for sundries received by **Samuel Thompson-** water bucket @ 3 shillings/2 pence; gouges @ 1 shilling/9pence; 1 pair snuffers @ 9 shillings; 1 trowel @ 1 shilling/6 pence; 1 blanket @ 3 shilling/10 pence; 2 dishes @ 5 shillings; 9 plates @ 3 shillings/6 pence; 1 lot sundries @ 2 shillings/6 pence; 1 lot ditto @ 4 shillings/1 pence; 1 ladder @ 14 shillings; 1 ladder @ 16 shillings/6 pence; sundries per Wm. Russell @ 34 shillings; 3 lbs. tea @ 9 shillings; 300 nails @ 3 shillings/3 pence = £ 5: 2: 8

William Hough- 1 adz @ 1 shilling/6 pence; 1 mason trowel @ 1 shilling/8 pence = £ 0: 3: 2

John Morris- 1 mason trowel @ 1 shilling/6 pence; 2 chisels @ 1 shilling/3 pence = £ 0: 2: 9

Job Cooper- 12½ yards sagathy @ 4 shillings/1 pence = £ 2:11: 0

Charles Crimm- 24 yards everlasting @ 2 shillings; 1½ yards durant @ 2 shillings = £ 2:10: 0

Amount brought up £ 1,131: 1: 1

Benjamin Whitaker- 17½ yards Durant at 1 shilling/8 pence; ½ dozen pewter plates @ 9 shillings/8 pence = £ 1:18:10

James Heaton- 2¼ yards of duffle @ 4 shillings/6 pence = £ 0:10:1½

Joseph Sophers- 3 hand irons @ 7 shillings/1 pence; 2 snuffers @ 1 shilling/6 pence; 1 trowel @ 1 shilling/7 pence; 3 augers @ 5 shillings/4 pence; 1 gouge @ 1 shilling/6 pence; 7 plates @ 3 shillings; dish and plates @ 4 shillings/9 pence; 5 pewter plates @ 7 shillings/2 pence; 1 ladder @ 2 shillings/6 pence = £ 1:14 5

William Wright- 10 yards plaid @ 1 shilling/3 pence; ½ dozen pewter plates @ 9 shillings/1pence = £ 1: 1: 7

Peter Neville- 1 set curtains @ 12 shillings; 1 lot sundries @ 2 shillings; 1 lot ditto @ 1 shilling = £ 0:15: 0

Christian Climmer- 1 coverlid @ 18 shillings = £ 0:10: 1

Nathan Smith- 1 pair hand irons @ 10 shillings/1 pence

James Tucker- 1 ladder @ 14 shillings

Stephen Roberts- 1 ladder @ 16 shillings/6 pence

Samuel Clendenen- 17¾ yards @ 1 shilling/8 pence = £ 1: 9: 7

Benjamin Murphey- 3½ yards @ 5 shillings = £ 0:17: 6

Archibald Morrison- 3 parcels cloth @ 9 shillings/6 pence; 1 3/8 yards ditto @ 12 shillings = £ 2: 5: 0

John Love- 1 smith vise @ £ 2: 5: 0

Richard Mathews- 1 blanket @ 5 shillings; 3 ounces thread @ 1 shilling/6 pence; 1 candle stick @ 1 shilling; 450 nails @ 2 shillings/3 pence; 1 funnel @ 6 shillings; 1 tea pot @ 4 shillings/6 pence; turbenlone(?) balsam @ 2 shillings/1 pence = £ 0: 7: 6

James Newhouse- 1 tea pot @ 3 shillings/9 pence; 1 chisel @ 7 shillings = £ 0: 9: 3

cash for lot of cohea tea @ 52 shillings/6 pence; tanbark @ 60 shillings received per **Jonah Thompson**   = £ 5:12: 6

Garlock Sickler- 5 lbs. nails @ £ 0: 5: 0

John Redman- 1 set desk mounting @ £ 1:10:11

Sarah Thompson- 1 complete set of tea china @ 60 shillings; 1 silver soup ladle @ £ 2; 1 pair silver sugar tongs @ 15 shillings; 6 silver tea spoons @ 25 shillings; 1 family Bible @ 10 shillings; 1 soup tureen @ 6 shillings; 1 set casters @ 36 shillings; 1 sugar glass @ 2 shillings/6 pence; 1 tea kettle @ 12 shillings; 1 cider tub @ 6 shillings; 1 tin bucket @ 6 shillings; 1 tub @ 6 shillings; 1 iron kettle @ 16 shillings; 1 coffee mill @ 7 shillings/6 pence; 1 pair fire tongs @ 36 shillings; 1 walnut table @ 42 shillings; 1 pair low bedsteads @ 12 shillings; 1 tin coffee pot @ 3 shillings/6 pence; 1large trunk @ 20 shillings; 1 small ditto @ 12 shillings; 1 table (&) 3 chairs @ 24 shillings = £ 20:16: 6

1 saddle @ 80 shillings; 1 little wheel @ 16 shillings per daughter **Nancy** = £ 4:16: 0

1 saddle @ 80 shillings; 1 little wheel @ 16 shillings per daughter **Betsey** = £ 4:16: 0

1 pot rack @ 24 shillings; 1 per pot hooks @ 3 shillings/9 pence; 1 pair trammels @ 10 shillings = £ 1:17: 9

1 sacking bottom bedstead & feather bed & furniture devised to the **widow** = £ 14: 0: 0

1	ditto	ditto	ditto	to daughter **Nancy** = £ 14: 0: 0
1	ditto	ditto	ditto	to daughter **Betsey** = £ 14: 0: 0
1	ditto	ditto	ditto	to son **Israel** = £ 16: 0: 0
1	ditto	ditto	ditto	to daughter **Sally** = £ 16: 0: 0
1	ditto	ditto	ditto	to daughter **Pleasant** = £ 16: 0: 0
1 18 day clock and case			ditto	to son **Israel** = £ 15: 0: 0

1 silver watch @ £ 5; six table & six teaspoons IST @ £ 5: 0: 0 to son **Israel** = £ 10: 0: 0

To amount brought over £ 1,132:11:11½

Jonah Thompson- to amount of sundries particularly devised-
1 black mare @ 240 shillings; 1 table & cloth @ 60 shillings; 1 set drawers @ 120 shillings; 1 saddle & bridle @ 80 shillings; 6 pewter plates @ 18 shillings; 3 basins @ 18 shillings; 1 looking glass @ 36 shillings; 6 chairs and 1 armed ditto @ 36 shillings; several under-beds = £ 31: 6: 0

Samuel Thompson- devised to him- 1 feather bed & furniture & bedstead £ 14: 0: 0; 6 silver tea & 6 table spoons 120 shillings; 1 silver table spoon @ 6 shilling; 7 yards silk @ 4 shilling; 1 (?) silk handkerchief @ 4 shillings; 1 per salts @ 6 shillings; 1 pewter tankard @ 7 shillings/6 pence; cash for I yard of cambric @ 12 shillings; (?) @ 3 shillings; 9 ditto @ 3 shillings/4 pence; 500 nails @ 5 shillings; 1 side leather @ 11 shillings/3 pence = £ 26: 1: 0

James Brown- 1 wagon with three wheels @ £ 3:11: 0

Note- 3 cotton counter-pins @ 24 shillings; 3 bed quilts @ 15 shillings; 2 pair of fine cotton sheets @ 60 shillings; 5 homemade linen sheets @ 12 shillings/6 pence; 10 homemade ditto @ 10 shillings; 1 set window curtains @ 20 shillings; 2 blue and white coverlids @ 54 shillings; 1 mixed ditto @ 20 shillings; 1 blue quilt @ 45 shillings: The above items retained by the **widow Thompson**

At a Court held for Loudoun County December the 14th 1804 this inventory and sale amount of the estate of **Israel Thompson deceased** was returned into Court and ordered to be recorded. Examined, **Chas. Binns** Clerk of Court.

(Loudoun County Will Book F, pp. 396-403)

Appendix V

This Indenture made this 5/1/1743 between William Fairfax Esq. of the County of Fairfax of the one part and George Griffeth (Griffith) of County aforesaid of the other part, 100 Acre-lot, Lease for Lives, bounded as by a survey made thereof by Amos Janney as followeth Viz. Beginning at a white oak standing by the east side of a drain of the North Fork of Kittockton and extending thence west one hundred poles to a stake by a swale crossing a swamp, crossing a creek at forty eight poles and again at ninety two poles, then south one hundred and sixty poles to a stake & stones crossing a creek at two poles then east one hundred poles to a stake crossing a drain at sixty poles thence north one hundred and sixty poles to the first station, Fairfax County Deed Book A, Part 2, pp. 330-334

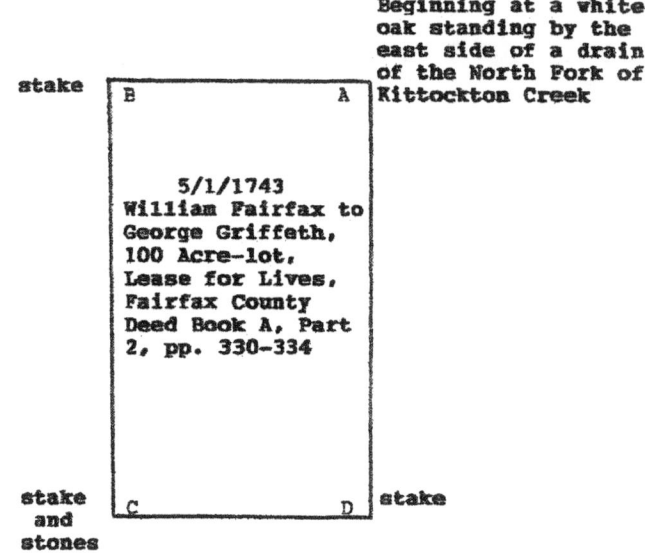

one inch = fifty poles

This Indenture made this 5/1/1743 between William Fairfax Esq. of the County of Fairfax of the one part and Jonathan Richardson of the County of Loudoun of the other part, 100 Acre-lot, Lease for lives, bounded as by a survey thereof by Amos Janney as followeth Viz. Beginning at a white oak & black oak standing by small drain of the North Fork of Kittockton & extending thence south one hundred and sixty poles to a stake near a small marked hickory thence east one hundred poles to a stake near a marked white oak thence north one hundred & sixty poles to a stake by a marked box oak thence west one hundred poles to the first station, Fairfax County Deed Book A, Part 2, pp. 337-339

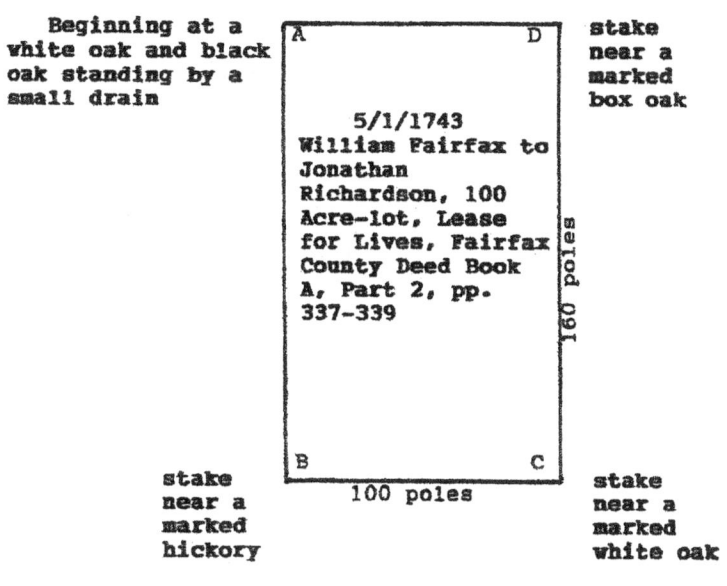

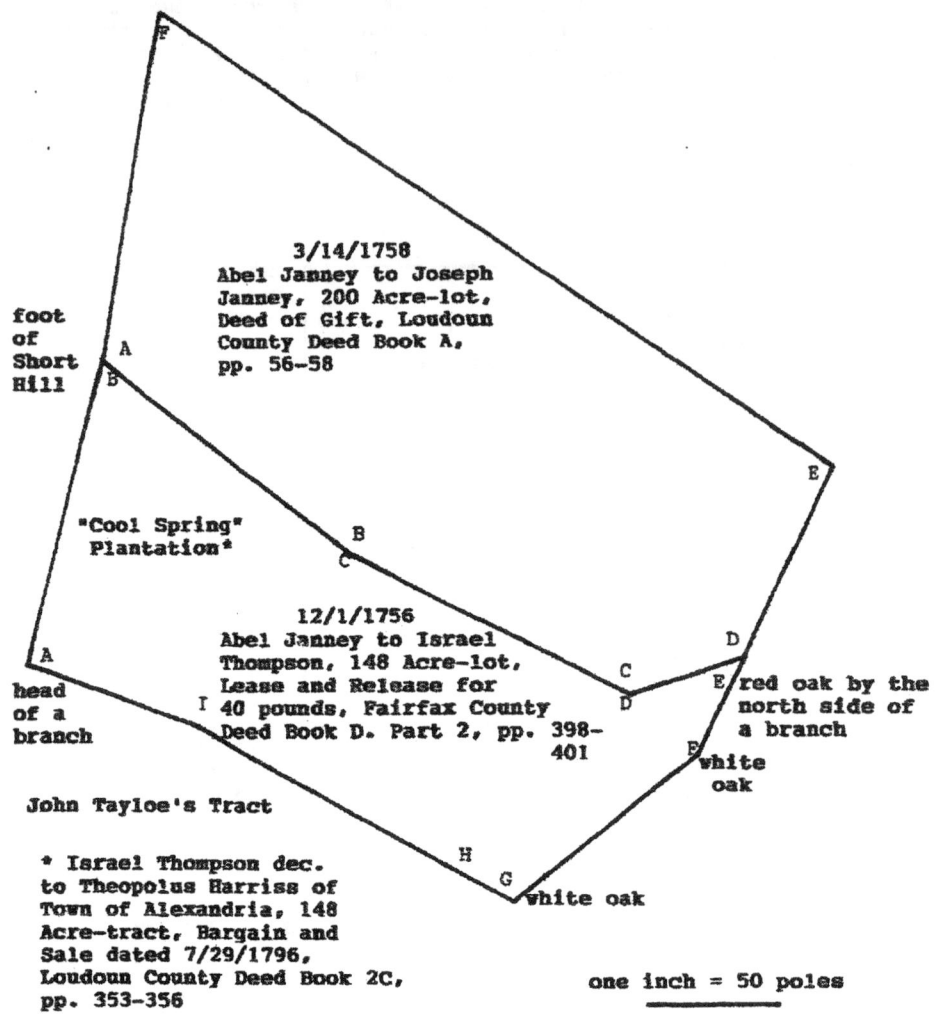

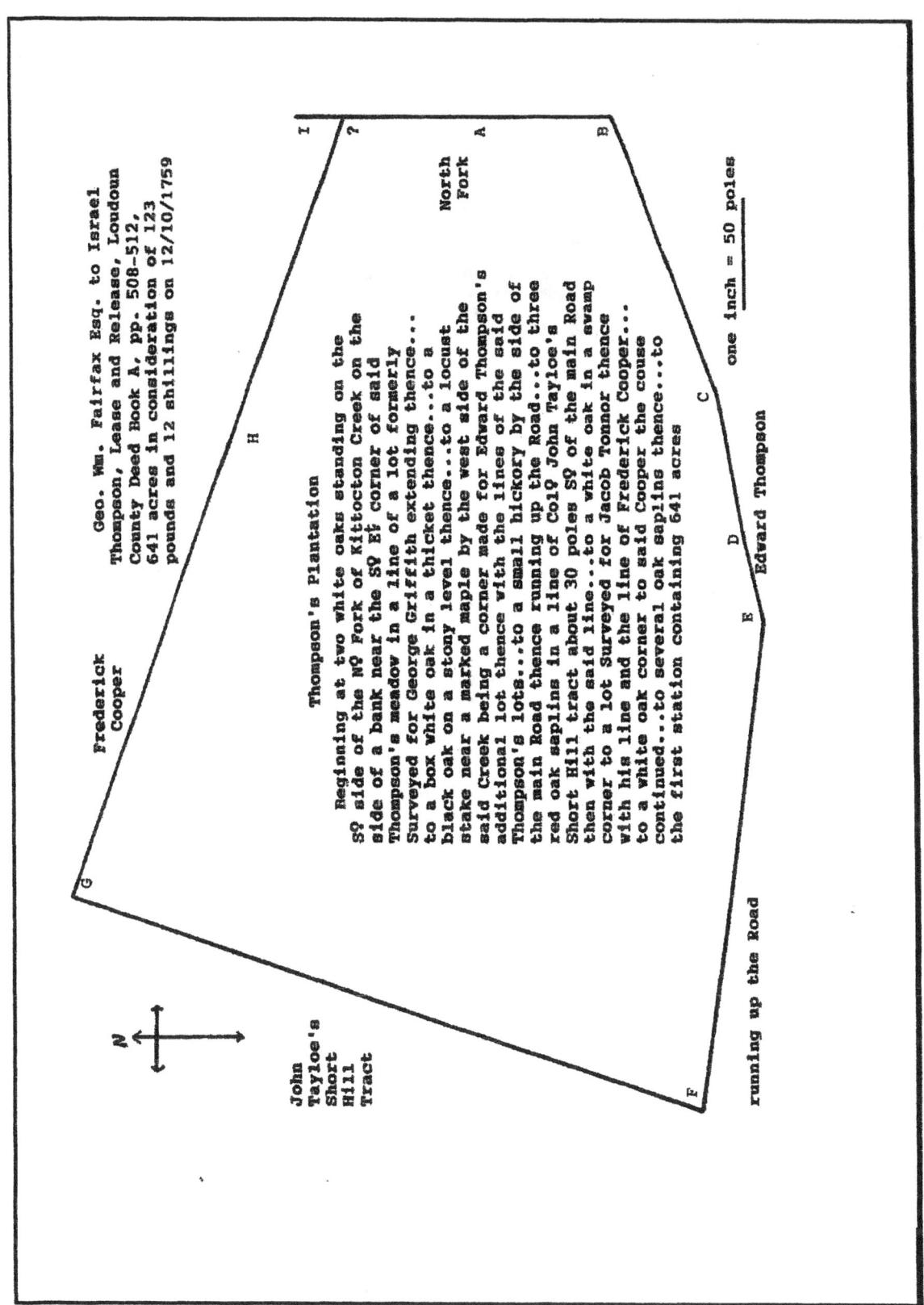

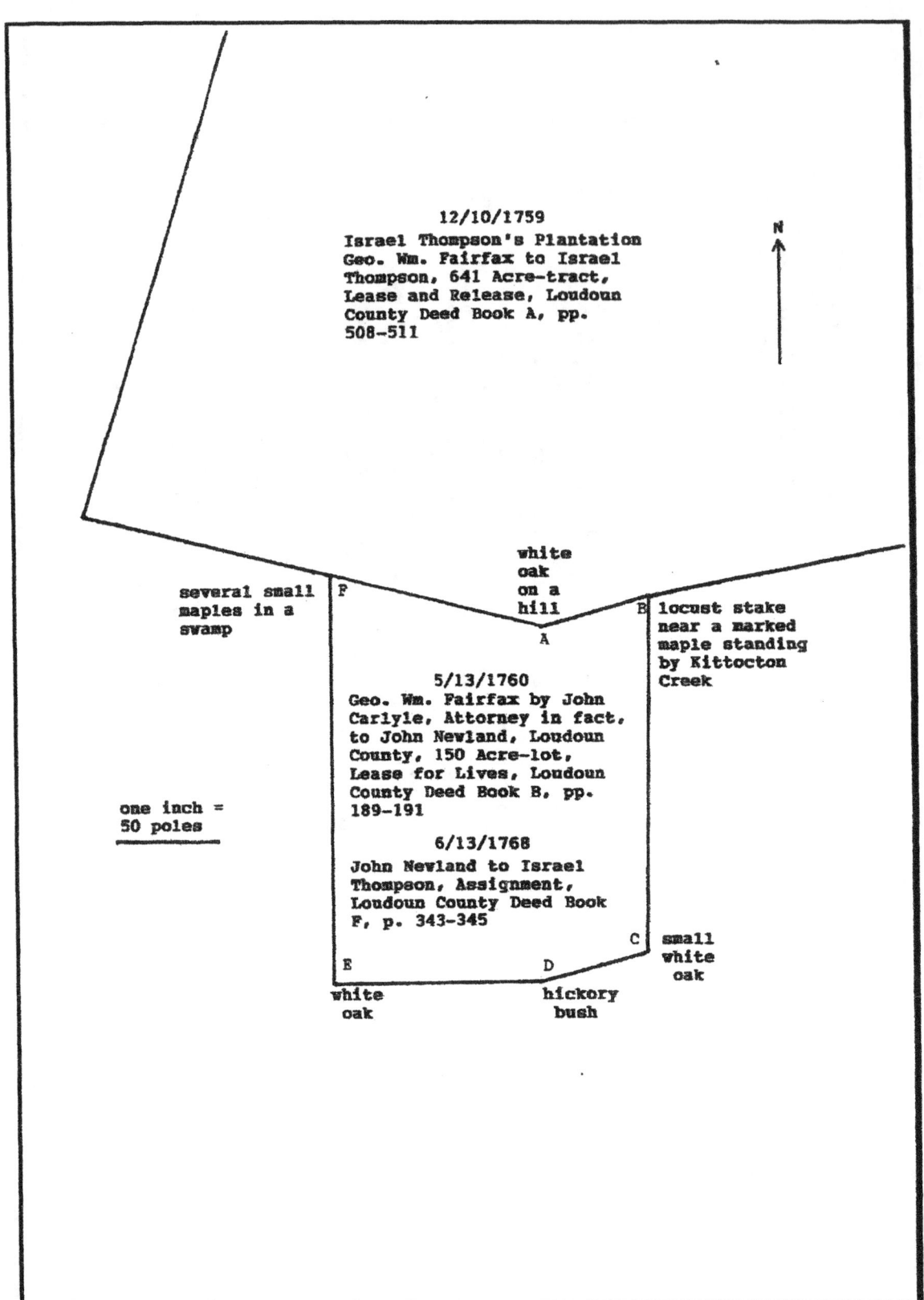

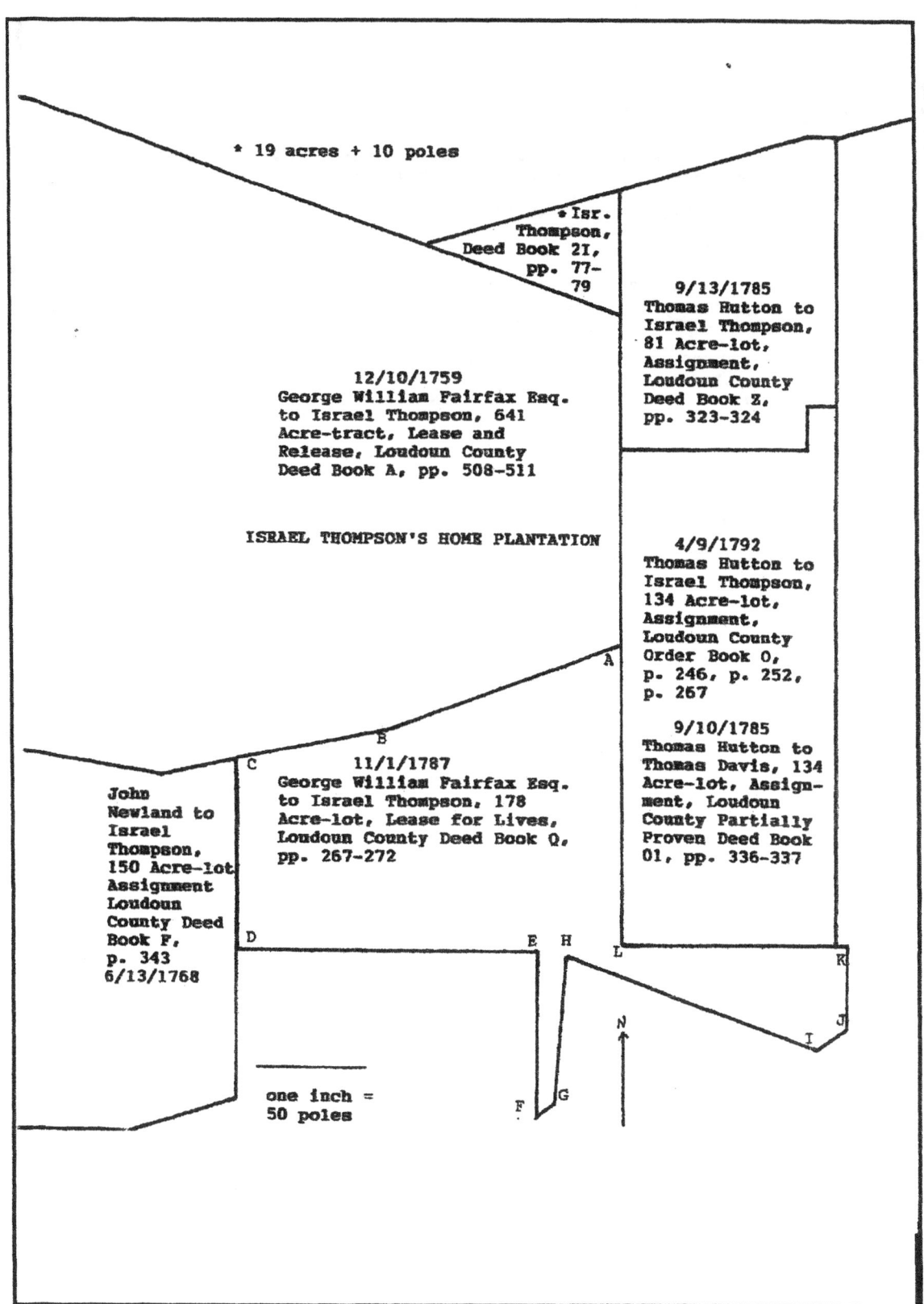

9/2/1745, William Janney to Joseph Yates, 165 Acre-lot, Assignment, see Loudoun County Deed Book V , pp. 152-154

8/29/1761, Joseph Yates to Robert Yates, 165 Acre-lot or Plantation "Get", Last Will and Testament, Loudoun County Will Book A, pp. 43-44

10/14/1793, Robert Yates to Israel Thompson, 165 Acre-lot, Assignment in consideration of 200 pounds, Loudoun County Deed Book V, pp. 152-154

4/7/1803, Ferdinando Fairfax to Sandford Ramey, 300 Acre-lot (including the subject 165 Acre-lot), Bargain and Sale, Loudoun County Deed Book 2C, pp. 304-306 (Loudoun County Deed Book 3R, pp. 38-41 dated 4/22/1828)

Israel Thompson, Administrative Account, Loudoun County Will Book F, pp. 327 - 330

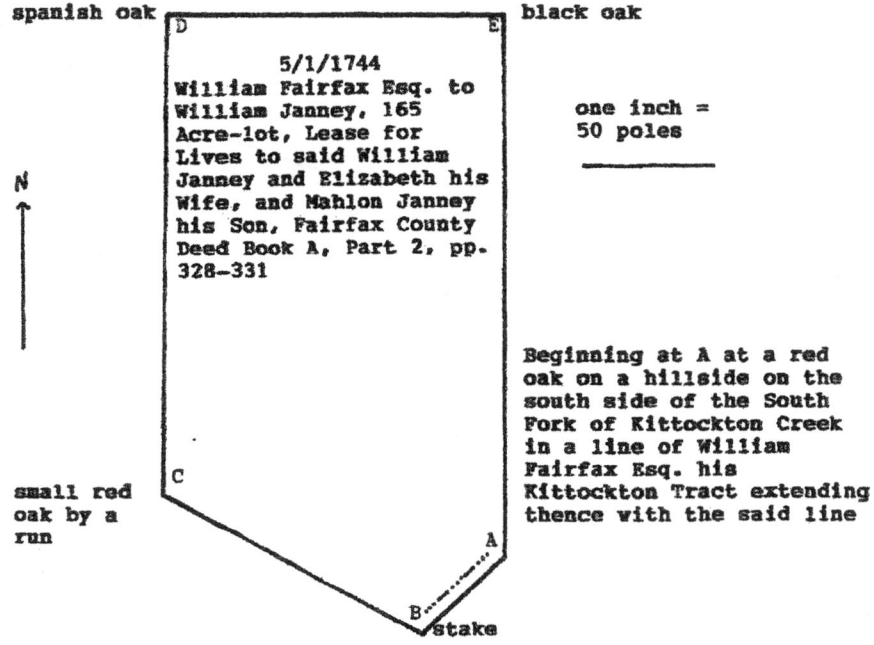

Bounded as by a Survey thereof made by Amos Janney

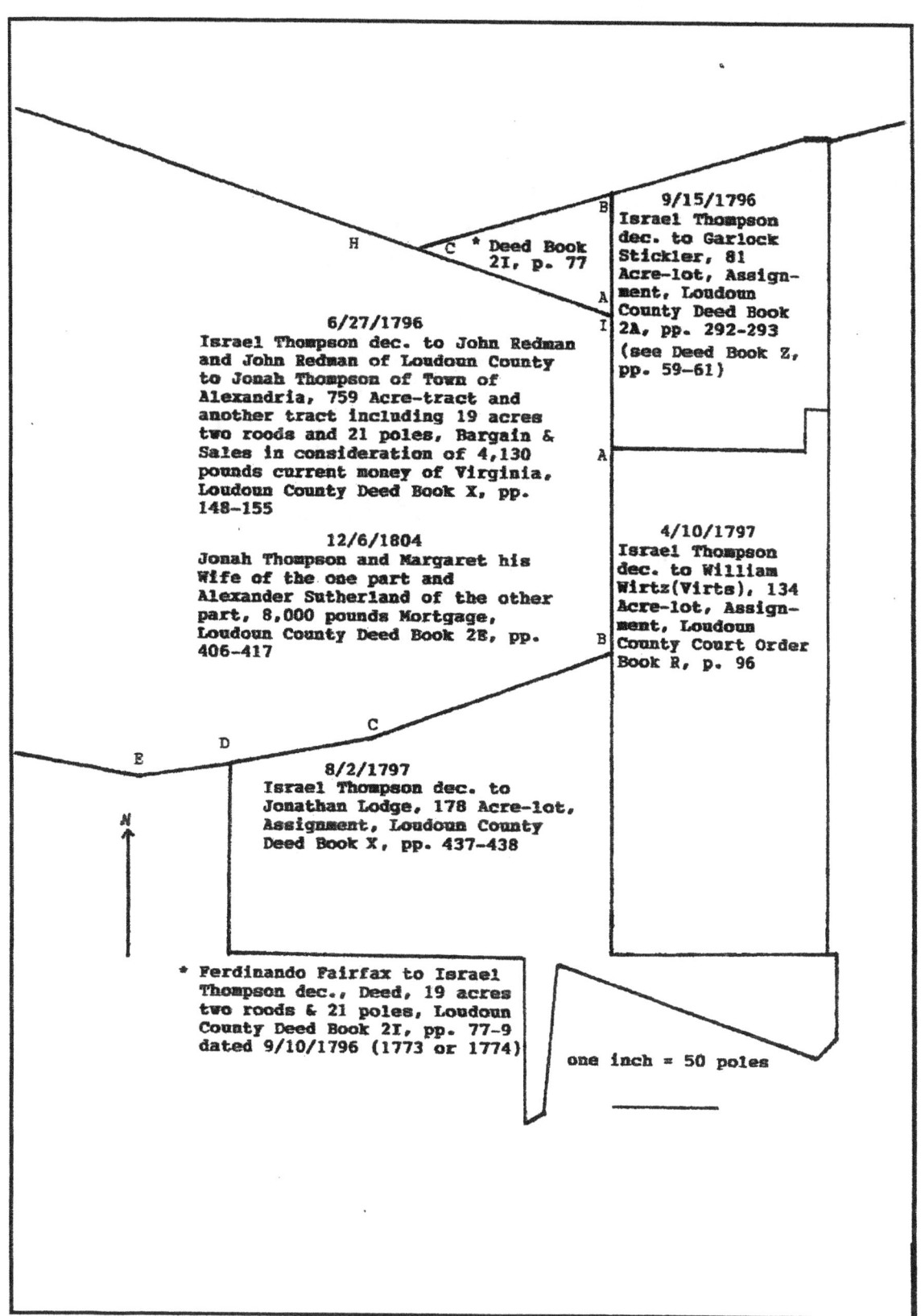

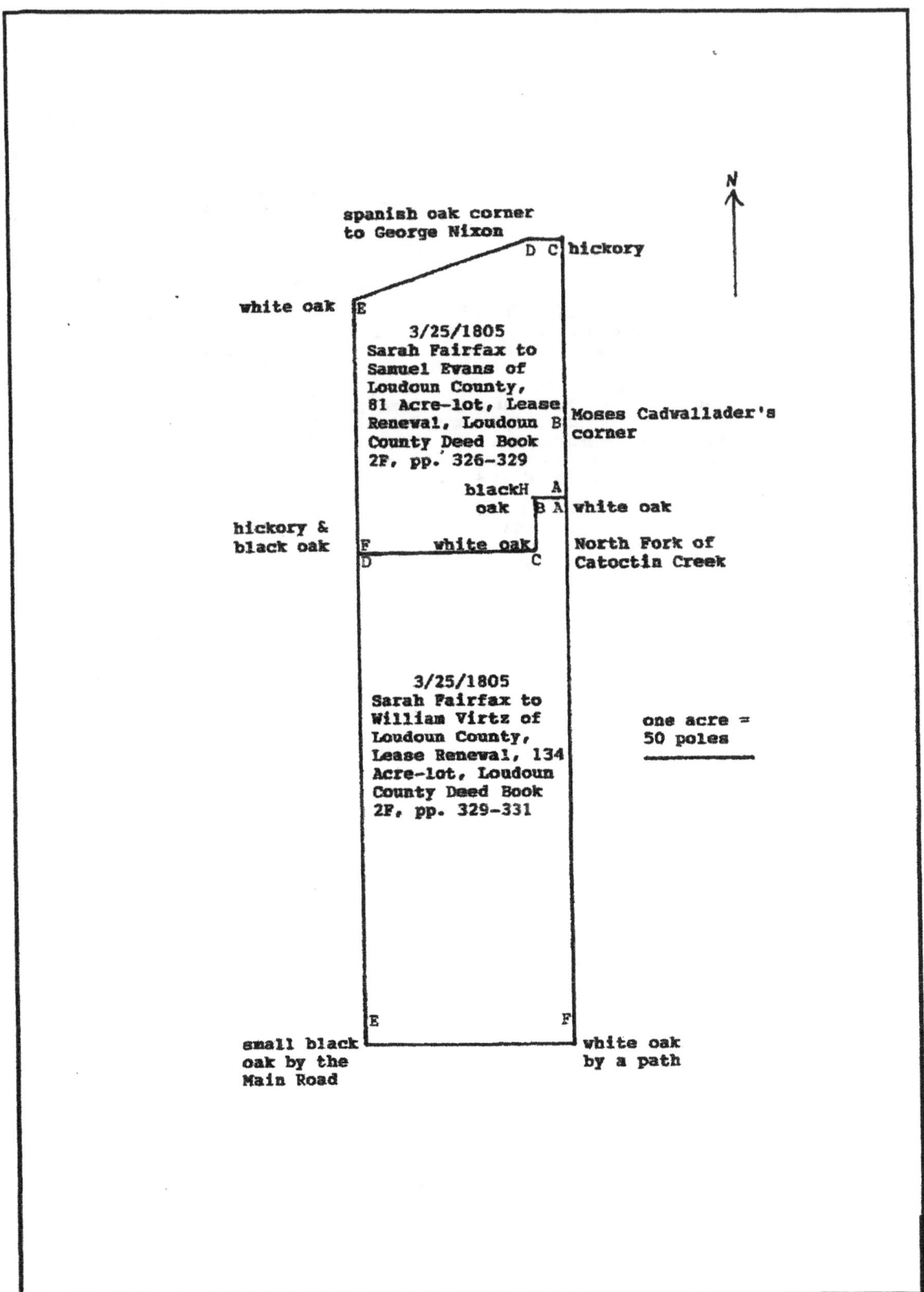

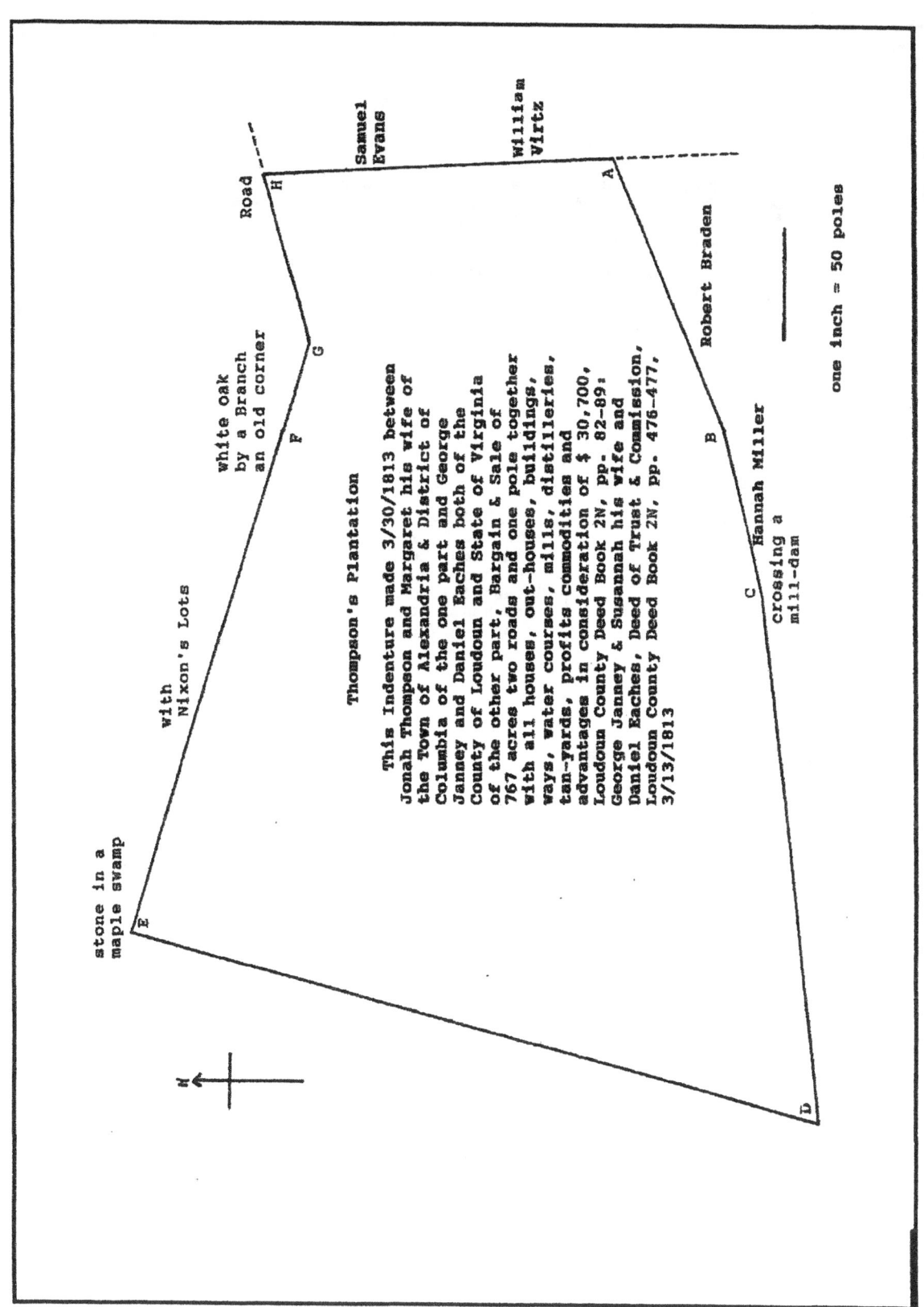

*This Indenture made this eleventh day of June, 1787, between George William Fairfax Esq. by George Nicholas his Attorney in fact of the one part and Andrew Copeland of the County of Loudoun of the other part, 18 Acre-lot, Lease for Lives including the said Andrew Copeland and Jacob Copeland and Jonathan Copeland his Sons and the longest liver of them, Loudoun County Deed Book P, pp. 587-592

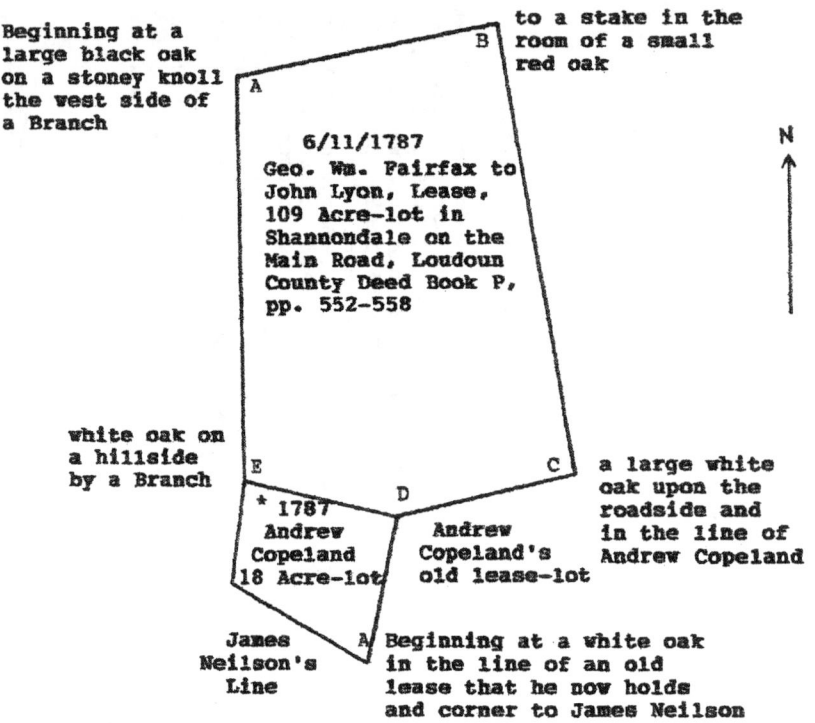

one inch = fifty poles

This Indenture made 8/15/1805 between Jonah Thompson, Richard Griffith and Mary his wife, William Hamilton and Elizabeth his wife, Israel Hague Thompson, John Vandeventer and Pleasant his wife and Sarah Thompson of the one part and Thomas Hough of the County of Loudoun & State of Virginia of the other part, Assignment of 109 Acre-lot by lease in consideration of 137 pounds and 10 shillings, Loudoun County Deed Book Z, pp. 87-89

Antecedents: 2/28/1791, John Lyons to Samuel Thompson, Assignment of 109 Acre-lot by lease, Loudoun County Deed Book U, pp. 190-192; 6/11/1787, Geo. Wm. Fairfax to John Lyon, 109 Acre-lot, Lease, Loudoun County Deed Book P, pp. 552-558

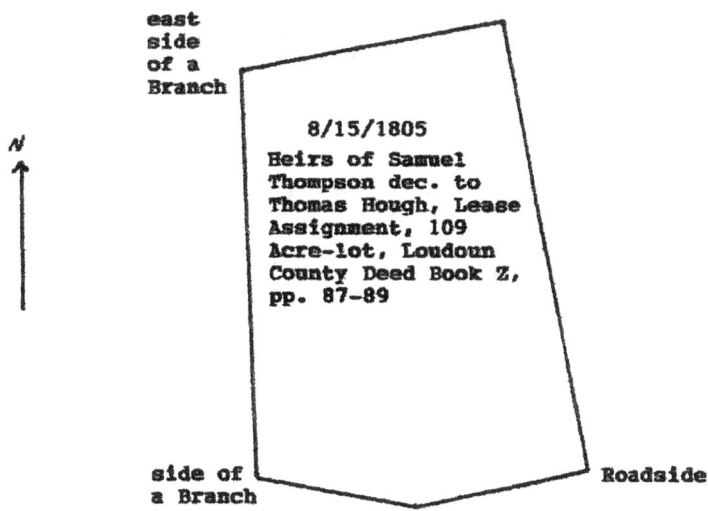

one inch = fifty poles

7/12/1811, Ferdinando Fairfax and William Bird Page of the County's of Jefferson and Frederick to Jonathan Mathews (Mathew) of the County of Loudoun, 125 Acre-lot, Bargain and Sale in consideration of $ 1,250.06, Loudoun County Deed Book 2N, pp. 393-396

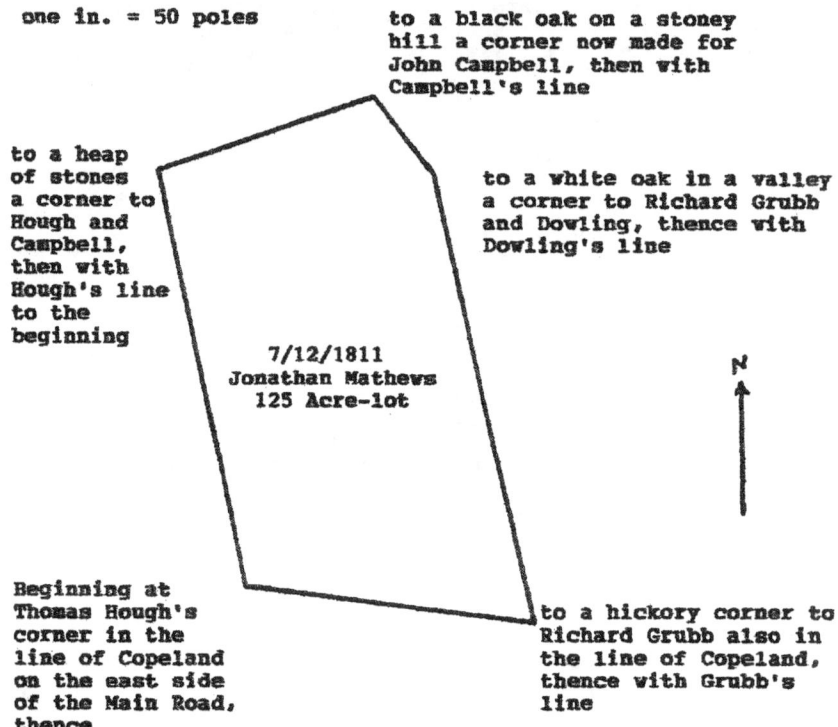

one in. = 50 poles

to a black oak on a stoney hill a corner now made for John Campbell, then with Campbell's line

to a heap of stones a corner to Hough and Campbell, then with Hough's line to the beginning

to a white oak in a valley a corner to Richard Grubb and Dowling, thence with Dowling's line

7/12/1811
Jonathan Mathews
125 Acre-lot

Beginning at Thomas Hough's corner in the line of Copeland on the east side of the Main Road, thence

to a hickory corner to Richard Grubb also in the line of Copeland, thence with Grubb's line

Antecedents: 5/1/1761, Geo. Wm. Fairfax to Samuel Phillips, 100 Acre-lot, Lease for Lives, Loudoun County Deed Book B, pp. 186-189: 8/6/1773, Samuel Phillips to Thomas Smith, Assignment, Loudoun County Deed Book K, pp. 169-171: 4/9/1789, Thomas Smith to Jesse Mathews, Assignment, Loudoun County Deed R, pp. 165-6: 9/12/1795, Jesse Mathews to Jonathan Mathews, Assignment, Loudoun County Deed Book X, pp. 158-160

Endnotes

[2] Albert Cook Myers, pp. 32-37
[3] Albert Cook Myers, pp. 41-49
[4] Carl R. Lounsbury, Editor, An Illustrated Glossary of early Southern Architecture & Landscape, The Colonial Williamsburg Foundation, Oxford University Press, New York, 1994, p. 279
[5] Asa Moore Janney and Werner Janney, Ye Meetg Hous Smal: A Short Account of Friends in Loudoun County, Virginia 1732-1980, Goose Creek Monthly Meeting of the Society of Friends(United), Lincoln, Virginia, 1980, p. 5
[6] Lawrence Washington, Administrative Account, Fairfax County Will Book 1, Part 2, pp. 536-539
[7] Carol Bryant, Abstracts of Chester County, Pennsylvania, Land Records, Volume 1 1681-1730, Willow Bend Books, Westminster, MD, 2000: Carol Bryant, Abstracts of Chester County, Pennsylvania, Land Records, Volume 2, 1729-1745, Willow Bend Books, 1999
[8] John Pitts Launey and F. Edward Wright, Early Church Records of Delaware County, Pennsylvania, Volume 1, Family Line Publications, Westminster, Maryland, 1997
[9] Charlotte Meldum & Martha Reamy, Early Church Records of Chester County, Pennsylvania, Volume 2, Family Line Publications, Westminster, Maryland, 1997
[10] Albert Cook Myers, p. 303, 329
[11] Henry C. Peden Jr., M.A. and John Pitts Launey, Early Church Records of Delaware County, Pennsylvania, Volume 2, Family Line Publications, Westminster, Maryland, 1997
[12] William Wade Hinshaw, Encyclopedia of American Quaker Genealogy, Volume II; Philadelphia Monthly Meeting, Friends Book and Supply House, Richmond, Indiana, 1938
[13] John Pitts Launey, Early Church Records of Delaware County, Pennsylvania, Volume 3, The Welsh Tract, Family Line Publications, Westminster, Maryland, 1997
[14] Martha Reamy, Early Church Records of Chester County, Pennsylvania: Volume 1, Quaker Records of Bradford Monthly Meeting, Willow Bend Books, Westminster, Maryland, 2000
[15] William Wade Hinshaw, Encyclopedia of American Quaker Genealogy; Fairfax Monthly Meeting, Friends Book and Supply House, Richmond, Indiana
[16] Albert Cook Myers, p. 60
[17] Albert Cook Myers, pp. 86-7
[18] William Wade Hinshaw, Encyclopedia of American Quaker Genealogy, Philadelphia Monthly Meeting, Friends Book and Supply House, Richmond, Indiana, 1938
[19] Albert Cook Myers, p. 17
[20] 3/15/1741, Proprietor's Office to Amos Janney of Fairfax County, Patent, Proprietor's Office, Book E, Folio 425: 4/2/1744, Amos Janney to Jacob Janney, Lease and Release, 580 Acre-tract, Fairfax County Deed Book A, Part 2, pp. 278-281
[21] 4/20/1742, Proprietor's Office to Joseph Hollingsworth of Fairfax County, Patent, 360 acres, Proprietor's Office, Book E, p. 453: 8/20/1745, Joseph Hollingsworth and Martha his wife to William Ferrall, Lease and Release of 360 acre-lot in consideration of £ 20: 0: 0, Fairfax County Deed Book A, Part 2, pp. 460-462: 4/17/1750, William Ferrall (Farrell) of Christiana Hundred in New Castle upon Delaware, miller, and Martha his wife, to Thomas Willson (Wilson) of Fairfax County, Lease and Release of 360 acre-lot in consideration of £ 40: 0: 0 as witnessed by Thomas John, Thomas Gore, Israel Thompson, Fairfax County Deed Book C, Part 1, pp. 70-73: 9/17/1754, Thomas Willson to Francis Willson, Lease and Release of 100 acre-lot (Division) as witnesses by William Wildman, Cornelius Donohoe, Israel Thompson, Stephen Peters, Fairfax County Deed Book C, Drawer X: 11/18/1755, Thomas Willson to George Cunningham, Lease and Release of 100 acre-lot (Division), Fairfax County Deed Book D, Part 1, pp. 163-165: 11/11/1764, Thomas Willson to Jonas Potts, Lease and Release of 260 acre-lot in consideration of

£ 113, Loudoun County Deed Book D, pp. 347-350; 3/5/1770, Robert Rutherford to Moses Cadwallader, Lease and Release of 100 acre-lot (Division), Loudoun County Deed Book H, pp. 209-211; 4/11/1787, Moses Cadwallader to Henry Nichols, Lease and Release of 100 acre-lot in consideration of £ 250 (Division), Loudoun County Deed Book Q, pp. 165-167

[22] Marty Hiatt, Early Church Records of Loudoun County, Virginia, 1745-1800, Willow Bend Books, Westminster, Maryland 2002, p. 108

[23] Martha Reamy, Early Church Records of Chester Count, Pennsylvania, Volume 1: Quaker Records of Bradford Monthly Meeting, Willow Bend Books, Westminster, Maryland, 2000, p. 128

[24] Martha Reamy, p. 133

[25] William Thompson may have been the son of John and Jacomintye (Elting) Thompson of Frederick County, Maryland: See John Thompson's last will and testament dated on 9/5/1748 and proven on 3/17/1750-1, Frederick County, Maryland, Will Book A1, p. 2. A certain William Thompson witnessed an indenture of lease from George William Fairfax to Francis Lamb dated 7/20/1756, for 175 acres of land on the Beaverdam Branch of Catoctin Creek, Fairfax County Deed Book R, pp. 202-204. For Forest Thompson, see Marty Hiatt, p. 64

[26] John Pitts Launey & F. Edward Wright, Early Church Records of Delaware County, Pennsylvania, Volume 1, Family Line Publications, 1997, p. 69

[27] Marty Hiatt, p. 65

[28] Charlotte Meldum & Martha Reamy, Early Church Records of Chester County, Pennsylvania, Volume 2, Family Line Publications, Westminster, Maryland, 1997, p. 20, p. 42

[29] Marty Hiatt, p. 118

[30] John Pitts Launey, First Families of Chester County, Pennsylvania, Volume 2, Willow Bend Books, Westminster, Maryland, p. 152

[31] 5/9/1759, Mahlon Janney to Edward Thompson, Lease and Release, Loudoun County Deed Book A, pp. 311-3

[32] Edward Thompson, Last Will and Testament, Loudoun County Will Book B, p. 75

[33] Israel Thompson, Last Will and Testament, Loudoun County Will Book E, p. 87

[34] Edward Thompson to Jesse Woodward Jr., Power of Attorney, Loudoun County Deed Book H, pp. 1-2

[35] Harrison Williams, Legends of Loudoun: An Account of the History and Homes of a Border County of Virginia's Northern Neck, Garrett and Massie, Inc., Richmond, Virginia, 1938, pp. 88-92

"(1755), June the 4…March'd 14 Miles and halted at an old age Quaker's with silver locks. His wife on my coming in accosted me in the following manner: 'Welcome Friend set down, thou seem full bulky to travel, but thou art young and that will enable thee. We were once so ourselves but we have been married 44 years & may say we have lived to see the Days that we have no pleasure therein'. We had recourse to our old Dish Gammon, nothing else to be had; but they had some liquor called whiskey which was made of Peaches. My Friend Thompson being a preacher, when the soldiers came in as the Spirit mov'd him, held forth to them and told them the great Virtue of Temperance. They all stared at him like pigs, but had not a word to say in their justification."

"June the 5. My lodgings not being very clean, I had so many close companions call'd Ticks that deprived me of my Night's rest, but I indulg'd till 7. We halted this day all the Nurses Baking Bread and Boiling Beef for the march to Morrow. A fine regale 2 Chickens with Milk and Water to Drink, which my friend Thompson said was fine temperate liquor. Several things lost out of my Wagon, amongst the rest they took 2 hams, which my Coach man said was an Abomination to him, and if he could find out who took them he would make them remember taking the next."

"June the 6. Took my leave of my Friend Thompson, who bid me farewell."

[36] 1749 Fairfax County Court Order Book (1749-1754), p. 52, p. 129, p. 138, p. 163, p. 171, p. 206, p. 223, p. 243, p. 271, p. 452, p. 502, p. 502: 1754 Fairfax County Court Order Book (1754-1755), p. 298, p. 379: See 3/24/1750, Lewis Ellzey to Thomas Davis, Lease for Lives, 159 acre lot of land on the west side of Kitockton Mountain (Catoctin Mountain), Fairfax County Deed Book C, pp. 156-157

[38] John Pitts Launey and F. Edward Wright, Early Church Records of Delaware County, Pennsylvania, Volume 1, Family Line Publications, 1997, p. 69 : Carol Bryant, Abstracts of Chester County, Pennsylvania Land Records, Volume 1 1681-1730, Willow Bend Books, Westminster, Maryland, 2000, p. 216

[39] Margaret Lail Hopkins, Cameron Parish in Colonial Virginia, Lynchburg, Virginia, 1988, p. 85 ("Edward Thomson")

[40] Alice Morse Earle, Forward by James Baker, American Classics: Home Life in Colonial America, Berkshire House Publishers, Stockbridge, Massachusetts, 1993, pp. 212-251

[41] Margaret Lail Hopkins, Cameron Parish in Colonial Virginia, Lynchburg, VA, 1988

[42] Roberto Costantino, Miscellaneous Road Cases, 1758-1782, Loudoun County Circuit Court, Archives, Files No. 38-48, Leesburg, Virginia, Heritage Books, Inc., Bowie, Maryland, 2003, pp. 164-165

[43] 3/6/1755, Mahlon Janney of Fairfax County to Francis Hague, Joseph Yates, John Hough, Edward Norton, and Mercer Brown, Fairfax County Deed Book D, Part 1, pp. 135-138

[44] David Hackett Fischer, Albion's Seed: Four British Folkways in America, Oxford University Press, New York, 1989, pp. 530-538

[45] Albert Cook Myers, pp. 235-236

[46] Israel Thompson, Administrative Accounts, Loudoun County Will Book F, pp. 392-395, pp. 396-403

[47] Israel Thompson, Administrative Accounts, Loudoun County Will Book F, pp. 392-395, pp. 396-403

[48] Marty Hiatt, Early Church Records of Loudoun County, Virginia 1745-1800, Family Line Publications, Westminster, Maryland, 1995, p. 63

[49] Marty Hiatt, p. 66

[50] Marty Hiatt, p. 67

[51] Marty Hiatt, p. 69

[52] Marty Hiatt, p. 77

[53] Albert Cook Myers, pp. 209-215

[54] David Hackett Fischer, pp. 485-490

[55] William Wade Hinshaw, Encyclopedia of American Quaker Genealogy, Fairfax Monthly Meeting, Friends Book and Supply House, Richmond, Indiana, 1938, pp. 551-552: Henry C. Peden, Jr., Quaker Records of Southern Maryland: Births, Deaths, Marriages and Abstracts from the Minutes, 1658-1800, pp. 34-5, p. 81

[56] Elise Grenup Jourdan, Early Families of Southern Maryland, Volume 7, Willow Bend Books and Family Line Publications, Westminster, Maryland, 1999, pp. 299-324 (pp. 305-306)

[57] Grace L. Tracey and John P. Dern, Pioneers of Old Monocacy: The Early Settlement of Frederick County, Maryland 1721-1743, Genealogical Publishing Company, Baltimore, Maryland, 1989, p. 83

[58] William Henry Farquhar, Annals of Sandy Spring: Twenty Years History of a Rural Community in Maryland, Cushings & Bailey, Baltimore, 1884, A Facsimile Reprint by Heritage Books, Inc., Westminster, Maryland, 1999, p. viiv-xxv

[59] Henry C. Peden, Jr. pp. 34-5

[60] Margaret Lail Hopkins, Cameron Parish in Colonial Virginia, Lynchburg, VA, p. 85 ("Edward Thomson")

[61] Albert Cook Myers, pp. 7-12

[62] Jay Worrall, Jr., The Friendly Virginians: America's First Quakers, Iberian Publishing Company, Athens, Georgia, 1994, p. 54

[63] John Pitts Launey and F. Edward Wright, Volume 1, pp. 91-2

[64] John Pitts Launey and F. Edward Wright, Volume 1, p. 69

[65] Vouchers for charges v. the estate of Israel Thompson from 1797 to 1801, Will Book F, Loudoun County Courthouse, Circuit Court, Archives, Leesburg, Virginia

[66] Administrative Accounts, Liber A, Volume 1, pp. 79-82, Frederick County, Maryland

[67] Vouchers for charges v. the estate of Israel Thompson from 1797 to 1801, Will Book F, Loudoun County Courthouse, Circuit Court, Archives, Leesburg, Virginia: "Births and deaths of my children with some remarks".

[68] In the estimation of the author the said lease lot was in the same place as a later land conveyance via Lease and Release from George William Fairfax to Israel Thompson which would comprise his Home Plantation. See 12/10/1759, George William Fairfax to Israel Thompson, Lease and Release, Loudoun County Deed Book A, pp. 509-513. Such a sequence of indentures from a lease lot recorded in Fairfax County, firstly, to a lease and release overlaying the earlier lease lot recorded in Loudoun County, secondly, was undertaken nearly contemporaneously between George William Fairfax and John Hough. See 6/18/1755, George William Fairfax to John Hough, Lease, Fairfax County Deed Book D, Part 1, pp. 104-106: 4/19/1759, George William Fairfax to John Hough, Lease and Release, Loudoun County Deed Book A, pp. 263-267

[69] Stuart E. Brown Jr., Virginia baron: The Story of Thomas 6th Lord Fairfax, Chesapeake Book Company, Berryville, Virginia, 1965, p. 102

[70] The private land holding named "Merryland" in Maryland, was surveyed to be a 5,000 acre-tract of land for Benjamin Tasker on 11/14/1730. Tasker assigned the certificate of survey to John Colvill. Colvill, in turn, had the "Merryland" tract resurveyed dated 2/14/1732, to be a 6,300 acre-tract of land. The "Merryland" Tract was ultimately conveyed intact on 1/23/1772 by Francis Colville, George Washington, and John West, executors to the estate of Thomas Colvill, to men named Adam Stewart, Thomas Montgomery, and Cumberland Wilson. The modern towns of Petersville, Weaverton, Brunswick, and Knoxville, have since been built in whole or in part over old "Merryland", in the most southwesterly part of Frederick County, Maryland. See Garce L. Tracey and John P. Dern, Pioneers of Old Monocacy: The early Settlement of Frederick County, Maryland 1721-1743, Reprinted for Clearfield Company, Inc. by Genealogical Publishing Company, Inc., Baltimore, Maryland, 1989, p. 37

[71] Stuart E. Brown, Jr., p. 103

[72] 5/27/1772, George William Fairfax to Michael Brown, Lease for Lives, Loudoun County Deed Book H, pp. 448-452

[73] 5/1/1743, William Fairfax to George Griffith, Lease for Lives, Fairfax County Deed Book A, Part 2, pp. 330-334

[74] 8/12/1745, George Griffeth to Samuel Mead, Lease Assignment, Fairfax County Deed Book A, Part 2, pp. 488-489

[75] 5/1/1743, William Fairfax to Jonathan Richardson, Lease for Lives, Fairfax County Deed Book A, Part 2, pp. 337-339

[76] 5/1/1744, William Fairfax to Samuel Gregg, Lease for Lives, Fairfax County Deed Book A, Part 2, pp. 334-336

[77] 5/1/1744, William Fairfax to John Hough, Lease for Lives, Fairfax County Deed Book A, Part 2, pp. 340-342

[78] 5/1/1744, William Fairfax to John Bishop, Lease for Lives, Fairfax County Deed Book A, Part 2, pp. 342-344

[79] 5/1/1744, William Fairfax to William Janney, Lease for Lives, Fairfax County Deed Book A, Part 2, pp. 328-331

[80] 9/2/1745, William Janney to Joseph Yates, Assignment, Loudoun County Deed Book 2E, pp. 152-154

[81] 6/18/1755, George William Fairfax to John Hough, Lease for Lives unto John Hough, Amos Hough, and Samuel Hough, 150 acres of land on the North Fork of Catoctin Creek near the Great Gap in the Short Hill, Fairfax County Deed Book D, Part 1, pp. 104-106: 9/10/1755, George William Fairfax to Samuel Smith, Lease for Lives unto Samuel Smith, Sarah Smith, and Mary Ann Smith his daughter, 150 acres of land on Dutchmans Run, Fairfax County Deed Book D, Part 1, pp. 189-191: 7/16/1756, George William Fairfax to Andrew Redman, Lease for Lives, 100 acres of land unto Andrew Redman, Mary Redman his wife, and William Redman his son, Fairfax County Deed Book D, Part 1, pp. 293-296: 7/20/1756, George William Fairfax to Thomas Lamb, Lease for Lives unto Thomas Lamb, Ossi Lamb his wife, Thomas Lamb his son, 150 acres on the Beaverdam Branch of Catoctin Creek, witnessed by John Hough, William Thompson, Benjamin Harris, Fairfax County Deed Book D, Part 1, pp. 294-296.

[82] 12/1/1756, Abel Janney to Israel Thompson, Lease and Release, Fairfax County Deed Book D, Part 2, pp. 398-401

[83] Israel Thompson's Last Will and Testament, Loudoun County Will Book E, pp. 87-93: 7/29/1796, Jonah Thompson, Samuel Thompson, and William Hough, Executors of Israel Thompson deceased to Theopulus Harriss, Bargain and Sale, Loudoun County Deed Book 2C, pp. 353-356

[84] Roberto Costantino, pp. 49-50

[85] Edited by Lois Green Carr, Philip D. Morgan, and Jean B. Russo, Colonial Chesapeake Society: "Slave Life in Piedmont, Virginia 1720-1800", by Philip D. Morgan, The Institute of Early American History and Culture, Williamsburg, Virginia, The University of North Carolina Press, Chapel Hill, North Carolina, 1988, pp. 433-484

[86] Karen Mauer Green, The Maryland Gazette 1727-1761: Genealogical and Historical Abstracts, The Frontier Press, Galveston, Texas, 1989, p. 247

[87] 7/17/1757, George William Fairfax to Isaac Hollingsworth, Lease and Release, 300 acres of land on the south side of the Beaverdam Branch of Catoctin Creek, Loudoun County Deed Book A, pp. 7-9: 4/9/1759, George William Fairfax to John Hough, Release, 150 acre lot of land on the North Fork of Catoctin Creek below the Gap in the Short Hill, Loudoun County Deed Book A, pp. 263-265: 4/10/1759, George William Fairfax to Stephen Harlan, Lease for Lives, 140 acre lot of land, Loudoun County Deed Book A, pp. 268-271: 12/10/1759, George William Fairfax to Ellen Poultney, Lease and Release, 200 acre lot of land, Loudoun County Deed Book A, pp. 347-351

[88] Karen Mauer Green, p. 252

[89] Israel Thompson, Administrative Accounts, Loudoun County Will Book F, pp. 392-395

[90] Israel Thompson, Administrative Accounts, Loudoun County Will Book F, pp. 392-395, pp. 396-403

[91] Israel Thompson, Administrative Accounts, Loudoun County Will Book F, pp. 392-395, pp. 396-403

[92] 2/13/1758, Nicholas Minor to Israel Thompson, Feoffment, Loudoun County Deed Book A, pp. 66-67

[93] Sarah S. Hughes, Surveyors & Statesmen: Land Measuring in Colonial Virginia, The Virginia Surveyors Foundation, Ltd. And The Virginia Association of Surveyors, Inc. 1979, p. 136

[94] 12/11/1759, George William Fairfax Esquire to Israel Thompson, Lease and Release, Loudoun County Deed Book A, pp. 509-513.

[95] 5/1/1743, William Fairfax to George Griffith, Lease for Lives, Fairfax County Deed Book A, Part 2, pp. 330-334

[96] Fairfax Harrison, Landmarks of Old Prince William: A Study of Origins in Northern Virginia in Two Volumes, Chesapeake Book Company, Berryville, Virginia, 1964, Footnote No. 130, p. 512 (Writings of Washington, ed. Ford, ii, 181)

[97] The Snickers's Gap ("Sniggers Gap")was previously known as the William's or Williams's Gap

[98] Carl R. Lounsbury, pp. 300-301

[99] Carl R. Lounsbury, pp. 300-301

[100] 1/22/1744, Joseph Richardson to Israel Thompson, Bill of Sale, Loudoun County Deed Book K, p. 283

[101] Loudoun County Court Order Book A, p. 584

[102] Carl R. Lounsbury, p. 168

[103] Carl R. Lounsbury, p. 232

[104] Carl R. Lounsbury, p. 399

[105] Loudoun County Court Order Book D 1767-1770, p. 23

[106] Roberto Costantino, p. 49, p. 120

[107] Roberto Costantino, p. 91

[108] 5/13/1761, John Newland to Israel Thompson, Assignment, Loudoun County Deed Book F, pp. 393-395. Note: It is the author's estimation that this land would become the property of one or more of Israel Thompson's near relatives. See Israel Thompson, Administrative Accounts, Loudoun County Will Book F, pp. 327-330 (p. 328). Also, 5/5/1796, Penelope Tucker of Loudoun County & Lomax Thompson of Fayette County, Pennsylvania, executors of Andrew Thompson, to Michael Virts of Loudoun County, Assignment, Loudoun County Deed Book X, pp. 31-33: 4/9/1805, Ferdinando Fairfax to Joseph Lewis Junior, Bargain and Sale, Loudoun County Deed Book 2C, pp. 388-392 ("Road corner to Andrew Thompson's Lot"; "Joseph Thompson's Field his corner stone"; "Jonah Thompson's mill pond"; "corner in Jonah Thompson's line"; "the line of Jonathan Lodge and Edward McDaniel"; "Thomas Tribbe's lot"; "line to Richard Brown thence with his line"; "line of James Clendenning")

[109] 12/11/1770, George Tingle to Israel Thompson, Bill of Sale, Loudoun County Deed Book H, p. 166. Note: It is the author's estimation that this land would become the property of one of the above listed relatives of Israel Thompson's, as above (Endnote No. 89).

[110] Roberto Costantino, pp. 122-3

[111] 6/14/1762, Francis Hague and Jane his wife to Mahlon Janney, Lease and Release, Loudoun County Deed Book C, Part 1, pp. 367-372

[113] 6/14/1762, Francis Hague and Jane his wife to Mahlon Janney, Lease and Release, Loudoun County Deed Book C, Part 1, pp. 367-372

[114] 8/28/1731, Proprietor's Office Patent for 703 acres of land to Catesby Cocke: 11/20/1733, Catesby Cocke to John Mead, Lease and Release, 703 acre-lot of land, Liber B, Folio 187: 2/16/1742, John Mead, carpenter, to David Griffeth, Lease and Release, 147 acre-lot in consideration of £ 12, Fairfax County Deed Book A, Part 1, pp. 13-15: 3/19/1743, John Mead, carpenter, to Francis Hague, yeoman, 303 acre-lot in consideration of £ 30 ("the remaining part"), Fairfax County Deed Book A, Part 2, pp. 282-285. Amos Janney possessed a land holding on Francis Hague's southern boundary line. Also, Francis Hague would acquire adjacent land from Amos Janney; land that Mary McGeach had purchased from John Mercer and Sons (See Thomas Hague, Samuel Hague, and Israel Thompson, Executors of Francis Hague deceased to William Hough on 6/7/1788, Lease and Release, 406 acre tract of land in consideration of £ 900, Loudoun County Deed Book Z, pp. 80-86).

[115] 5/4/1770, John Hough to Mahlon Janney, Lease and Release, 155 acre lot of land, Loudoun County Deed Book H, pp. 34-37

[116] 7/20/1761, Charles Earl of Tankerville to John Patterson, Letter of Attorney, Loudoun County Deed Book C, pp. 98-109: 7/12/1761, John West and Catharine his wife to John Hough, Loudoun County Deed Book B, pp. 242-7, Deed Book C, pp. 270-272.

[118] 3/12/1773, Francis Hague to Thomas Hague, Lease and Release, Loudoun County Deed Book I, pp. 168-173

[120] 2/16/1791, Joseph Janney and Hannah his wife to Stephen Wilson, Bargain and Sale, Loudoun County Deed Book S, pp. 325-328: 4/18/1794, John Janney and John Janney Junior, Executors of Joseph Janney dec. to John Williams, Bargain and Sale, Loudoun County Deed Book 2C, pp. 21-23

[121] George William Fairfax to Joseph Miers (Myers), Lease for Lives, Loudoun County Deed Book C, pp. 235-238

[122] Yardley Taylor, Memoir of Loudoun County, Virginia: To accompany The Map of Loudoun County by Yardley Taylor, Surveyor, Thomas Reynolds, Publisher, Leesburg, Robert Pearsall Smith, No. 15 Minor Street, Philadelphia, 1853, p. 22

[124] 4/24/1761, John Patterson attorney in fact for the Right Honorable Charles Earl of Tankerville of Great Britain to Samuel Schooley, Lease for Lives unto said Samuel Schooley for and during the natural lives of Garret Albertson aged 24 years, and William Schooley aged 5 years, and Nicholas Schooley aged one year, Loudoun County Deed Book C, pp. 5-10: 4/24/1761, John Patterson attorney in fact for the right Honorable Charles Earl of Tankerville of Great Britain to Samuel Schooley, Lease for Lives unto Samuel Schooley aged 32, and for Dorothy Schooley aged 24, and Garrett Schooley aged three, Loudoun County Deed Book C, pp. 10-14

[125] Roberto Costantino, p. 7, p. 9, p. 80, p. 83

[126] Roberto Costantino, p. 7, p. 41

[127] 6/9/1766, Joseph Hough to John Hough, Lease and Release, Loudoun County Deed Book E, pp. 77-81

[128] Roberto Costantino, p. 128, p. 146

[129] 5/8/1770, Mahlon Janney to John Hough, 150 acre lot of land, Lease and Release, Loudoun County Deed Book H, pp. 29-33

[130] Roberto Costantino, p. 91

[131] 4/9/1759, George William Fairfax to John Hough, Lease and Release, Loudoun County Deed Book A, pp. 263-267

[132] A plat of Col. John Tayloe's Kittockton Land by Col. Bertrand Ewell, Loudoun County Deed Book A, p. 232

[133] Roberto Costantino, p. 174

[134] 12/2/1749, Henry Brown to Edward Norton, Lease and Release, 100 acre-lot of land, Fairfax County Deed Book C, Part 1, pp. 35-38 ("about 20 poles from line surveyed for Saml. Mayberry now William Kirk extending thence parallel with Kirk's Line"): 9/22/1793, Richard Williams to Thomas Taylor, 135 acre-lot of land, Lease and Release, Loudoun County Deed Book V, pp. 138-142 (Beginning at a black oak standing in a line of Thomas Taylor which he purchased of Mercer Brown formerly one Maybury's land extending thence with the said line") Note: The said Saml. Mayberry (Maxberry) may have been in the iron monger business, possibly, as there was a contemporary Thomas Mayberry who had agreed to erect a 'bloomery for making bar iron on the plantation of William Vestal, lying upon Shunnandore' for William Vestal, John Fraden, Richard Stephenson and Daniel Burnett. See Norris, J.E., History of The Lower Shenandoah Valley Counties of Frederick, Berkeley, Jefferson, and Clark, Virginia, A Heritage Classic (facsimile reprint) Heritage Books, Inc., Bowie, Maryland 20716

[135] 5/21/1745, Richard Brown's Last Will and Testament, Fairfax County Will Book A, Part 1, p. 110: 11/5/1745, Hugh West to Richard brown, Lease, 200 acre-lot, Fairfax County Deed Book A, Part 1, pp. 507-509: 1/6/1749, Henry Brown to Edmund Sands, Lease and Release of 304

acre-lot, Fairfax County Deed Book C, Part 1, pp. 32-34: 12/2/1749, Henry Brown and Esther his wife to Edward Norton, Lease and Release, 100 acre-lot, Fairfax County Deed Book C, Part 1, pp. 35-38: 9/19/1750, Edmund Sands to Richard Roach, 100 acre-lot (Division), Fairfax County Deed Book C, Part 1, pp. 67-70: 11/5/1750, Richard Brown to William Brown, Lease, Fairfax County Deed Book C, Part 1, pp. 22-23: 8/11/1754, Edmund Sands to Richard Roach, 23 acre-lot (Division), Fairfax County Deed Book C, Part 1, pp. 789-792: 6/15/1762, Edward Norton to Richard Williams of Bucks County, Pennsylvania, Lease and Release, 100 acre-lot (Henry Brown to Edward Norton) and a 400 acre-lot (Aneous Campbell for Catesby Cocke to Edward Norton), Loudoun County Deed Book C, Part 1, pp. 35-38: 8/11/1763, Henry Brown to Richard Williams, Lease and Release, 76 acre-lot of land, Loudoun County Deed Book C, Part 2, pp. 709-713: 6/10/1774, Richard Williams to Joseph Sands, Lease and Release, 73 acre-lot of land, Loudoun County Deed Book K, pp. 269-272: 10/8/1784, Mercer Brown to Thomas Taylor, Lease and Release 300 acre-lot of land in consideration of £ 1,600, Loudoun County Deed Book O, p. 141: 8/15/1785, Joseph Sands to Jacob Sands, Lease and Release, 80 acre-lot and 22 acre lot ("lying on the east side of the road leading from Thos. Taylor's Mill to Fairfax Meeting house"), Loudoun County Deed Book P, pp. 376-378: 8/17/1786, Joseph Sands to Isaac Sands, Bargain and Sale, 53 acre lot of land, Loudoun County Deed Book P, pp. 378-381: 5/16/1793, The Right Honorable Charles Earl of Tankerville & the Honorable Henry Ostley Bennett both of Great Britain to Moses Plummer, Bargain and Sale, 109½ acre-lot of land, Loudoun County Deed Book V, pp. 116-123 ("Henry Brown's Corner"); ("south side of Roaches Mill Road"): 9/22/1793, Richard Williams to Thomas Taylor, Lease and Release of 135 acre-lot of land, Loudoun County Deed Book V, pp. 138-142: 5/11/1803, Writ of Aquod damnum awarded to Adam Householder Jr. (Hamilton Mills), Loudoun County Deed Book 2D, pp. 110-114: 4/2/1810, William Brown and Hannah his wife to John Hamilton, Bargain and Sale of 224 acres of land, Loudoun County Deed Book 2O, pp. 321-324: 2/9/1829, Division of Henry Taylor's Land (plat), Loudoun County Deed Book 3T, pp. 107-109

[136] See Edmund Sands's Will ("I give and Bequeath to my Son Isaac Sands, all my land or that part of my land below the Bigg Road coming from Mercer Brown's Mill, from Henry Brown's corner near the said Road, to Richard Roach's corner at the cross roads down to Catockton Kreek, all below said Road"), Loudoun County Will Book B, pp. 102-104

[137] Forms of Declaration for Assurance, R1 V1 No. 55, 1796, Virginia State Library, Richmond

[138] Forms of Declaration for Assurance, R4 V37 No. 533, 1805, Virginia State Library, Richmond

[139] John Jay Janney's Virginia: An American Farm Lad's Life in the Early 19th Century, Edited by Werner L. Janney and Asa Moore Janney, p. 74

[140] Israel Thompson, Accounts, Loudoun County Will Book F, p. 395

[141] 3/29/1771, Thomas Shepherd to William Neilson, Lease, Loudoun County Deed Book H, pp. 131-135

[142] Loudoun County Court Order Book K, p. 54, Loudoun County Court Order Book L, p. 265, Loudoun County Court Order Book M, p. 111

[143] Vouchers for charges v. the estate of Israel Thompson from 1797 to 1801, Will Book F, Loudoun County Courthouse, Circuit Court, Archives, Leesburg, Virginia

[144] Vouchers for charges v. the estate of Israel Thompson from 1797 to 1801, Will Book F, Loudoun County Courthouse, Circuit Court, Archives, Leesburg, Virginia

[145] Vouchers for charges v. the estate of Israel Thompson from 1797 to 1801, Will Book F, Loudoun County Courthouse, Circuit Court, Archives, Leesburg, Virginia

[146] Vouchers for charges v. the estate of Israel Thompson from 1797 to 1801, Will Book F, Loudoun County Courthouse, Circuit Court, Archives, Leesburg, Virginia

[147] Edwin J. Perkins, The Economy of Colonial America, Second Edition, Columbia University Press, New York, 1988, p. 136-137

[148] Edwin J. Perkins, p. 63
[149] Vouchers for charges v. the estate of Israel Thompson from 1797 to 1801, Will Book F, Loudoun County Courthouse, Circuit Court, Archives, Leesburg, Virginia
[150] Vouchers for charges v. the estate of Israel Thompson from 1797 to 1801, Will Book F, Loudoun County Courthouse, Circuit Court, Archives, Leesburg, Virginia, "Births and deaths of my children with some remarks"
[151] David Hackett Fischer, pp. 517-522
[152] Vouchers for charges v. the estate of Israel Thompson from 1797 to 1801, Will Book F, Loudoun County Courthouse, Circuit Court, Archives, Leesburg, Virginia, "Births and deaths of my children with some remarks"
[153] Vouchers for charges v. the estate of Israel Thompson from 1797 to 1801, Will Book F, Loudoun County Courthouse, Circuit Court, Archives, Leesburg, Virginia, "Births and deaths of my children with some remarks"
[154] Marty Hiatt, Early Church Records of Loudoun County, Family Line Publications, Westminster, Maryland, 1995
[155] Israel Thompson, Last Will and Testament, Loudoun County Will Book E, pp. 87-92
[156] Edwin J. Perkins, p. 146
[157] Vouchers for charges v. the estate of Israel Thompson from 1797 to 1801, Will Book F, Loudoun County Courthouse, Circuit Court, Archives, Leesburg, Virginia, "Births and deaths of my children with some remarks"
[158] 5/7/1768, Samuel Harned to Israel Thompson, Bill of Sale, Loudoun County Deed Book D, pp. 37-38
[159] Israel Thompson, Administrative Accounts, Loudoun County Will Book F, pp. 392-395, pp. 396-403
[160] Boyd Crumrine, Virginia Court Records in Southwestern Pennsylvania: Records of the District of West Augusta and Ohio and Yohogania Counties, Virginia 1775-1780, Consolidated Edition, With an Index by Inez Waldenmaier, Genealogical Publishing Co., Inc., Baltimore, Maryland, 1974, p. 277, p. 362
[161] Chancery Suits, Loudoun County Circuit Court, Archives, Jacob Hite's Administrators versus Israel Thompson, 1788, M 7023
[162] Israel Thompson, Administrative Accounts, Loudoun County Will Book F, pp. 392-395
[163] Loudoun County Court Order Book F, p. 87, "Israel Thompson Hogs & Sheep"
[164] Israel Thompson, Administrative Accounts, Loudoun County Will Book F, pp. 392-395, pp. 396-403, Israel Thompson, Administrative Accounts, Loudoun County Will Book F, p. 307
[165] Israel Thompson, Accounts, Loudoun County Will Book F, pp. 392-395, pp. 396-403: Israel Thompson, Administrative Accounts, Loudoun County Will Book F, pp. 303-310 (p. 307)
[166] Jay Worrall, Jr., p. 300
[167] Israel Thompson's Last Will and Testament, Loudoun County Will Book E, pp. 87-92, Israel Thompson, Accounts, Loudoun County Will Book F, p. 304
[168] Archer Butler Hulbert, Washington and the West, The Century Co., New York, 1905, pp. 27-28
[169] William Wade Hinshaw, Fairfax Monthly Meeting, pp. 572-573
[170] Cameron Parish Tithing, microfiche records, Thomas Balch Library, Leesburg, Virginia
[171] Virginia Public Claims, Loudoun County Record Group 48, Virginia State Library and Archives, as compiled and transcribed by Janice L. Abercombie, p. 11, p. 39
[172] Wesley E. Pippenger and James D. Munson, Ph.D., Volume III, p. 254
[173] T.H.S. Boyd, The History of Montgomery County, Maryland: From its Earliest Settlement in 1650 to 1789, originally published in Clarksburg, Maryland, 1879: A facsimile reprint with a new index published by Heritage Books, Bowie, Maryland 2001: "Thomas Moore was a remarkable

man. His father, Thomas Moore, an Irish Quaker, came to this country early in the last century, settled first in Pennsylvania, where he married, and afterwards removed to Loudoun County, Virginia, where he built a residence and called the place Waterford, after his native home. Here the son Thomas for a time carried on the business of a cabinet-maker, which he had learned. He then engaged in milling and merchandizing in connection with his brother-in-law, James McCormick. About the year 1794 he removed to Maryland, having married Mary Brooke, daughter of Roger Brooke, of Brooke Grove, in Montgomery County. Here he commenced farming on the estate of his wife, and soon distinguished himself as a practical farmer", pp. 90-91

[174] Wesley E. Pippenger and James D. Munson, Ph.D., Volume IV, p. 218

[175] Marty Hiatt, Early Church Records of Loudoun County, Family Line Publications, Westminster, Maryland, 1995

[177] Israel Thompson, Administrative Accounts, Loudoun County Will Book F, pp. 392-395, pp. 396-403

[178] Israel Thompson, Administrative Accounts, Loudoun County Will Book F, pp. 392-395, pp. 396-403, pp. 303-310

[179] Israel Thompson, Administrative Accounts, Loudoun County Will Book F, pp. 392-395, pp. 396-403

[180] Israel Thompson, Last Will and Testament, Loudoun County Will Book E, pp. 87-92

[181] Carl R. Lounsbury, pp. 222-223

[182] Israel Thompson, Administrative Accounts, Loudoun County Will Book F, pp. 392-395, pp. 396-403

[183] Israel Thompson, Administrative Accounts, Loudoun County Will Book F, pp. 392-395, pp. 396-403

[184] Israel Thompson, Administrative Accounts, Loudoun County Will Book F, pp. 396-403: Vouchers for charges v. the estate of Israel Thompson from 1797 to 1801, Will Book F, Loudoun County Courthouse, Circuit Court, Archives, Leesburg, Virginia

[185] Israel Thompson, Administrative Accounts, Loudoun County Will Book F, pp. 396-403: Samuel Thompson, Administrative Accounts, Loudoun County Will Book F, pp. 389-390

[186] Israel Thompson, Administrative Accounts, Loudoun County Will Book F, pp. 392-395, pp. 396-403

[187] David Hackett Fischer, pp. 560-566

[188] Vouchers for charges v. the estate of Israel Thompson from 1797 to 1801, Will Book F, Loudoun County Courthouse, Circuit Court, Archives, Leesburg, Virginia, "Births and deaths of my children with some remarks"

[189] Israel Thompson, Administrative Accounts, Loudoun County Will Book F, pp. 392-395, pp. 396-403

[190] Sarah Thompson, Administrative Accounts, Loudoun County Will Book I, pp. 331-334

[191] Wesley E. Pippenger and James D. Munson, Ph.D., The Virginia Journal and Alexandria Advertiser, Volume IV (February 8,1787 to May 21,1789), Willow Bend Books, Westminster, Maryland, 2001, P. 37, p. 43, p. 48

[192] Israel Thompson, Administrative Accounts, Loudoun County Will Book F, pp. 392-395, pp. 396-403

[193] John Wolford Road (Route 694)

[194] "Thomas Hutton's Messuage", 38670 Old Wheatland Road (Route 698), Waterford, VA circa 1765 (See Virginia Historic Landmarks Commission Survey Form 53-593): The stone buildings and structures on Thomas Hutton's Messuage are especially interesting in the context of this discussion. The dwelling house is a simple hall-and-parlor house built into a bank, with a floor plan or footprint of 27 by 20 feet. The dimensions mirror some of Israel Thompson's most important buildings such as his gristmill building, and his later mansion house building; as they

were recorded for mutual assurance policies of fire insurance. The ground floor is the earliest part of the dwelling house c. 1775. The upper floor is about a generation later, and may have been built for William Virts of Loudoun County c. 1796. In fact, Israel Thompson had owned the indenture of lease for lives for the former Thomas Hutton's Messuage from circa 1785 to 1796. In the estimation of the author, Thomas Davis had resided here as well, probably, during the time period when it was under the control of Israel Thompson. Thomas Hutton's Messuage circa 1765 had been on a 134-acre lot of land on the North Fork of Catoctin Creek, which was adjacent to Thomas Hutton's additional lot of 81 acres of land on the North Fork of Catoctin Creek (circa 1765). The lot neighbored Israel Thompson's Home Plantation. Originally, this was on William Fairfax Esquire's Kittockton Tract (Piedmont Manor). It may have been on or about the site of the former survey made for George Griffith in 1743 (1743, Fairfax County Deed Book A, Part 2, pp. 330-334) and Jonathan Richardson's lot of land (1743, Fairfax County Deed Book A, Part 2, pp. 337-339).

[196] Israel Thompson, Administrative Account, Loudoun County Will Book F, pp. 392-395
[197] Carl R. Lounsbury, p. 157
[198] Carl R. Lounsbury, p. 19, p. 22
[199] Carl R. Lounsbury, p. 102
[200] Forms of Declaration for Assurance, R1 V1 No. 56, Virginia State Library, Richmond
[201] Forms of Declaration for Assurance, R4 V37 No. 538, Virginia State Library, Richmond
[202] Louisa Skinner Hutchison, Apprentices, Poor Children and Bastards Loudoun County, Virginia 1757-1850, Willow Bend Books, Westminster, Maryland, 2000, p. 15
[203] Louisa Skinner Hutchison, p. 32
[204] Louisa Skinner Hutchison, p. 33
[205] Louisa Skinner Hutchison, p. 51
[206] Louisa Skinner Hutchison, p. 55
[207] Louis Skinner Hutchison, p. 69
[208] Cameron Parish Tithing, Shelburne Parish Tithing, Loudoun County Personal Property Taxes, microfiche records, Thomas Balch Library, Leesburg, Virginia
[209] Loudoun County Personal Property Taxes, microfiche records, Thomas Balch Library, Leesburg
[210] 11/13/1769, William West, Last Will and Testament, Loudoun County Deed Book A, pp. 226-229: 9/10/1781, Craven Peyton, Last Will and Testament, Loudoun County Will Book B, pp. 378-381
[211] Townsend M. Lucas, p. 10, p. 12
[212] Israel Thompson's Last Will and Testament, Loudoun County Will Book E, pp. 87-92
[213] Nancy Griffith's Last Will and Testament, Loudoun County Will Book K, pp. 371-373
[214] Jonah Thompson to Sib, Fairfax County Deed Book N, p. 391
[215] Jonah Thompson to Daniel, Fairfax County Deed Book W, p. 382
[216] Townsend M. Lucas, Numbered Certificates of Free Negroes, Loudoun County, Va., p. 10, p. 12
[217] Dorothy S. Provine, Alexandria County, Virginia Free Negro Registers, Heritage Books, Inc., Bowie, Maryland, p. 25, p. 28, p. 58, p. 111, pp. 208-209
[218] 5/5/1744, William Fairfax to William Janney, Lease for Lives, Fairfax County Deed Book A, Part 2, pp. 328-331: 8/29/1761, Joseph Yates, Last Will and Testament, Loudoun County Will Book A, pp. 43-45 (William Janney to Joseph Yates, Assignment, two lease lots comprising a plantation named "Get")
[219] 8/29/1761, Joseph Yates's Last Will and Testament, Loudoun County Will Book A, pp. 43-45

[220] 10/14/1793, Robert Yates to Israel Thompson, Assignment, Loudoun County Deed Book V, pp. 152-154: Also, see George William Fairfax to James Ross, Lease for Lives, Loudoun County Deed Book B, pp. 303-305, Sarah Fairfax to Anthony Wright, Lease Renewal, Loudoun County Deed Book X, pp. 176-179

[221] Israel Thompson's Last Will and Testament, Loudoun County Will Book E, pp. 87-92

[222] Vouchers for charges v. the estate of Israel Thompson from 1797 to 1801, Will Book F, Loudoun County Courthouse, Circuit Court, Archives, Leesburg, Virginia

[223] Vouchers for charges v. the estate of Israel Thompson from 1797 to 1801, Will Book F, Loudoun County Courthouse, Circuit Court, Archives, Leesburg, Virginia

[224] Vouchers for charges v. the estate of Israel Thompson from 1797 to 1801, Will Book F, Loudoun County Courthouse, Circuit Court, Archives, Leesburg, Virginia

[225] Israel Thompson, Accounts, Loudoun County Will Book F, p. 400

[226] Vouchers for charges v. the estate of Israel Thompson from 1797 to 1801, Will Book F, Loudoun County Courthouse, Circuit Court, Archives, Leesburg, Virginia: Israel Thompson, Administrative Account, Loudoun County Will Book F, p. 303-310 (p. 303: "To cash Sebastian Thatcher 6/ Henry Burket for coffin 36/ (=) £ 2: 2: 0")

[227] Loudoun County Court Order Book Q, p. 84

[228] David Hackett Fischer, pp. 566-573

[229] Israel Thompson, Administrative Accounts, Loudoun County Will Book F, p. 303, p. 305

[230] Israel Thompson, Administrative Accounts, Loudoun County Will Book F, p. 304

[231] Israel Thompson, Administrative Accounts, Loudoun County Will Book F, p. 304

[232] Israel Thompson's Last Will and Testament, Loudoun County Will Book E, pp. 87-92

[233] Israel Thompson's Last Will and Testament, Loudoun County Will Book E, pp. 87-92

[234] Israel Thompson's Last Will and Testament, Loudoun County Will Book E, pp. 87-92

[235] Israel Thompson's Last Will and Testament, Loudoun County Will Book E, pp. 87-92

[236] Israel Thompson's Last Will and Testament, Loudoun County Will Book E, pp. 87-92

[237] Israel Thompson's Last Will and Testament, Loudoun County Will Book E, pp. 87-92

[238] Israel Thompson, Administrative Accounts, Loudoun County Will Book F, p. 307

[239] Israel Thompson, Administrative Accounts, Loudoun County Will Book F, p. 306

[240] Israel Thompson, Administrative Accounts, Loudoun County Will Book F, pp. 392-395, pp. 396-403

[241] Israel Thompson's Executors to Hugh Douglas, Bargain and Sale, Loudoun County Deed Book 2I, pp. 122-124

[242] Joseph McGeath (McGeach) to Israel Thompson, Lease and Release, Loudoun County Deed Book W, pp. 162-163

[243] William Wade Hinshaw, Volume II, Philadelphia Monthly Meeting, p. 667

[244] William Wade Hinshaw, Fairfax Monthly Meeting, p. 573

[245] Our Town at Gadsby's Tavern, Alexandria, Virginia, The Alexandria Association, 1956, Alexandria, p. 58

[246] Wesley E. Pippenger and James D. Munson, The Virginia Journal and the Alexandria Advertiser, Volume I (February 5,1784 to January 27, 1785), Willow Bend Books and Family Line Publications, 1998, p. 99

[247] 3/2/1789, Jonah Thompson of the Town of Alexandria and Margaret his wife to Pierce Bayley, Bargain and Sale, Loudoun County Deed Book R, pp. 223-227

[248] Mary G. Powell, The History of Old Alexandria, Virginia, The William Byrd Press, Inc., Richmond, Virginia, 1928, Chapter XIX

[249] F. Edward Wright and Wesley E. Pippenger, Early Church Records of Alexandria City and Fairfax County, Family Line Publications, Westminster, Maryland, p. 82

[250] Wesley E. Pippenger, Tombstone Inscriptions: of Alexandria, Virginia, Volume 3, p. 118

[251] Robert H. Wilson, "The Story of Old Town & Gentry Row" in Alexandria, Virginia, Distributed by Norma W. Dempsey, 214 Prince Street, Alexandria, VA 22314, p. 20

[252] Wesley E. Pippenger, Tombstone Inscriptions: of Alexandria, Virginia, Volume 3, p. 118

[253] The Fireside Sentinel, January-December 1989 Issues, Alexandria Library, Alexandria, pp. 6-11

[254] 6/11/1787, George William Fairfax to John Lyon, Lease, Loudoun County Deed Book P, pp. 552-558: 2/28/1791, John Lyon to Samuel Thompson, Assignment, Loudoun County Deed Book U, pp. 190-192: 8/15/1805, Jonah Thompson, Richard Griffith and Nancy his wife, William Hamilton and Elizabeth his wife, Israel Hague Thompson, John Vandeventer and Pleasant his wife, and Sarah Thompson, to Thomas Hough, Assignment, Loudoun County Deed Book Z, pp. 87-89

[255] Samuel Thompson, Accounts, Loudoun County Will Book F, pp. 389-391

[256] William Wade Hinshaw, Fairfax Monthly Meeting, p. 573

[257] 6/27/1796, Israel Thompson Executors to John Redman, Bargain and Sale, Loudoun County Deed Book X, pp. 148-151

[258] 6/28/1796, John Redman to Jonah Thompson, Bargain and Sale, Loudoun County Deed Book X, pp. 152-155: 9/10/1796, Ferdinando Fairfax to Israel Thompson's Executors, Bargain and Sale, Loudoun County Deed Book 2I, pp. 77-79 ("which part is said to be the parcel of land sold by George William Fairfax to said Israel Thompson about the year one thousand seven hundred and seventy three or seventy four joining the land formerly sold by said Fairfax to Thompson and is bounded as by a survey thereof made by Craven Peyton about the year one thousand seven hundred and seventy four in manner following.")

[259] 7/29/1796, Israel Thompson's Executors to Theopulus Harris, Loudoun County Deed Book 2C, pp. 353-355: Loudoun County Court Order Book T, p. 37: Loudoun County Court Order Book W, p. 136: Israel Thompson, Administrative Accounts, Loudoun County Will Book F, pp. 303-310, pp. 327-330

[260] 7/9/1797, Israel Thompson Executors to Isaac Miller, Assignment, Loudoun County Deed Book X, pp. 435-436: Loudoun County Court Order Book R, p. 159: Israel Thompson, Administrative Accounts, Loudoun County Will Book F, pp. 303-310, pp.327-330.

[261] 11/1/1787, George William Fairfax to Israel Thompson, Lease for Lives, Loudoun County Will Book Q, pp. 272-276

[262] Israel Thompson's Last Will and Testament, Loudoun County Will Book E, pp. 87-92

[263] Israel Thompson, Administrative Accounts, Loudoun County Will Book F, pp. 327-330. See p. 328: "(To cash paid) Harding for surveying two lots sold Ramy (Ramey). We know the services to have been perfd. & the a/c mislaid? £ 3: 9: 0". See p. 330: "(To cash received) Sanford Ramy (Ramey) at sundry times in pt. (part) payt. (payment) Lease Lot, (Voucher No.) 41, £ 249:18:10, (balance outstanding) £ 51: 2: 6"

[264] 4/7/1803, Ferdinando Fairfax to Sanford Ramey, Bargain and Sale, Loudoun County Deed Book 2C, pp. 304-306

[265] 8/8/1797, Israel Thompson's Executors to Jonathan Lodge, Assignment, Loudoun County Deed Book X, pp. 437-438: Loudoun County Order Book R, p. 159: Israel Thompson, Administrative Accounts, Loudoun County Will Book F, pp. 303-310, pp. 327-330.

[266] 12/11/1759, George William Fairfax to Israel Thompson, Lease and Release, Loudoun County Deed Book A, pp. 509-513 ("Edward Thompson's Additional lott")

[267] 11/1/1787, George William Fairfax to Israel Thompson, Lease for Lives, Loudoun County Deed Book Q, pp. 265-271

[268] 12/11/1759, George William Fairfax to Israel Thompson, Lease and Release, Loudoun County Deed Book A, pp. 509-513 ("in a line of a lott formerly surveyed for George Griffith"). See 5/1/1743, William Fairfax to George Griffeth (Griffith), Lease for Lives, Fairfax County Deed

Book A, pp. 330-334: 5/1/1743, William Fairfax to Jonathan Richardson, Lease for Lives, Fairfax County Deed Book A, pp. 337-339: See 8/12/1745, George Griffieth to Samuel Mead, Lease Assignment, Fairfax County Deed Book A, Part 2, pp. 488-489

[269] 9/13/1785, Thomas Hutton to Israel Thompson, Assignment, Loudoun County Deed Book Z, p. 323-325

[270] Loudoun County Court Order Book O, p. 246, p. 252, p. 267

[271] 9/12/1785, Thomas Hutton to Thomas Davis, Assignment, Partially Proven Deed Book 01, pp. 336-337

[272] 4/10/1797, Loudoun County Court Order Book R, p. 96: Israel Thompson, Administrative Accounts, Loudoun County Will Book F, pp. 303-310 (p. 308), pp. 327-330 (p. 328): 3/25/1805, Sarah Fairfax to William Virtz, Lease Renewal ("Thomas Hutton's Messuage"), Loudoun County Deed Book 2F, pp. 329-331: 10/24/1810, Peter R. Beverly and Lovely his wife to William Vertz, Bargain and Sale, Loudoun County Deed Book 2F, pp. 329-331: 6/23/1815, William Virts & Phebe his wife to Robert Braden, Bargain and Sale of 4 acre-lot (Division), Book 2S, Folio 483: 5/16/1828, William Virtz and Phebe his wife to Jesse Tribby, Bargain and Sale of 8 acres and 21 poles (Division), Book 3R, Folio 9: 3/17/1854, Jacob Virts and others to Albert J. Best and Elizabeth R. White, Loudoun County Deed Book 3R, pp. 21-23: 4/30/1856, Albert J. Best and Elizabeth R. White to Uriah Beans, Bargain and Sale (plat), Loudoun County Deed Book 5N, pp. 119-120 (Also, Albert J. Best and Elizabeth R. White's Reserved Lot): 3/18/1874, Uriah Beans and Martha-Jane his wife to Harrison Butler, Bargain and Sale of 4 acre-lot (Division): 4/1/1896, Martha J. Beans et al to John McGavack, Bargain and Sale, Loudoun County Deed Book 7M, pp. 158-159 (Norman and Betty Redman Mitchell's tenant farm): 11/15/1913, John McGavack to John W. Orrison, Bargain and Sale, Loudoun County Deed Book 8W, Folio 484: 5/22/1947, John W. Orrison and Judith M. Orrison his wife to Elmer G. Pauly and Charlotte May Pauly his wife, Bargain and Sale, Loudoun County Deed Book 12-O, pp. 90-93: 12/6/1948, Elmer G. Pauly and Charlotte May Pauly his wife to James B. Light and Elsie K. Light, Bargain and Sale, Loudoun County Deed Book 12-Y, pp. 235-237: 4/1/1749, James B. Light and Elsie K. Light to Fleet H. James and Emily T. James, Bargain and Sale, Loudoun County Deed Book 12-Z, pp. 424-425: 4/5/1950, Fleet H. James and Emily T. James to Mary F. Spratt, Bargain and Sale, Loudoun County Deed Book 13-G, pp. 15-18: 8/11/1958, Mary F. Spratt to Alfred T. Meschter and Florence Meschter, Bargain and Sale, Loudoun County Deed Book 379, pp.396-398: 1/2/1964, Alfred T. Meschter and Florence T. Meschter to Lena D. Moore, Bargain and Sale, Loudoun County Deed Book 431, pp. 309-313: 6/24/1976, Lena D. Moore to Randal D. Boone and Mary U. Boone, Bargain and Sale, Bargain and Sale (Division with plat), Loudoun County Deed Book 643, pp. 232-237: 3/27/1984, Randal D. Boone and Mary U. Boone to Nancy C. McCormick and Sally A. McCormick, Bargain and Sale, Loudoun County Deed Book 839, pp. 1093-1095: 2/29/1988, Sally A. McCormick and Nancy C. McCormick to Patricia A. Costantino, Bargain and Sale, Loudoun County Deed Book 980, pp. 187-189

[273] 9/13/1785, Thomas Hutton to Israel Thompson, Assignment, Loudoun County Deed Book Z, pp. 323-324: 9/15/1796, Israel Thompson's Executors to Garlock Stickler, Assignment, Loudoun County Deed Book 2A, pp. 292-293: 12/12/1796, Loudoun County Court Order Book R, p. 35: Loudoun County Court Order Book U, p. 194: Israel Thompson, Administrative Accounts, Loudoun County Will Book F, pp. 303-310 (p. 306), pp. 327-330 (p. 329): 1/14/1799, John Stigler to Samuel Evans, Assignment, Loudoun County Deed Book Z, pp. 59-61: 3/25/1805, Sarah Fairfax to Samuel Evans, Lease Renewal, Loudoun County Deed Book 2F, pp. 326-329: 8/3/1811, Peter R. Beverly and Lovely his wife to Robert Braden, Bargain and sale, Loudoun County Deed Book 2N, pp. 65-67

[274] 9/11/1797, Israel Thompson's Executors to Stephen Wilson, Bargain and Sale, Loudoun County Deed Book Y, pp. 13-15: 9/11/1797, Samuel Wilson to Stephen Wilson, Bargain and Sale, Loudoun County Deed Book Y, pp. 17-19

[275] 9/11/1797, Stephen Wilson to Sarah Thompson, Assignment, Loudoun County Deed Book Y, pp. 16-17

[276] Israel Thompson, Administrative Accounts, Loudoun County Will Book F, pp. 327-330 (See p. 330, "(Cash received) Stephen Wilson for exchange in Land £ 10: 0: 0"

[277] Israel Thompson, Last Will and Testament, Loudoun County Will Book E, pp. 87-92

[278] 4/8/1799, Stephen Wilson and his wife to Sarah Thompson, Bargain and Sale, Loudoun County Deed Book Z, pp. 164-166

[279] The Alexandria Gazette, January 31, 1798

[280] 12/6/1804, Jonah Thompson and Margaret his wife to Alexander Sutherland, Deed, Loudoun County Deed Book 2E, pp. 406-411: Alexander Sutherland and Nancy his wife to Jonah Thompson, Mortgage, Loudoun County Deed Book 2E, pp. 411-416: Alexander Sutherland to Jonah Thompson, Deed, Loudoun County Deed Book 2G, p. 134

[281] Jay Worrall, Jr., The Friendly Virginians, Iberian Publishing Company, Athens, Georgia, 1994, p. 252

[282] A Brief History of the Westtown Boarding School, Fourth Edition, Sherman & Co., Philadelphia, 1888

[283] Israel (H.) Thompson, minor in account with Asa Moore, Guardian Accounts, Book 1, Loudoun County, Virginia, p. 159

[284] Henry C. Peden, Jr., M.A. and John Pitts Launey, Early Church Records of Delaware County, Pennsylvania, Volume 2, Family Line Publications, Westminster, Maryland, 1997, p. 172, p. 176. This is pure speculation on the part of the author but he may have even fathered twins either legitimately or illegitimately, which may have been related somehow to his disownment by the Concord Monthly Meeting, Society of Friends, p. 302.

[285] 4/11/1806, Israel H. Thompson to Benjamin H. Canby, Bargain and Sale, Loudoun County Deed Book 2G, pp. 226-227. See Israel Thompson, Administrative Accounts, Loudoun County Will Book F, pp. 327-330 ("To Israel Thompson Junier (sic) for 3 years rent of lot in Leesburg")

[286] Israel H. Thompson, Last Will and Testament, Loudoun County Will Book M, p. 154

[287] Sally W. Thompson, Last Will and Testament, Loudoun County Will Book H, pp. 125-126: Sarah Thompson, Administrative Accounts, Loudoun County Will Book I, pp. 234-236

[288] Nancy Griffith, Last Will and Testament, Loudoun County Will Book K, pp. 371-373

[289] Sarah Thompson, Accounts, Loudoun County Will Book I, pp. 331-334: Sarah Thompson, Administrative Accounts, Loudoun County Will Book K, pp. 86-88

[290] 3/13/1813, Jonah Thompson and Margaret his wife to George Janney & Daniel Eaches, Bargain and Sale, Loudoun County Deed Book 2N, pp. 82-85: 3/13/1813, George Janney and Susannah his wife and Daniel Eaches of the first part and Thomas Swann of the second part and Jonah Thompson of the third part, Deed of Trust and Commission, Loudoun County Deed Book 2P, pp. 471-477

[291] Eugene M. Scheel, "Wheatland", Loudoun Times Mirror, Leesburg, Virginia

[292] T. Michael Miller, Artisans and Merchants of Alexandria, Virginia, 1780-1820, Volume 1, Heritage Books, Inc., Bowie, Maryland, 1991: T. Michael Miller, Artisans and Merchants of Alexandria, Virginia, Volume 2, Heritage Books, Inc., Bowie, Maryland, 1992

[293] There is a portrait alleged to be an image of Jonah Thompson's mentioned in the publication, Our Town 1749-1865 at Gadsby's Tavern, Alexandria, Virginia, The Alexandria Association, Alexandria, Virginia, 1956, p. 57. In fact, according to the owner of the painting, Taylor Burke Junior, who the author interviewed for this work, the painting was probably of an image of Jonah

and Margaret Thompson's son, Samuel Thompson of Alexandria made c. 1815 (oil on canvas, 27½ x 21 inches, Artist unknown).
[294] T. Michael Miller, Portrait of a Town, Alexandria, District of Columbia (Virginia) 1820-1830, Heritage Books, Inc., Bowie, Maryland, 1995
[295] Joan M. Dixon, National Intelligencer Newspaper Abstracts 1834-1835, Heritage Books, 2000, p. 21
[296] Wesley E. Pippenger, Tombstone Inscriptions of Alexandria, Virginia, Volume 3, Family Line Publications, Westminster, 1992, p. 118

A

Abel Jeneys Road (Abel Janney's Road), 19
Abraham, 41
Adams, Andrew, merchant in Leesburg, 20
Addison, Joseph, 21
additional lot, Thomas Hutton's, 49
additional lott, Edward Thompson's, 48
adjacent lot to Cold Spring, Joseph Janney to Israel Thompson, 48
adjacent lot to Cold Spring, Shannondale Tract, 48
Africa, 19, 52
African American, 19
Africans, 19
Alexandria, 6, 20, 22, 29, 30, 34, 37, 42, 47, 48, 49, 52, 53, 54
Alexandria & Washington Turnpike Co., 54
Alexandria Academy, 54
Alexandria Canal, 53
Alexandria County, retrocession, 52
Alexandria Road, 22
Alexandria, County of, 52
Alexandria, District of Columbia, 42, 49
Alexandria, occupied by British forces, 52
Alexandria, port of, 6, 16
Alexandria, port town, 29
Alexandria, port town of, 52
Alexandria, Town of, 52
America, 8, 15, 37
American, 13
American Colonies, 7
American Indian, 19
American Revolution, 36
Anabaptists, 11
Anglican Church, 8, 37
Anglicans, 11
Anglo-Dutch, 13
Anglo-Irish, 6, 7, 13, 15
Anne Arundel County, Maryland, 14
annexed parcel of land, Jonah Thompson's plantation (Israel Thompson's plantation), 48
Apology for the True Christian Divinity, by Robert Barclay, 21
apprentices, labor, 41
apron-maker, 13
Armagh, County of, Ireland, 9, 15
Armstrong, George, 68
Ashby, John, 22
Ashby's Gap, 19
Atlantic Coastal Seaboard, 34

Atlantic Eastern Seaboard, 6, 13
Atlantic Ocean, 52
Atlantic Ocean, trade interests, 52
Awbrey, Francis, 8

B

Bakehouse, Thomas, 72
Baker, 33
Ball, Farling, 27, 67
Ball, Isaac, 67
Ball, Nathan, 69
Ball, Stephen, 72
Bank of Alexandria, 47, 48, 51, 52
Baptists, 6
Barbados, 34
Barclay, Robert, 21
bark & millhouse, 49
bark-mill, 13, 26
barn, Israel Thompson's, 40
Barrett, Giles, 15
Barrett, Mary, 15
Barrett, Mary (wife of Giles), 15
bastards, labor, 41
Bath, The, 22
Beaverdam Branch of Catoctin Creek, 7, 18, 19
Beaverdam Branch of Catoctin Creek, mouth of, 27
Belfast, 7
Bell, Robert, 41
Belvoir, 16
Bennett Senior, Charles, 43
Bennett, Charles, 69, 71
Berkley Springs, WV, 22
Bermuda, 19, 52
Bible, family, 21
Bible, small, 21
Bible, the, 13
Binns, Chas., 61, 74
Bird, Catherine, 47
Bird, William, 47
Bishop, Elizabeth, 18
Bishop, John, 18, 24
Bishop, Samuel, 18
black locust trees, 7
black walnut trees, 7
Blakely, William, 67
Blue Ridge, 19, 22
Blue Ridge Mountain, 6, 8
Blue Ridge Mountain System, 8
Blue Ridge Mountain, summit of the, 19
Blue Ridge Uplands, 7, 19, 34

boards of wood, 29
bolting chest and bolting cloth, mill, 23
bolting mill, 26
book binder, 13
bookkeeping, 21
Boston, 34
Braddock, General, 10
Bradford Monthly Meeting, 8, 9
Branches of Catoctin Creek, 7, 19, 26
Brandywine Creek, 8
breeches-maker, 13
brew-house, Richard Brown's, 27
bridge over Kittockton, subscription for building, 44
Bristol, 7
British, 19
British goods, competition with, 13
Broad Run, Catoctin Creek (Milltown Creek), 26
Brook, 15
Brook or Brooke, 15
Brooke, 15
Brookeville, Maryland, 15
Brown, James, 74
Brown, John, & others, new mill, 24
Brown, John, and others, 27
Brown, Mary (Norton), 27
Brown, Mercer, 27
Brown, Richard, 27
Browne, Mrs., 10
Bucks County, Pennsylvania, 14
Bull Run, 19, 20
Bull Run Mountain, 19, 47
Burke Jr., Taylor, 53
Burke, Julia Thompson, 54
Burkitt, Henry, 43
Burns, Nathan, 41
Butcher, John, 27

C

Cadwalader, Moses, 14
Calender, Samuel, 68
Cameron Parish, 6, 10, 11, 15, 36, 41
Cameron Street, Alexandria, 47, 48
Cammell, Elizabeth, 41
Campbell, Aneous, 20
Campbell, Elizabeth, 41
Campbell, John, Earl of Loudoun, Captain General and Governor in Chief, 19
Canada, 52
Canby, Benjamin, 67
Canby, Samuel, 33
Caribbean ports, 29
Carlyle & Dalton, 20
Carlyle, John, 20
Carolina, 7
Carolina Road, 22, 47
Carr, Thomas, 66
Carr, William, 68
Catesby Cocke & John Mercer, 8

Catholics, 11
Catoctin Creek, 8, 10, 18, 20, 24, 27
Catoctin Creek, mouth of, 26
Catoctin Mountain, 6, 7, 8, 19, 22, 44
Catoctin Mountain woodland lot, Israel Thompson's, 45
Channel, Doctor James, 43
Chapman, Thomas, 67
Charlemont, Ireland, 9
Charles Earl of Tankerville, 20, 26
Charles Town Pike, 7, 22
Chesapeake Bay, 7, 52
Chester County, 9
Chester County, Pennsylvania, 9, 15, 49, 51
Chester Monthly Meeting, 8, 15
children, labor, 41
Christ (Episcopal) Church, 47, 54
Christ Episcopal Cemetery, 54
Christiana River, 8
Christians, 19
Church of England, 6, 11
cider-mill, 26
City Hotel, Alexandria, 54
Civil War, 52
Clapham, Josias, 61, 66
Clendenen, Samuel, 73
Clendenin, Samuel, 71
Climmer, Christian, 73
Clinter, John, 70
Cocke, Catesby, 8, 20
Coffee, John, 37
Cold Spring Plantation, 7, 19
Cold Spring Plantation, Israel Thompson's, 44, 48
Coldwell (Caldwell), Joseph, 59
Colony of Virginia, 6, 15
Colvill, John, 8, 9, 18, 20, 26
Colvill, Thomas, 20
Concord Monthly Meeting, 8, 9, 50, 51
Cook, Captain James, 20
Cook's Voyages, a book, 20
Coolidge, Capt. Judion, 20
Cooper, Frederick, 22
Cooper, Job, 72
cooper's shop, 28
cooper's shop, fireplace, 28
Copeland, Andrew, 66, 70
Copeland, John, 69
Cork, 7
County Court, Loudoun, 23
cowhouse, Israel Thompson's, 40
Creoles, 19
Crimm, Charles, 72
Cromwell, Lord Lieutenant, 15
Cromwell, Oliver, 15
Crouch, Walter, 71
Cummings, John, 66
Cunnard, Anthony, 72
Cunnard, Edward, 67
Cunningham, George, 90
Currel, James, 72

currier, the, 13
curry shop, 49
curry shop, Israel Thompson's, 14

D

Dalton, (John), 20
dam and floodgates, mill, 23
dam and race, water grist or merchant mill, 28
dam, as bridge, 49
dam, John Hough's, 27
dam, Jonah Thompson's, 49
dam, mill, 27, 28
dam, sawmill, 29
Daniel, 42
Davis, Abraham, 68
Davis, Anne, 15
Davis, Ignatius, 67
Davis, John, 24, 67
Davis, Thomas, 10, 15, 49, 68, 71
Delaware, 8
Delaware County, 9, 15
Delaware River Valley, 6, 8, 15, 32, 40
Dern, John P., 15
Dickinson, John, 49
dictionary, 21
Difficult Run, 19
Dillon, James, 37
distilleries, 49
District of Columbia, 49, 52
Donaldson, Stephen, 39
Donohoe, Cornelius, 90
Doughty, Reuben, 67
Douglas, H., 66
Douglas, Hugh, 45
Douglass, 68
Douglass, Capt. Hugh, 68
dry goods and hardware store, Jonah Thompson's, 48
Dublin, 7
Dutch, 13
Dutchmans Branch, 19
Dutchmans Creek, 18
Dutchmans Run, 27
Duval, 15
dwelling house, 28
dwelling house, tanyard, 49
dwelling house, Thomas Davis's, 10

E

Eaches, Daniel, 52
Earle, Alice Morse, 10
Edgmont, 8
Edmundson, William, 15, 21
Edwards, Thomas, 45, 61
England, 13, 15, 20
English, 6, 13, 15, 21, 22
English grammar, a book, 21

Europe, 52
Europe, Continental, 29
European, 19
Evans, Samuel, 71

F

Fairfax County, 10, 15, 16, 18, 19, 42
Fairfax County, Virginia, 14, 16, 18
Fairfax County, western, 19
Fairfax Meetinghouse, 6, 13, 26
Fairfax Meetinghouse, neighborhood about, 6, 24, 26
Fairfax Monthly Meeting, 6, 7, 8, 9, 13, 14, 33, 37, 48, 51
Fairfax Monthly Meeting overseer, Israel Thompson, 14
Fairfax Monthly Meeting, payment towards, 44
Fairfax Monthly Meting, 47
Fairfax Monthly Meting, Fairfax Meetinghouse, 13
Fairfax Parish, 47
Fairfax Preparative Meeting, 6
Fairfax Street, Alexandria, 47
Fairfax, Bryant, 20
Fairfax, County of, 6
Fairfax, Ferdinando, 35, 48
Fairfax, George William, 16, 18, 20, 22, 48
Fairfax, George William, and family, 20
Fairfax, William, 8, 9, 16, 18, 20, 22, 42
Fairfax, William Henry, 8
Falls Monthly Meeting, Pennsylvania, 14
farmer or planter, 13
Farquhar, William Henry, 15
Federal Government, 52
Ferrall, William, 90
Ferrall, William and Martha, 90
ferry traffic, Potomac River, 22
Ferry, Robert Harper's, 19
Finley, David, 47
Fischer, David Hackett, 33
flood gate, water grist or merchant mill, 28
flood gates, dam, 23
ford, crossing the South Fork of Catoctin Creek, 26
ford, old, 24
Fort Cumberland, Maryland, 10
Fox, George, 15
Fox, William, 69
framed house, 28
framed house, cellar, 28
framed house, door and glass windows, 28
framed house, stone chimney, 28
France, Mr., 67
Frederick County Court (Maryland), 15
Frederick County, Maryland, 14, 15, 18, 20
Frederick County, Virginia, 8, 9, 14
French and Indian War, 10, 19, 33
Friends, 6, 13, 14, 15, 18, 39, 42, 44
Friends books, 13
Friends, Irish, 7
fulling mill, 26

G

Gadsby's Tavern, Alexandria, 53
garret, Israel Thompson's mansion house, 40
gears, mill, 23
George Town (Leesburg), 22
George, John, 27
Georgetown Bridge Co., 54
German, 13
Get Plantation, 44, 48
Get Plantation, Israel Thompson's, 43
Get Plantation, Joseph Yates, 42
Get Plantation, Robert Yates, 43
Gilpin, George, Commissioner, 22
glover or glove-maker, 13
Goose Creek, 10, 11, 27
Goose Creek Meeting, 7
Goose Creek Meeting House, 9
Goose Creek Meetinghouse, 9, 44, 49
Goose Creek Meetinghouse, neighborhood about, 24
Goose Creek Monthly Meeting, 14
goose pond, Nathan Spencer's, 24
Gore, Joshua, 37
Gore, Thomas, 90
Grange Monthly Meeting, 9
Grange, Ireland, 9
Great Britain, 29
Great Gap, 8
Great Gap in Short Hill, settlement about, 48
Great Gap in the Short Hill, 27, 48
Great Gap, Short Hill Mountain, 7, 14
Great Lakes Region, 36
Greater Catoctin Creek, 18, 20, 27
Greater Pennsylvania, 19
Green, Parson Charles, 22
Green, Reverend Charles, 10
Gregg, Elizabeth, 18
Gregg, George, 20, 27, 68
Gregg, John, 70
Gregg, Samuel, 18, 41, 69
Gregg, Thomas (son of Samuel), 18
Griffith (Griffeth), George, 22
Griffith (Griffeth), George, survey for, 22
Griffith, Ann Thompson, 42
Griffith, Banjamin (son of George), 18
Griffith, George, 18, 22, 49
Griffith, George (son of George), 18
Griffith, Israel Thompson, 51
Griffith, Nancy, 51
Griffith, Richard, 68, 72
Griffith, Sarah Pleasant, 51
grist mill, 28
grist or merchant mill, Israel Thompson's, 28
gristmill, 6, 23, 26
gristmill, Israel Thompson dec., 27
gristmill, Israel Thompson's, 27
gristmill, Richard Roach's, 27
gun, powder horn, and shot pouch, Samuel Thompson's, 39

H

Hague, 33
Hague, Amos, 69, 70
Hague, Francis, 13, 14, 26, 33, 51, 64
Hague, Francis and Jane, 64
Hague, Jane, 26, 33, 64
Hague, Sarah, 33, 45, 61
Hague, Sarah, daughter of Francis and Jane Hague, 64
Hague, Thomas, 26, 44, 60
Halkett, Peter, 10
Hamilton, Betsy, 51
Hamilton, Betsy Thompson, 54
Hamilton, Elizabeth, 54
Hanes, Jno., 70
Hanks, William, 67
Hannah, 42, 45, 60
harness-maker, 13
Harper's Ferry, 19
Harris, 15
Harris, Anne, 15
Harris, Theopulus, 48
Harrison, William, 71
Hatcher, Joshua, 66
hater, 13
Haverford Monthly Meeting, 8, 9
Heaton, Doctor, 51
Heaton, Doctor James, 43, 68
Heaton, James, 61, 72
Hillsboro, 48
Hillsborough, 48
Hillsborough (Hillsboro), 27
Hinshaw, William Wade, 48
Hite Junior, Isaac, 36
Hite Junr., Isaac, 60
Hite, Isaac, 60
Hite, Jacob, 34
Hodge, Edward, 67
Hoge, Morgan, 41
Holland, 15
Holland, Benjamin, 66
Hollingsworth, Joseph, 20, 90
Hollingsworth, Joseph and Martha, 90
Homan, Samuel, 41
home industry, Israel Thompson's plantation, 35
Hopewell Monthly Meeting, 9, 14
Hough, 33
Hough, Ann H., 51
Hough, Doctor (Isaac), 51
Hough, Eleanor Hite, 51
Hough, John, 14, 18, 20, 22, 26, 27, 51
Hough, John (blacksmith), 18
Hough, John, surveyor, 20, 22
Hough, Joseph, 68
Hough, Joseph (son of John), 18
Hough, Sarah (wife of John), 18
Hough, William, 43, 51, 60, 61, 68, 72
Hough, Wm., 61
house, Richard Brown's, 27

houses, 49
Howell, 33
Hufty, Benjamin, 72
Hutton, Thomas, 49

I

Independents, 6
intersection of roads under Short Hill Mountain, 19
Intersection, Little River Turnpike and Carolina Road, 47
Ireland, 6, 7, 8, 9, 15, 21
Ireland, Quaker Church, 15
Irish, 6
Irish Quaker, 37
Irish Quakers, 15
Israel Thompson & Company, 13

J

Janney, 33
Janney, Abel, 19, 20
Janney, Amos, 20, 90
Janney, Amos, surveyor, 18
Janney, Asa Moore, 7
Janney, Elizabeth (wife of William), 18
Janney, George, 52
Janney, Jacob, 9, 90
Janney, Jos., 14
Janney, Joseph, 48, 49, 59
Janney, Mahlon, 9, 13, 26, 43, 60, 61, 66
Janney, Mahlon (son of William), 18
Janney, Susannah, 52
Janney, Werner, 7
Janney, William, 18, 42
Jeneys, Abel, 19
John, 41
John Wolford Road (Route 694), 40
John, Thomas, 90
Johnson, David, 67, 71
Johnston, David, 29
joists, 29
Joseph & Ann, son and daughter of William Richardson, 64
Joseph Smith, partnership, 36
Jourdan, Elise Greenup, 15
journeyman and apprentice, 41

K

Kennett Monthly Meeting, 8, 15
Kentucky, 44
Kentucky, District of, 7, 36, 44
Keyes Gap Road, 34
Key's Ferry (Keyes Ferry), 49
Key's Gap (Keye's Gap) Turnpike Road, 22
Key's Gap Turnpike Road, 34
King Street, Alexandria, 47

King, Osburne, 71
Kirk, William, 20, 26, 27
kitchen or kitchens, Israel Thompson's home plantation, 38
kitchen, Israel Thompson's, 40
Kittockton Creek, 23
Kittockton Creek, William Kirk's on, 20
Kittockton Land, John Tayloe's, 27
Kittockton Tract, 18
Kleinhoff, John, 49
Kuykendal, Benj., 34

L

laborers and servants, 41
Lacy, David, 68
Lambag, Joseph, 69
land, Israel Thompson dec. to Thomas Hague, 44
lane to mill, Israel Thompson's, 24
Larrow, Isaac, 69
lath, 29
Latin America, 52
Latin testament, 21
Latrobe, Benjamin, 48
law book, old, 21
Lee's burg (Leesburg), 22
Leesburg, 7, 10, 20, 22, 36, 40, 47, 49, 51
Leesburg (George Town), Israel Thompson's half-acre lot, 22
Leesburg to Snickers's Gap Road, 24
Leesburg, a marketplace, 22
Leesburg, at intersection, 22
Leesburg, building and development of new stone gaol, 40
Leesburg, Courthouse, 42
Leesburg, Francis Hague's currying shop, 51
Leesburg, Israel H. Thompson's two acre lot with a dwelling house, 51
Leesburg, Jacob Towner's tanyard lot, 51
Leesburg, John Hough's lot, 51
Leesburg, seat of the Court, 22
Leesburg, town spring, 51
Leesburg, William Peyton's lot, 51
Leslie, Thomas, 72
licensed retailer, Israel Thompson, 28
Life of Edmund. (Edmundson), a book, 21
Life of John Richardson, a book, 21
Lincoln, 7, 9, 44
lintel, 29
Little River Turnpike, 47
Little River Turnpike Co., 53
Little, Charles, Commissioner, 22
Littlejohn, John, 40
Liverpool, 7
Lodge, Jonathan, 48
lodging, Israel Thompson's plantation, 36
London, 20
London, England, 10
Long Bridge, over Potomac River, 54

lot in George Town (Leesburg), Israel Thompson's, 22
lot on Catoctin Mountain, Israel Thompson's, 44
lot, annexed, 49
lot, George Tingle to Israel Thompson, 24
lot, Israel Thompson dec. to Garlock Stickler, 49
lot, Israel Thompson dec. to Jonathan Lodge, 48
lot, Israel Thompson dec. to Wm. Wirtz (William Virts), 49
lot, John Newland to Israel Thompson, 24
lot, Samuel Thompson's, 48
Loudoun County, 6, 8, 18, 19, 20, 21, 26, 34, 37, 45, 47, 49, 51
Loudoun County, western, 30
Loudoun Street, Leesburg, 22
Loudoun Valley, 6, 8, 10, 18, 20, 27, 32
Loudoun, County of, 22
Love, John, 73
Lurgan Meeting, Ireland, 15
Lurgan Monthly Meeting, 15
Lurgan, Ireland, County Armagh, 15
Lynn, Adam & Thompson, Jonah, 47
Lyons, James, 66

M

machinery, mill, 23
main road, the (Vestal's Gap Road), 22
mansion house, 38
mansion house and other houses, Israel Thompson's, 38
mansion house, Israel Thompson's, 6, 38, 40, 44
mansion house, kitchen, barn, cowhouse, Israel Thompson's deceased, 41
mansion house, kitchen, barn, cowhouse, Jonah Thompson's, 41
manteltree, 29
Marks, Thomas, 71
marriage contract, 45
marriage contract, Israel Thompson and Sarah Hague, 33
Maryland, 7, 14, 15, 19, 23
Maryland Gazette, 20
Masonic Lodge, Jonah Thompson member, 54
Massey, 15
Massey, Aquila, 14
Massey, Lee, 22
Mathews, 15, 33
Mathews, Richard, 69, 71, 73
Mayberry (Maxberry), Saml., 27
McCarty, John, 66
McDonald, Edward, 71
McGeach, William, 59
McGeach's, 59
McGeath, John, 45
McGeath, Joseph, 45
McGeath, Wm., 45
McIlhaney, James, 20, 35, 61
McIlhaney, John, 43
McKemie, James, 41
McLean, Duncan, 67

McPherson & Thompson, 47
Mead, John, 20
Mead, Samuel, 14, 18
Meade, Benjamin, 69
measurements, 21
Meeting at Sandy Spring, 15
Mekenney, Sarah, 14
Mercer, John, 8
Mercer, John, and sons, 20
merchant mill, 6, 27, 30
merchant mill, Israel Thompson's, 27
merchant mill, Jonah Thompson's, 27, 28
merchant miller, 23, 30
merchant miller, the, 13
merchant or grist mill, 28
Meredith, Benjamin, 69
messuage, 49
messuage, Sarah Thompson's, 49
messuage, Thomas Hutton's, 49
Middle Atlantic Region, 13
Middle English from Norman French, 49
Middle Turnpike Co., 53
militia, 36
mill, 26
mill and store, Farling Ball's, 27
mill dam, 28
mill dam, John Hough's, 27
mill dam, Jonah Thompson's plantation, 49
mill house, 28
mill lot, 27
mill lot, Mahlon Janney's, 26
mill lot, Thomas Shepherd's, 28
mill lot, William Nielson's, 28
mill seat, North Fork of Catoctin Creek, 23
mill tailrace, 26
mill, bolting cloth and bolting chest, 28
mill, Buchers, 27
mill, door, 28
mill, grinding stones, 28
mill, hoisting gears, 28
mill, Israel Thompson's, 6, 23, 24, 26, 29, 44
mill, Israel Thompson's deceased, 27
mill, John Brown & others, 24, 27
mill, John Butcher's (Buchers Mill), 27
mill, John George's, 27
mill, landscape site, 23
mill, Mahlon Janney's, 26
mill, Mercer Brown's, 27
mill, planning and development, 28
mill, plantation, 27
mill, Richard Brown's, 27
mill, Richard Roach's, 27
mill, stone chimney, 28
mill, William Kirk's, 26, 27
miller, 23
Miller, Isaac, 48
miller, the, 13, 27
miller's dwelling house, Israel Thompson's deceased, 27
miller's dwelling house, Jonah Thompson's, 27

millhouse (other), Richard Brown's, 27
millhouse, Richard Brown's, 27
milling, 23
millrace, 26, 28
mill-race, 23
millrace, Mahlon Janney's, 26
mills, 49
millseat, 6, 27
millseat locality, Mahlon Janney's, 26
millseat, Israel Thompson's, 24
mill-seat, Israel Thompson's, 24
mill-seat, Israel Thompson's, 24
millseat, John Tayloe's Kittockton Land, 27
millseat, Mahlon Janney's, 26
mill-seat, Richard Brown's, 27
millstones, 23, 27
Milltown Creek, 26
millwright, 23
Milton, John, 21
Minor, Nicholas, 22
Minor's place, Mr., 10
Minta, 41
Monocacy Meeting, 8, 15
Monongahela River, 7, 36, 44
Montgomery County, Maryland, 15
Moore & Phillips, 51
Moore (Senior), Thomas, 37
Moore, Asa, 37, 43, 51, 68, 72
Moore, James, 37, 67
Moore, Thomas (Junior), 37
Moore, Thomas (Senior), 37
Morgan, Ann H. Thompson, 54
Morgan, Eugenia Thompson, 54
Morris, John, 72
Morrison, Archibald, 73
Morrisonville, 19
Morriss, Edward, 69
Morriss, John, 71
mouth of tailrace, Mahlon Janney's mill, 26
M'shony, James, 40
Murphey, Benjamin, 69, 73
Murphy, Darby, 69
Mutual Assurance Society, 47
Myers, 33
Myers, Albert Cooke, 6, 8, 14, 15
Myers, Jonathan, 14

N

N. Fairfax Street, Alexandria, 47, 48
Nancey, 15
Negro, numbered certificate of free, 42
neighborhood, tanyard, 49
Neville, Peter, 73
New Castle County, 15
New Castle County, Pennsylvania, 9
New Castle, Delaware River, 7
New England, 13, 34

New Model officers and soldiers, Oliver Cromwell's, 15
New York Times, 52
Newark Monthly Meeting, 8, 15
Newhouse, James, 73
Newland, John, 24
Nicholas, George, 48
Nicholas, Samuel, 66
Nichols, Thomas, 67
Nicklin Junior, John, 71
Nicklin, Doctor John, 43, 68
Nicklin, Dr. John, of Waterford, 20
Nicklin, John, 43, 45, 61
Nielson, William, 28
Nixon, James, 68
North America, 19
North Fork of Catoctin Creek, 6, 7, 8, 10, 18, 22, 23, 27, 29, 49
North Fork of Catoctin Creek, mouth of, 27
Northern Ireland, 9, 15
Northern Neck Proprietary, 8, 18
Northern Virginia, 6, 10, 16, 18, 30, 32, 52
Northwest Fork of Goose Creek, 7, 9, 28

O

oak bark, 13
oak-hickory flora community, 8
Occoquan River, 19
Ohio River Valley, 34, 36
old smooth (bore) gun, Israel Thompson's, 39
Old Wheatland Road (Rt. 698), 26
ordinary, Leesburg, 47
ordinary, Nicholas Minor's, 22
Osburne, Abner, 68
Osburne, William, 72
outbuildings, 49
outhouses of all kinds, Richard Brown's, 27
Oxley, Bridain, 69
Oxley, Everit, 66

P

Pacific Ocean, 20
Pain's Ferry (Payne's Ferry), 19
Pains Ferry (Payne's Ferry), road to and from, 24
pamphlets, sundry, 21
Papists (Catholic), 11
Paradise Lost, by John Milton, 21
Patterson, John, 20, 26
Patuxent River, 20
Paxson, William, 37
Pennsylvania, 6, 7, 8, 9, 14, 15, 34, 37, 49
Pennsylvania barn with forebay, 40
Pennsylvania style barn with forebay, 29
Pennsylvania, Province of, 6, 8
Perry, Samuel, 66, 68
Peter, 23, 41

Peters, Stephen, 90
pew, Jonah Thompson's, 47
Peyton (Payton), William, 41
Peyton Colonel Francis, 47
Peyton family, 47
Peyton, Craven, 24, 47
Peyton, Francis, 37, 47
Peyton, Margaret, 42, 47
Peyton, William, 51
Peyton's Grove, Alexandria, 47
Philadelphia, 9, 37, 47, 49
Philadelphia Monthly Meeting, 8, 9, 47
Philadelphia, port of, 7
Phillis, 41
Piedmont Manor, 18
Piedmont Region, 7, 19, 30
Piedmont Region, slave population, 19
Plan of Leesburg, plat by John Hough, 22
plank, 29
plantation, 7
plantation near Goose Creek Meetinghouse, Israel Thompson's, 44, 49
plantation near Goose Creek Meetinghouse, Stephen Wilson's, 49
plantation, Edward Thompson deceased, 49
plantation, Edward Thompson's, 7, 9
plantation, George Janney and Daniel Eaches, 52
plantation, Israel Thompson's, 6, 7, 10, 18, 20, 22, 23, 24, 26, 29, 30, 34, 36, 37, 38, 40, 41, 42, 44, 48
plantation, Jonah Thompson's, 48, 49, 51
plantation, Thomas Willson's, 9
Pope, Alexander, 21
Popham, Mary Ann Thompson, 54
Potomac River, 8, 19, 20, 26, 47, 52, 53, 54
Potomac River canal scheme, George Washington's, 53
Potomac River Valley, 8, 29, 36
Potomac River Valley Region, 36
Potomac River, over, ferry traffic, 22
Potomac River, western shore of, 20
Potowmack (Company), 41
Potowmack Canal, 36
Potowmack Navigation Co., 44
Potts, John, 71
Powell, Burr, 36, 60
Powell, Leven, 36, 37, 40, 60
Poyer, Philip & Thompson, Jonah, 47
Presbyterians, 6, 11
Price, John, 51
Prince William County, 19
Protestant, 6, 20
Protestant Episcopal Church (Anglican Church), 47
Province of Pennsylvania, 8
Purdum, Benjamin, 43, 60, 61
Purer Translation of the Bible, a book, 21
Puritan movement, 15
Pursell (Purcell), Thos., 45

Q

Quaker, 7, 8, 10, 11, 13, 14, 15, 33, 37, 39, 42, 43
Quaker Church, 21
Quaker Meeting, above Great Gap, 14
Quaker Meeting, Sandy Spring Meetinghouse, 14
Quaker Meetings, 42
Quaker, Irish, 9
Quakerism, 6, 15
Quakers, 6, 11, 13, 14, 32, 33, 39, 43, 44
Quakers, in Ireland, 6
Quakers, Irish, 7, 8
Quakers, watchfulness, 37
quarter, 23
quartering house, 23
Queen Street, Alexandria, 47

R

rafters, 29
Ramey, Sanford, 48
Rateken, Capt. James, 36
real estate, Margaret Peyton's, 47
Red Lion, Leesburg, 47
Redman, John, 48, 60, 61, 69, 70, 73
Redmond (Redman), John, 43
residence, Thomas Moore's, 37
Respass, Col. Thomas, 66
Respass, Thomas, 34
Revolutionary war, 39
Revolutionary War, 36, 41, 42, 47
Richardson, 15
Richardson, Ann, 14, 15, 23, 64
Richardson, Ann (daughter of William), 15, 33
Richardson, Elizabeth, 18
Richardson, John, 69
Richardson, Jonathan, 18
Richardson, Joseph, 15, 44, 59, 64
Richardson, Joseph (son of Jonathan), 18
Richardson, Joseph (son of William), 23, 33
Richardson, William, 14, 15, 23, 38, 64
Ridley Township, 15
Rinker, Edward, 66
Risby, Beck, 42
Roach, James, 69
Roach, Richard, 27
road corner to Mahlon Janney's mill lot, 26
road corner, Mahlon Janney's mill lot, 26
Road to Pains Ferry, 19
Road, Israel Thompson's lane to the Leesburg to Snickers's Gap Road, 24
Roberts, Joseph, 68, 71
Roberts, Stephen, 73
Rosemont, 48
Royal Street, Leesburg, 22
Ruse, Michael, 70
Russell, William, 67

S

saddler, 13
Sanders, Nicholas, 66
Sandy Spring Meetinghouse, 14, 15
Sandy Spring, Meeting at, 15
Sarah, 41
sash window, four-light, 29
saw mill, 26
sawmill, 26, 28
sawmill dam, Israel Thompson's, 29
sawmill, all her gears, wheels, saws and appurtenances, 28
sawmill, corner to Mahlon Janney's mill lot, 26
sawmill, George Gregg's, 27
sawmill, Israel Thompson's, 29
sawmill, Mahlon Janney's, 26
sawmill, Richard Brown's, 27
sawmill, Thomas Shepherd to William Nielson, 28
Saxton, John, 41
scantling, 29
Scatterday, Aaron, 67
Schooley, 33
Schooley, Samuel, 26
schoolhouse, subscription for building, 44
Scot, 6, 13
Scotland, 19
Sebastian, Benjamin, 22
Sectarians, 11
Sewel, William, Dutch Quaker historian, 21
Shaffer, George, 72
Shannondale Manor, 18
Shannondale Tract, 48
Sheane (Shinn, Shene), Ann, 33
Sheane, Ann, 33, 61
Sheane, Ann, Israel and the late Ann Thompson's adopted daughter, 45
Shelburne Parish, 6, 37, 41
Shenandoah River, 8, 22
Shenandoah Valley, 36
Shepherd, Thomas, 28
Shieds, Thomas, 67
Shipman, William, 69
shoemaker or cordwainer, 13
Shoemaker, George, 67
shoemaker's shop, tanyard, 49
Short Hill, 22
Short Hill Mountain, 7, 8, 14, 19, 48
Short Hill Tract, John Tayloe's, 22
Shunk, Isaac, 72
Sib, 42
Sickler, Garlock, 73
slave, 42
slave labor, 41
slavery, 19, 42
slavery, Israel Thompson's engagement in, 22
slaves, 11, 42
slaves, as payment for cargoes, 29
Smith, Joseph, 60
Smith, Nathan, 73
Smith, Thomas, 68, 71, 72
Snickers's (Snickers) Gap, 22
Snickers's Gap Road, 22
Snowden, 15
Society of Friends, 7, 14, 32, 36, 37
Sopher, Joseph, 71
Sophers, Joseph, 72
South Fork of Catoctin Creek, 9, 18, 19, 24, 26, 27, 37, 42, 44, 48
South Fork of the Beaverdam Branch of Catoctin Creek, 22
South, the edge of the, 6
South, the upper, 7
Southern Maryland, 13
Spencer, Nathan, 9, 24, 59
spring water, 8
springhouse, 34
State Government, Virginia, 22
Statlar, John, 66
Steer, Isaac, 51
Stevens, Thomas D., 71
Stickler, Garlock, 49
store, Farling Ball's, 27
store, Israel Thompson's, 29, 39
storehouse, Israel Thompson's, 28, 44
sumac leaves, 13
surveyor of the road, Israel Thompson, 24
Sutherland, Alexander, 49
Swann, Thomas, 52
system of damming and channeling waters, mill, 23

T

tailrace, Mahlon Janney's, 26
tan-bark, 49
tanner & currier, 13
tanner and currier, 14
tanner and shoemaker, apprentice, 41
tanner, apprentice, 41
tanner, the, 13
tanning and currying, 13
tanyard, 49
tanyard solution for soaking hide or skin, 29
tanyard vats, 13
tanyard, Israel Thompson deceased, 49
tanyard, Israel Thompson's, 6, 13, 29, 44
tanyards, 49
Tayloe, John, 8, 20, 22, 27
Tayloe, John (son of John), 20
Taylor, Mahlon, 68
Taylor, Richard, 66
Taylor, Stacy, 61, 69
Taylor, Timothy, 66
Taylor, Yardley, 26
textile goods, Israel Thompson's, 39
The Daily National Intelligencer of Washington, D.C., 54

The Farmer's Wife or The Complete Country Housewife, a book, 21, 38
The History of the Rise, Increase and Progress of the Christian People called Quakers, by William Sewel, 21
The Married Houses, Alexandria, 47
The Virginia Journal and Alexandria Advertiser, 36
theater, Alexandria, 54
Thomas, 15
Thomas, Lord Fairfax, 27
Thomas, Lord Fairfax and Baron Cameron, 8, 18
Thompson, 9, 33
Thompson & Peyton, 47
Thompson & Veitch, 47
Thompson deceased, Israel, 43, 45, 66, 74
Thompson deceased, Jonah, 54
Thompson deceased, Margaret Peyton, 54
Thompson House, Alexandria, 47
Thompson Jr., Isaac, 33
Thompson Jr., Sarah (daughter of Isaac), 33
Thompson Mill, 28, 29, 30, 49
Thompson Mill, headrace, 28
Thompson Mill, razed, 28
Thompson Mill, settlement cluster about it, 27
Thompson of Louden County, Israel, 34
Thompson, Ann, 15, 23, 32, 33, 44, 64
Thompson, Ann (daughter of Israel and Sarah), 33
Thompson, Ann (Nancy), 44
Thompson, Ann, the late, 44
Thompson, Betsey, 73
Thompson, Betsey, daughter of Israel and Sarah Thompson, 64
Thompson, Betsy, 68
Thompson, Betzey, 59, 60
Thompson, C. & Thompson, J.P., 47
Thompson, Craven Peyton, 54
Thompson, deceased, Sarah, 51
Thompson, Edward, 7, 9, 10, 15, 22, 32, 44, 48, 49
Thompson, Edward (son of Edward), 9
Thompson, Edward (son of Israel and Ann), 33
Thompson, Edward and Mary, 10
Thompson, Edward, son of Israel & Ann Thompson, 63
Thompson, Edward, wife and sons, 9
Thompson, Elizabeth, 33, 43, 44
Thompson, Elizabeth (Betsy), 44
Thompson, Forest, 9
Thompson, Hannah, 9
Thompson, Henry, 15
Thompson, Isaac, 9, 24, 33
Thompson, Israel, 6, 7, 8, 9, 10, 13, 14, 15, 16, 18, 19, 20, 21, 22, 23, 24, 26, 27, 28, 29, 30, 32, 33, 34, 35, 36, 37, 38, 39, 40, 41, 42, 43, 44, 45, 48, 49, 51, 52, 59, 60, 61, 90
Thompson, Israel & Ann, 63
Thompson, Israel (H.), 59, 60, 61, 73
Thompson, Israel (H.), son of Israel and Sarah Thompson, 64
Thompson, Israel (Issey), son of Israel & Ann Thompson, 63

Thompson, Israel (son of Israel and Ann), 32, 33
Thompson, Israel (son of Israel and Sarah), 33
Thompson, Israel and Joseph, 9
Thompson, Israel H., 33, 40, 43, 44, 45, 49, 50, 51
Thompson, Israel P., 54
Thompson, Israel, Commissioner, 40
Thompson, Israel, son of Israel & Ann Thompson, 63
Thompson, Israel, son of Israel and Sarah Thompson, 64
Thompson, Israel, the late, 44
Thompson, Issac, 9
Thompson, J.P., 54
Thompson, Jane, 9
Thompson, John, 54
Thompson, Jonah, 27, 33, 36, 41, 42, 43, 44, 45, 47, 48, 49, 51, 52, 53, 54, 59, 60, 61, 63, 64, 66, 69, 72, 73
Thompson, Jonah & Son, 47
Thompson, Jonah, alderman, 52
Thompson, Jonah, justice of the peace, 52
Thompson, Jonah, Mayor of Alexandria, 47, 52
Thompson, Jonah, President, Bank of Alexandria, 47
Thompson, Jonah, served on the vestry, 54
Thompson, Jonah, son of Israel & Ann Thompson, 63
Thompson, Jonah, trustee poor house, 52
Thompson, Jonah, vigilance committee, 52
Thompson, Joseph, 9, 29
Thompson, Joseph (son of Isaac), 33
Thompson, Joshua, 9
Thompson, Margaret, 42, 47, 49, 52, 54
Thompson, Margaret, daughter of Jonah and Margaret Thompson, 54
Thompson, Mary, 9, 10
Thompson, Mary (Barrett), 15
Thompson, Mary (daughter of Israel and Ann), 33
Thompson, Mary, daughter of Israel & Ann Thompson, 63
Thompson, Nancey, 59, 60
Thompson, Nancy, 51, 68, 73
Thompson, Nancy, daughter of Israel and Sarah Thompson, 64
Thompson, Pleasant, 33, 44, 50, 59, 60, 73
Thompson, Pleasant, daughter of Israel and Sarah Thompson, 64
Thompson, Prudence, 9
Thompson, Prudence (wife of Henry), 15
Thompson, Rebecca, 9
Thompson, Sally, 59, 60, 73
Thompson, Sally Eleanor, 51
Thompson, Sally, daughter of Israel and Sarah Thompson, 64
Thompson, Samuel, 32, 33, 38, 39, 41, 43, 44, 48, 59, 60, 61, 68, 70, 71, 72, 74
Thompson, Samuel (son of Jonah), 54
Thompson, Samuel, son of Israel & Ann Thompson, 63
Thompson, Samuel, son of Jonah and Margaret Thompson, 53
Thompson, Sarah, 37, 40, 44, 49, 50, 51, 59, 61, 66, 70, 73
Thompson, Sarah (daughter of Edward), 9

Thompson, Sarah (Hague), 33, 44
Thompson, Sarah Hague, 44
Thompson, Sarah W., 33, 51
Thompson, Sarah W. (Sally), 44
Thompson, Sarah, widow, 49
Thompson, widow (Sarah), 73, 74
Thompson, William, 9
Thompson, William Edward, 54
Thompson's additional lot, Edward, 22
Thompson's house in Alexandria, Jonah, 52
Thompsons in Lowden County, Israel, 34
Thompson's Meadow, 22
Thompson's place, Edward and Mary, 10
Thompson's Wharf, Alexandria, 52
Thompsons, Israel, 34
Thomson, Edward, 11
Thomson, Edward, he and wife both preachers, 11
three adjacent lots, Israel Thompson's, 44
Three Volume Dictionary of Arts and Sciences, 20
Tidewater Region, 36
Tiffin, Doctor Edward, 43
Tingle, George, 24
Towner, Jacob, 51
Townsend, Thomas, 24
Tracey, Grace L., 15
tract, Abel Janney's, 19
Tribbe, Joseph, 69
Truro Parish, 6, 10
Tucker & Thompson, 47
Tucker, James, 73
Tucker, Nicholas, 71
turnpike road, Alexandria to Keys (Keyes) Ferry, 49
turnpikes, 22
Tuscarora Creek, 22
two adjacent lots, Israel Thompson's, 44

U

Underwood, Stephen, 69
United States, 36, 37, 42, 47, 52
United States, President of, 52
Upper Potomac River Valley, 6
Upper Providence Township, Chester County (Delaware County), 15
Uwchlan Monthly Meeting, 8, 9

V

Vandeventer, Doctor John, 51
Vandeventer, Isaac, 68
Vandeventer, Pleasant, 51, 54
Vandeventer, Pleasant Thompson, 54
Vestal's Gap, 22
Vestal's Gap Road, 7, 22, 34
Virginia, 6, 7, 9, 19, 32, 47
Virginia Assembly, 47
Virginia Journal and Alexandria Advertiser, 37
Virginia Yearly Meeting for 1757, 42

Virginia, Commonwealth of, 52
Vitus, Pompy, 70

W

War of 1812, 51, 52
Ware, Robert, 68
warehouse facilities, Thompson's Wharf, 52
Warrington Monthly Meeting, 9
Washington, D.C., invasion of by British, 52
Washington, District of Columbia, 52
Washington, General George, 36, 37
Washington, George, 7, 22, 36, 53
Washington, Lawrence, 7, 8
Washington, Pennsylvania, 34
water courses, 49
water courses, mill, 23
water suit mill, 26
water, soft, 37
water, supply of running, 13
Waterford, 7, 13, 20, 26, 36, 37, 43, 49, 51
Waterford, house and lot of land where John Nicklin lived, 45
Waterford, Ireland, 7
Waterford, Joseph Janney's division numbered 9, 10 & 11, 49
Waterford, Loudoun County, 37
Waterford, Sarah Thompson's messuage of land, 49
Waterford, Thomas Moore's (Senior) residence, 37
Waterford, three lots, Stephen Wilson to Sarah Thompson, 49
Waterford, two lots of ground nearly opposite Stephen Wilson possessed by indenture of lease, 45
watermill, 6, 27, 29
water-mill, 23
waterpower, 23, 27
waterwheel, 23
ways, 49
Welsh, 6, 13
west gate, Israel Thompson's, 29
West Indian markets, 29
West Indies, 16, 19, 29, 30, 52
West Jersey, 7
West River Meeting, 14, 15
West River Monthly Meeting, 14
West, John, 26, 69
West, Thomas, 47
Western Branch Meetinghouse, 42
western lands, Israel Thompson's, 44
Westmorland, 15
Westtown Boarding School, 49, 50, 51
Westtown, Chester County, 49
Wetherly, Mathew, 69
Wheatland, 6, 7, 30, 52
Wheatland post master, Robert Heard, 52
Wheatland post master, Samuel Nixon, 52
Wheatland post office, 7, 52
Wheatland, half dozen or more houses including flourishing mill and store, 52

Wheatland, secessionist hamlet, 52
Whitaker, Benjamin, 72
White, James, 67, 71
White, Josiah, 72
Whitehaven, 7
Wildman, 33
Wildman, Joshua, 69
Wildman, William, 68, 90
Will, 42
Will, Negro boy, 45
William (Will), 45, 61
Williams, 33
Williams, David, 14
Williams, John, 71
Will's Creek, 10
Willson (Wilson), Thomas, 90
Willson, Francis, 90
Willson, Rebecca, 9
Willson, Thomas, 9, 90
Wilmouth, William, 67
Wils, Elizabet, 14
Wilson, Ebenezer, 68
Wilson, Joseph, 69
Wilson, Samuel, 67
Wilson, Stephen, 45, 49, 61, 66
Wilson, the ship, 20
Winchester, 8, 14

Wine, Jacob, 71
Wirtz (Virts), Wm., 49
Wood, Joseph, 69
Wood, Josiah, 66
Wood, Richard, 20
Woodward Jr., Jesse, 9
Woodward, Jesse, 9, 43
Woodward, Joseph, 68
Woodward, Prudence, 9, 32, 44, 59
Woolman, John, 42
Wright, Anthony, 68
Wright, Patterson, 66
Wright, William, 66, 73
Wrightstown Monthly Meeting, 9
Wrigley, Lawrence, 69

Y

Yates, Alice, 43
Yates, Benjamin, 42
Yates, Joseph, 42, 43, 48
Yates, Robert, 18, 29, 42, 43, 48, 59, 71
Yohogania County, Virginia Court held for, 34
York County, Pennsylvania, 9
Young's Night Thoughts, a book, 21

Roberto Costantino

My reasons for having undertaken this project of recording a historical site are varied. In part, it happened as a consequence of my circumstances at the time. But, much more so, this resulted from my fascination with and curiosity about a certain landscape on and about Wheatland, on the North Fork of Catoctin Creek and under the Short Hill Mountain. Here historical events and patterns of events have made a significant contribution to American history.

Much as planner and author Fredrick Gutheim wrote about the Greater Potomac River Valley as a whole, which this site is parcel of; it has been colored by the East and the West, the North and the South, and in the process has become a cross section of the nation and to a lesser extent of the world. Its people have adapted themselves to changing needs and changing times in terms with the natural facts of the region.

Roberto (Robert) Valerio John Costantino is a graduate of Langley High School, McLean, Virginia. He attended college at Indiana University, Bloomington, for two and one half years and then transferred to and graduated from Loyola University, New Orleans, where he majored in political science. Afterwards, he earned an undergraduate certificate in accounting from The American University, Washington, D.C. Additionally, Robert holds a graduate degree in urban and environmental planning with a concentration in preservation planning from the University of Virginia, School of Architecture.

Robert is the author or editor of two other books on Virginia history. In fact, this book publication is an outgrowth of a two volume non circulating book recording a historical landscape site in Virginia, published in 1994 by the School of Architecture and in the collection of the University of Virginia Fine Arts Library, which he prepared under the direction of Professor K. Edward Lay, entitled, Israel Thompson's Plantation (AIV No. 149). The other book was published by Heritage Books in 2003, entitled, Miscellaneous Road Cases, Loudoun County, Virginia, 1758-1782.

Currently, in addition to his ongoing work as a research historian, Robert is a retail merchant in the art and antique business and he works for the Loudoun County School System, Department of Transportation. He lives with his sweetheart and wife, Patty, and their children, Julie and Marc, on the road between Waterford and Wheatland, Loudoun County, Virginia.

www.ingramcontent.com/pod-product-compliance
Lightning Source LLC
Chambersburg PA
CBHW081148230426
43664CB00018B/2851